We'll Support Y

C000096965

We'll Support You Evermore

edited by David Bull

Duckworth

This book is dedicated to love and loyalty, as exhibited by so many. With thanks to my father, for giving me an early lead, and in memory of my mother, who constantly demonstrated, by example, the all-round importance of these qualities.

First published in 1992 by
Gerald Duckworth & Co. Ltd.
The Old Piano Factory
48 Hoxton Square, London N1 6PB
Tel: 071 729 5986
Fax: 071 729 0015

© 1992 by the Child Poverty Action Group

All rights reserved. No part of this publication
may be reproduced, stored in a retrieval system, or
transmitted, in any form or by any means, electronic,
mechanical, photocopying, recording or otherwise,
without the prior permission of the publisher.

A catalogue record for this book is available
from the British Library

ISBN 0 7156 2447 4

Picture credits

The publishers thank the following for supplying and giving permission to reproduce illustrations: David Bull for pp. 59 (below), 71, 83, 107, 179 (below), 207, 217; Colorsport for pp. 3, 27 (below), 37 (below), 43 (below), 67, 74, 79, 86, 101 (below), 111, 121 (below), 133, 136, 155 (below), 163, 171, 179 (above), 184, 195, 203; Harry Fletcher for pp. 27 (above), 141; Hulton Picture Company for pp. 37 (above), 43 (above), 48, 51, 101 (above), 115, 121 (above), 147, 160, 168, 187, 221; Martin Lacey for pp. 95, 96; Liverpool Anti-Racist Arts and Community Association for p. 200. Every effort has been made to trace the owners of illustrations, but this has sometimes proved impossible. Copyright owners are invited to contact the publishers.

Typeset by Ray Davies
Printed in Great Britain by
Redwood Press Limited, Melksham

Contents

Acknowledgments

To edit a collection of 24 plentifully illustrated chapters is to run up several debts. Mine are four-fold.

First, formal acknowledgments for permission to reproduce previously published material and to use illustrations appear at the end of the relevant chapters and on the imprint page. I am grateful also to Harry Fletcher, Syd Jeffers and Martin Lacey, whose football memorabilia (cards, programmes, photos and fanzines) included various items missing from my collection.

Secondly, I am grateful to friends and colleagues who provided encouragement, advice or technical assistance and to my family for their tolerance, as the scripts took over the basement and as messages from their authors invaded the kitchen – even if word that 'No. 10 rang – *again!*' invariably offered light relief.

Next, it was reassuring to work, again, with Duckworth. Despite a break of 20 years, I was unlikely to forget that Colin Haycraft is never one to let ignorance of a subject get in the way of his judgment. Who better, then, to approach with an idea for a book on watching football? When he interrupted my review of soccer milestones in order to enquire 'Munich? What's 1938 got to do with football?', I *knew* that I was with the right publisher. That view has been splendidly confirmed by the assiduous, supportive and expeditious editing of Deborah Blake (on blue pencil) and Ray Davies (on floppy disk) and by Jonathan Earl, who knows his football, made finding photos fun and enthusiastically sustained my belief in our venture.

Finally, my 23 fellow-contributors. It would be invidious to name names, but I should like to issue four particular 'thankyou's: to Mrs Pat Arlott, for enduring, on behalf of her late husband, my many enquiries; to the handful who understood the concept of 'deadline' (including all three school-teachers: such discipline!); to others who came with a late acceleration worthy of Linford Christie; and to all the social scientists who made the supreme sacrifice – for our non-academic text – of forgoing footnotes.

And I want to thank all the contributors for giving generously of their time. It is, of course, the lot of football fans to make a disproportionate, often unappreciated, contribution to the game – a point made a few times in this book. The fans' labour of love that I have in mind here is that of agreeing to waive royalties in favour of the Child Poverty Action Group – coupled, in three instances, with requests that donations be made to other causes: the British Lung Foundation, for Pat Arlott; Christies Hospital,

Manchester, for Rob Behrens; and Family Action in Rogerfield and Easterhouse, for Bob Holman.

And I've had *such* fun, swapping so many good yarns with contributors, some of which I've enjoyed seeing in writing. I do hope that these stories have a similar impact on you, whether your perspective be that of a fellow-fan or that of somebody who shares, as I do, John Gaustad's maxim – in the frontispiece to all his Sportspages classics – that, in order to work, a sports book should be 'as much about life as about sport'. Several contributors have indeed shared with us a slice or two of their lives – from passed-down memories of the 1923 Cup Final (fancy Jean Thomasson and Bob Holman each having a father at Wembley that day!) to aspirations for the next generation of fans.

So it is, I hope, appropriate both to acknowledge the contribution of those who introduced these story-tellers to the role of fan – especially those who came to the rescue of the surprisingly large minority whose dads disliked football – and to offer best wishes to the young followers to whom readers are so affectionately introduced in many a chapter. And perhaps I might also be permitted to say a word, in conclusion, about those who cannot look forward with us in that way. Thus, I am sad that the two chapters (5 and 15) that salute the teams of two fans within my extended family, Jack Holton and Clive Fowler, also report their funerals. And I wish that John Arlott had lived to judge whether the above efforts have furthered the 'literature for soccer' for which he hoped and whether our collection is worthy of his supportive letter, in September 1991, wishing us 'luck with the book, for many people of different ages feel similarly to you about ordinary small football clubs'.

I hope that the book reaches and pleases such a range of people, thus rewarding the many acknowledged above.

August 1992   David Bull

Contributors

Pete Alcock: Principal Lecturer in Social Policy and Acting Head of Applied Social Science at Sheffield City Polytechnic (becoming Sheffield Hallam University), he is a member of the Child Poverty Action Group's executive and a specialist in social security policy. He lives in Sheffield and is a season-ticket-holder at Hillsborough.

John Arlott: Best known as *the* cricket commentator and writer, John Arlott had many other lives – from policeman to BBC literary producer – as recounted in his autobiography, *Basingstoke Boy*. He even commentated on, and wrote about, football: see especially *Concerning Soccer*, from which his contribution to this book has been excerpted. He died in December 1991.

Rob Behrens: Principal Lecturer in Social Policy at the Civil Service College, Sunningdale. Educated at Burnage Grammar School, Manchester – where he came nowhere near to winning the Roger Byrne Trophy – and at the Universities of Nottingham and Exeter, he spent 12 years as an academic in exile in the West Midlands, before becoming a civil servant in 1988.

David Bull: Senior Lecturer in Socio-Legal Studies at Bristol University, he formerly worked in the Universities of Exeter and Manchester. He has served, since 1967, on the executive, latterly as Chair, of the Child Poverty Action Group. In recent seasons, his work has consistently taken him to the USA at Semi-Final time; Southampton FC has consistently avoided a conflict.

Roger Bullock: Senior Research Fellow at the Dartington Social Research Unit. Although this child-care research centre of the University of Bristol is based in Devon, its research covers the whole of the country, ensuring that he regularly passes the Hawthorns.

Alastair Campbell: Political Editor of the *Daily Mirror* and *Sunday Mirror* columnist, he started out as a *Mirror* trainee on the *Tavistock Times*, where his writing included a sports column. He is a regular contributor to BBC and Independent TV and radio. Burnley's chairman has been known to complain that his club gets more coverage on the *Mirror*'s political pages than in its sports section.

Tessa Davies: Having qualified and practised as a nurse at the John Radcliffe Hospital, Oxford, she studied, then temporarily taught, Social Policy at the University of Bristol. She is now a full-time mother of two pre-school children, a part-time Lecturer in Sociology and Social Policy at the University of Southampton and a TV-time football fan.

Geoff Fimister: Adviser and writer on welfare rights. He studied at Liverpool and Loughborough and has worked, in some capacity, with Glasgow University, Newcastle City Council, the Association of Metropolitan Authorities, the European Economic and Social Committee, and the Child Poverty Action Group. Into football, music (various) and scrambling about in the hills.

Harry Fletcher: Assistant General Secretary, National Association of Probation Officers, since 1984. Born in Stockport and educated at Ladybarn Secondary Modern, Burnage Grammar and the University of East Anglia, he qualified in Social Work at the University of Bristol, practised for Waltham Forest Council and was Senior Social Worker, One Parent Families, 1977-84.

Bruce George: Has represented Walsall South since 1974, having won more elections (six) than football matches. Despite his appalling record as a goalkeeper, he is a defence specialist. He is Vice Chairman of the Commons Defence Select Committee and has written six books – including three Jane's *Nato Handbooks* – and over 150 articles on related issues.

Cyril Gibson: Having worked in the electricity industry all his life, apart from six years in the army, he retired, in 1979, to chair the Bristol Citizens Advice Bureau and to put in 10 years of voluntary work with the Avon Social Services Department and the Probation Service, advising on debt and benefit problems and representing at tribunals.

Bob Holman: Formerly Professor of Social Administration in the University of Bath, he has worked, for the last 16 years, for community projects on council estates, latterly in Easterhouse, Glasgow. He is the author of *Putting Families First* (Macmillan Education, 1988) and *Good Old George: the Life of George Lansbury* (Lion, 1990).

Jack House: Head of Humanities at Ashton Park Comprehensive School, Bristol and priest (non-stipendiary) at the Church of Saint Francis of Assisi, Ashton Gate, in the Parish of Bedminster. Bristol born and bred, he is a shareholder (minor) and lifelong supporter (avid) of Bristol City FC.

John Hughes: Freelance sports journalist since 1974. Born in Nottingham, he spent 14 years on the weekly *Worthing Herald*; *Rhodesia Herald* and *Morning Telegraph*, Sheffield (both mornings); and the *Southern Evening Echo*. He is now based in Southampton, working mainly for the BBC – including regular football coverage for Radio 5 – and editing the Southampton FC programme.

Syd Jeffers: A black '30-something', born in London, now living in Clapton. Studied at Sussex before becoming a researcher at Bristol University's School for Advanced Urban Studies. His main interests are in renewing his annual contract; 'race' and identity politics; homelessness; policy evaluation; and the currently popular notion of 'empowerment'.

Martin Lacey: Printer and publisher, Juma, Sheffield. Born in Pinner, he rotated between Sheffield, Canada (becoming ice-hockey fan of Calgary Flames) and London, before returning to Sheffield in 1988. Having printed early editions of *When Saturday Comes* (to which he occasionally contributes), he now prints 50-odd club fanzines each season.

Phil Lee: Born in Ashton-under-Lyne and educated at the Universities of Bradford, Kent and London. A lecturer and youth and community worker, he more usually writes on sociological and social policy issues. Until recently working in the School of Social Work at Leicester University, he has just been appointed Head of Applied Social Studies at Edgehill College, Ormskirk.

John Major: A Chelsea fan as long as he can remember, he was formerly a Lambeth councillor and became Member of Parliament for Huntingdonshire in 1979 (Huntingdon since 1983). He has served in a number of Ministerial posts, including Minister of Social Security and the Disabled, Chancellor of the Exchequer, Foreign Secretary and, since November 1990, Prime Minister.

Alan Plater: Born in Jarrow, adopted by Hull and living in London. Trained as an architect, he has been a writer since 1960, working in films, theatre, radio and TV (*A Very British Coup* and *Fortunes of War*; and versions of his novels *Misterioso* and the *Beiderbecke* trilogy). In his spare time he listens to jazz, is potty about his grown-up family and is President of the Writers' Guild.

Rob Pugh: Head of History at Dane Court Grammar School, Broadstairs, he previously taught in Ramsey, Cambridgeshire, where he became a part-time Peterborough supporter. Since the age of 14, though, his real sporting love has been Brighton and Hove Albion – leaving some room for other sports, politics, history, films and pub quiz evenings.

Eugene Ring: Born in London, he supports Surrey at cricket. He has travelled far afield to study (Universities of Liverpool and East Anglia), to teach (Universities of Keele, Birmingham and, since 1976, Bristol – in the School for Advanced Urban Studies) and to consult (Australia, Hungary, Turkey and Zimbabwe) in the fields of organisation and management.

Cherry Rowlings: Professor of Social Work at the University of Stirling. A Bristolian who has been a social worker in Croydon and Lewisham (although she never braved the Den) and then an academic in the Universities of Oxford, Keele and Bristol. She moved to Stirling in 1991 and is slowly adjusting to the Scottish League.

Jean Thomasson: Having taught in Whitehaven and given birth to three Bolton fans in Bradford, Walsall and Newcastle-upon-Tyne, she is now back home in Bolton, teaching Geography at Westhoughton High School. A local organiser for Christian Aid, she is also active in Amnesty International, Greenpeace and Friends of the Earth.

Stephen Wagg: Has lectured in further, higher and adult education since the mid-1970s and currently teaches at Leicester University. He wrote *The Football World* (1984) and, with John Williams, edited *British Football and Social Change* (1991). His latest book, *Come on Down?*, edited with Dominic Strinati and published in the autumn of 1992, deals with popular media culture.

Introduction

People speaking up on 'The People's Game'

David Bull

Forty years ago, John Arlott, taking time out from his massive contribution to the literature of cricket, put the case for a 'literature for soccer': while he felt it to be widely believed, within the game, that the literary appetite of 'football followers' could be satiated by 'brief match-accounts and dressing-room gossip', this great sports journalist wondered whether football might somehow rid itself of its image as 'The Craft Without an Art'.

For a few pages of his 1952 book, *Concerning Soccer*, John Arlott stepped out of his professional role to write 'A Supporter's Piece' – on his first love, Reading FC. I am so pleased that, shortly before his death in December 1991, he gave me permission to reproduce that elegiac memoir as the first of the 24 supporters' pieces in this book.

That is not to pretend that the reminiscences of John Arlott, the soccer fan, in any way inspired me to persuade fellow-enthusiasts to write, in a similar vein, about their 'careers' – as Eugene Ring puts it in his chapter – as supporters. On the contrary, I came across those recollections of Reading only in 1991 – tucked away, as the sole piece of its kind, in an excellent collection of soccer journalism assembled by Brian Glanville in 1962.

The inspiration for this book has come not from such professional contributions to the 'literature for soccer' but from people outside that world of football-reporting, taking time off from their various professional responsibilities in order to write, instead, about their loves and loyalties as football fans. My first encounter with that phenomenon was in 1959, when I read, in the *Listener* of 19 February, a 'requiem ... from the terraces' by Max Gluckman, the eminent anthropologist.

This famous observer was rather dismissive of his fellow-spectators, many of whom 'are not skilled judges of good football'. Despite this, I have ever since regarded that piece as a watershed: in order to contribute to the literature for soccer, you did not *have* to be a journalist in the Arlott/Glanville mode or a player/manager with a ghostwriter at hand; you could be a supporter, with publishable thoughts on your perspective from the terraces.

It is beyond the scope of this introduction to review the ways in which that non-professional soccer literature developed over the next 30 years. But take, if you will, the three hats that Max Gluckman was wearing: social scientist; writer on non-sporting matters; and terrace fanatic. I propose to adopt that three-fold classification here as a way of illustrating the kinds of writing that have encouraged me to think positively about what can be said, in publishable form, by those outside the triumvirate of player, manager and football reporter.

These three developments might be described as the *social science of soccer*; the *alternative journalism*, as non-sports writers take the field; and *spectator-speak*, as fans on the terraces (some of them social scientists or professional writers, of course) have their say. This collection owes something to each of those developments, especially in so far as football's followers have increasingly attracted the attention of the social scientists and the alternative journalists – sometimes as an integral part of an analysis that considers the game's many actors; occasionally as their prime focus (although we shall see that one has often had to be deemed a 'hooligan' or a 'thug' to merit such limelight).

The social science of soccer

The range of relevant academic enquiries is considerable. Leaving aside the economics of football (Arnold) and the several social histories of recent years – both of the game in general (Mason; Wagg) and of particular clubs (Korr; Arnold – again) – we can focus on three kinds of study (tribal, sociological and environmental) of football fans.

My initial exposure, within my undergraduate anthropology syllabus, to tribes came too soon to include the 'Soccer Tribe', which zoologist Desmond Morris later investigated at Oxford's Manor Ground and elsewhere. Whether his study qualifies as anthropology need not concern us here: the pity is that the outcome, in 1981, was hardly 'science' of any kind – social or otherwise. Unsubstantiated generalisations litter an exaggerated text, spoiling an outstanding collection of football photography. Gluckman's put-down of spectators is mild compared with the patronising nonsense that Morris offers. Thus we learn that 'the more progressive elements in the tribe', who want to see the game 'packaged as family entertainment, with the razzmatazz approach of show business', are having to contend with the romanticism of football's 'devout followers', whose 'typical week is spent in the factories and offices, the shops and streets of the busy urban world of the twentieth century. Their work lacks any sharp climax and is often monotonously repetitive, so that ... they eagerly anticipate the peaks of high tension and emotional drama that the game will bring, breaking their steady routine with surging moments of almost unbearable excitement.' The fact that most football followers are working-class males – see David Canter's demographic analysis, of which more below – does not justify Morris's sweeping depiction. And most of us – as Martin Lacey rationally explains, amid all the unashamed romanticism of his chapter – will often go to support our favourites with little hope of much excitement, even in *bearable* proportions.

Morris's lack of insight is compounded when he *does* attempt to forgo generalisation for a 17-fold categorisation of types 'who crop up again and again at each Tribal Gathering'. For instance, his distinction between 'Loyalists' and 'Jokers' takes no account of the way in which we faithful so often rely upon our cynicism –'gallows humour', as Rob Behrens puts it – to sustain our loyalty.

The sociological contribution – just about synonymous, surely, with the output of the Sir Norman Chester Centre for Football Research at the University of Leicester – has also suffered, in my view, from its pretension. I refer not to any Morris-style generalisations – the Centre's thorough scholarship is a strength on which I continue to draw – but to the draining effect of its sociological jargon. You have to have a special kind of immunity (with which my Sociology degree never provided me) to survive some of the impenetrable language of *Football on Trial* (1990). This book makes such an important research contribution yet its findings are too often buried in jargon. Its evidence that the media may have helped to *manufacture* hooliganism, and the proven deficiencies of all-seater stadia as a solution to the phenomenon, need to be made more accessible to those of us unversed in the Leicester lingo.

In its 1991 collection of essays on *British Football and Social Change* (edited by John Williams and Stephen Wagg), the Centre explicitly associates itself with the growth of 'jargon-free books by interested academics'. This does not, alas, prevent the senior editor from pondering the relationship between the 'new iconography' and 'bourgeois cultural hegemony'.

Finally, there are the analysts of the football environment, from the geographer, John Bale, to the environmental psychologists – David Canter and his team – who have much of importance to say about the viewpoint of the most pertinent 'expert' on the game: the fan.

Alternative journalism

The Glory Game, by Hunter Davies (1972), must be the undisputed proto-

type of the study to which I referred earlier, wherein all the key actors in a
club – in this case, Spurs – are identified.

His coverage of the fans interests me in two ways. First, he demonstrated
how it could be more interesting to read about a fan who had missed only
three Spurs' games in 40 years, than about new signing, Ralph Coates. The
process of *identification* that this involves is even more apparent in Davies's
subsequent collection, *My Life in Football* (1990). Most of his interviews
with the stars left me cold, compared with the pieces on being a fan –
especially the one headed 'Why I hate Spurs'. It is an essay on loyalty:
players are 'mercenaries [who] don't give a damn'; managers change clubs
so often that 'half of them don't know what town they're in' and the best
that can be said of directors is that 'they are less faithless than players or
managers'. That leaves the fans as 'the only people in football concerned
with moral or philosophical problems. You can go anywhere, as a fan. No
one is paying you. You have signed nothing. You have total free will. Yet
in your bones, you know you have no choice. You can't change colours.
For better or for worse. Your team is your team. Till death do you part.'

Hence, despite his hatred for commercial developments at White Hart
Lane – the very things that Desmond Morris tells us the 'progressive'
supporter wants – Davies has to keep on going there.

Secondly, it is interesting to note how, writing 20 years ago, Davies
thought it appropriate to devote separate chapters to 'The Supporters' and
'The Skinhead Special'. One cannot help wondering whether the ordinary
fans might have received *more* attention, these past 20 years, if the focus
had not been so heavily on hooligans. On the other hand, fanzines have
emerged as a reaction not only to the disdainful commercialism that caused
Hunter Davies to hate Spurs but also, as Martin Lacey explains in his
chapter, to the distorted media image of the hooligan fan. More of the
fanzine movement anon. Meanwhile, enter another journalist, running with
the mob. I refer, of course, to Bill Buford's sensational account, *Among the
Thugs* (1991). Setting the tone with a macho quotation from Baden-Powell
on teaching 'the lads ... to be manly', this American journalist proceeds to
describe, and attempts to explain, 'how normal English males behave ...
the domain of the male spectator has always been characterised by its
brutish masculine excesses'.

This special pleading enables Buford to arrive at the remarkable conclusion that events at Hillsborough in April 1989 were a product of 'how people
attend football matches. It is normal.' All of this sits oddly with his
observation of press photographers' trying to create a missile-throwing
event in the 'images ... they wanted'. In his brilliant coverage of Italia '90,

novelist Pete Davies likewise complains of the images created by the popular press, so that 99.9 per cent of football-goers are 'maligned ... because of every 10,000 who go, three are arrested'.

I do not share some of Davies's assumptions, especially the way in which he sees *playing* the game, as a boy, as an essential apprenticeship to being a fan; but, then, he hopes that readers who 'love football will ... enjoy vehemently disagreeing with at least half' of what he says in *All Played Out* (1990). *That* is, he argues, 'at least half of what being a fan is all about'.

I'll drink to that! What Pete Davies also demonstrates is the *place* of the fan, as just one of the actors in what he calls 'Planet Football'. It is a compelling piece of writing. So, too, is Dave Hill's '*Out of His Skin*' (1989), a devastating demonstration of racism in British soccer, not only on the terraces but in the Liverpool dressing room. I shall return to that theme below: my concern here was to illustrate the contribution to the soccer literature of four freelance writers.

Spectator-speak

And, finally, the also-rans: the fans speak up!

The obvious forum, here, has been that of the football fanzine, the development of which is described by Martin Lacey in his chapter. It was a development that initially passed me by – for two reasons.

The first was my 'can't beat 'em; join 'em' approach to club programmes. How could they be like *Pravda*, as Lansdown and Spillius put it, addressing me, in 'appalling prose, aimed at idiots' – to quote Hunter Davies on the 'mail order catalogue' that passed for a programme at White Hart Lane – and yet constantly invite my participation? When Southampton's marketing manager kept going on about our greater involvement in the club, I put it to him that this should include a fan's column in the official programme.

Taken up on that proposition, I ran foul, once or twice, of censorship. My first two pieces in 1981 were inoffensive, but I complained, in the third, that such craftsmen as Ardiles and Williams had spent too much of Saints v Spurs kicking each other. Censored! The players' committee had objected, I was told: it was bad for their image if the programme mentioned fouls. Sidelined, I made my comeback in October 1985, when a new marketing manager again invoked participation. So, until March 1987, I had my own regular column.

Despite modest interference – I was forbidden to *quote* the terrace usage of 'coon' – I was free to take on both racism and sexism (the latter when I reacted to the centenary event followed up by Tessa Davies). I could even criticise the manager: Chris Nicholl, a truly gentle man, welcomed 'open' comment. Unfortunately, his less liberal chairman rudely terminated my column when I aired the case for under-soil heating.

By the time a new editor offered me reinstatement in 1991 (contract renewed for 1992-93), this restricted notion of participation had been substantially overtaken by the burgeoning vogue for independent comment in fanzines. Indeed, invitations to participate were by now on the other foot, as the manager, chairman and selected players were offered opportunities to respond, in the fanzine, to their critics on the terraces. I am a convert to this medium: until I was asked, in 1990, to write for one of the Southampton fanzines, *On the March*, I had never so much as glanced at one.

This brings me to my second reason for neglecting this movement for so long. Quite simply, I had formed the bigoted notion that fanzines were trash. I had no idea that they could be as good as Martin Lacey claims – 'intelligent and knowledgable but also biased, committed, outspoken and irreverent' – everything I'd like this book to be. Martin has backed his judgment not only by becoming, as he explains, a central printer of local fanzines, but also, as he neglects to mention, by producing some excellent annual compendia of fanzine articles and illustrations. How I laughed at the idea – in his 1991 collection, *Get Your Writs Out!* – of the Leyland-Daf Riot Van Trophy sponsored by the police.

A different kind of collection appeared in 1990, when Harry Lansdown and Alex Spillius asked 20 men and a woman, 'most of whom do not make a living out of the game, to write about what football means to them ... to say ... this is what football is like'. The outcome, *Saturday's Boys*, was the immediate stimulus for this book. That stimulus was partly positive: their collection reinforced both my Gluckman lesson, of 1959, that you don't have to be a football writer to write well about football and the Canter thesis that the fans are the true 'experts'. But it was also negative, in that its range of football experiences was too wide for me, especially in that there were too many stories about *playing* football.

I have two problems with that emphasis. First, while incidents in the amateur game make for many a good oral yarn, they make tedious reading: in order to identify with a football report, I must know at least some of the actors. Thus, I can picture Bruce George being offered a contract by John Toshack. That is why I lifted my ban, for the purpose of his chapter in this book, on playing stories. The only other exception was for Bob Holman, so that he might develop his argument about football's role in neighbourhood social work. Secondly, playing memoirs exaggerate the macho image of the game. Lansdown and Spillius apologise for their sexist title, *Saturday's Boys*, and justify, as typical of the terraces, a ratio of one woman to 20 men – as in the Anfield photo on our cover. According to Canter, the ratio is nearer 1:5 or even 1:4. We've achieved 1:7 in this collection and would have done better; but female fans are so self-effacing ('who'd want to read what *I* have to say?') while men will pester you to be included.

I usually said 'No' to volunteers. A principal criterion was relevance: did the perspective of each contributor add variety, while fitting into the limited range of themes to which I felt a book on *watching* football should be confined? I need to say a little more about our focus, our style and my choice of appropriate contributors, before explaining the organisation of this book.

Our focus and style

Our starting point is *loyalty* to a club. While especially interested in how loyalty has been sustained against the pulls of geographical mobility, I invited contributions on a few related themes. What was the experience of immobile fans, within a 'divided city'? How, if at all, did race or gender affect one's commitment? And what conflicts were created by the competing loyalties of the next generation or by one's professional commitments?

My brief on style was simple: the story should be accessible. It should *include* the reader, inviting his or her identification with the places, personalities and events described. This required three constraints on contributors.

First, we needed no scientific analysis. Any social analysis should be not of the theoretical kind that excludes those unitiated in the ways and assumptions of social science, but in the introspective mode – see, for instance, the chapters by Alcock, Bullock, Jeffers and Wagg – that is geared to our goal of inviting *identification*. If analysis is to be non-scientific, it follows, secondly, that I did not require of authors the standards, in respect of generalisations, that I demanded of Desmond Morris. On the contrary, I was more than happy for colleagues to express unsubstantiated opinions. Canter observes that when 'normally sane and rational people start discussing football, reason and balanced judgment can fly out of the window'. I have encouraged that flight path.

Finally, I am satisfied that the writing is free of sociological jargon – although it does, of course, indulge in the in-group language of football itself. I am assured by non-football freaks, who have read a draft chapter or two, that this did not debar them. Recognising, though, that Rob Pugh's title is strictly for the fanzine fraternity, I've explained it in the 'Riddles' section at the end of the book.

The contributors

The most important qualification, as I indicated earlier, was not to be a soccer writer: I wanted football followers who wrote not as a profession, but from their passion. I have broken that self-imposed rule in two instances – both, I submit, for good reasons. First, as I intimated at the outset, the John Arlott who reminisces on Reading was very much Arlott, the young fan revisited, as opposed to Arlott, the seasoned reporter. We get a hint, in the final paragraph of his chapter, of how his professional responsibilities might impinge on his childhood loyalties. His autobiography is more explicit: 'with his transfer of work to Southampton, his loyalties were switched.'

This is a conflict I have discussed with John Hughes, who has likewise been drafted to the south coast. Readers will notice a nice irony about the way he discusses his dilemma: having no need, like us football reporters *manqués*, to indulge in match reports and player profiles, he manages to be somewhat briefer.

Those two professional linesmen apart, the 22 amateur players are mainly from the field of public policy, notably the 'helping professions' and the world of pressure group politics. An important link was the Child Poverty Action Group, of which three authors are executive members. And a few other contributors have a longstanding involvement in the Group. Upon becoming Prime Minister in 1990, John Major assured CPAG of his continuing interest in its activities. So I invited him to contribute to a book whose royalties would go to the Group. Despite the difficulties to which he refers in his chapter – how can a Prime Minister 'be expected to find time to be a football fan'? – I am so pleased that John Major could find time to report on his efforts to continue watching Chelsea.

Apart from John Arlott, John Major and Alan Plater, there are no 'household names' among our contributors. When inviting chapters, I was seeking not so much the great and the good, but people with something of interest to say about watching football.

Loyalty from afar

Each of the first 14 chapters discusses loyalty at a distance. The first nine are arranged in chronological order of the writer's introduction to his or her team – from John Arlott (Reading, 1923) to Martin Lacey (Wealdstone, 1971). The next two chapters are a bit different. Although some of us were exiled early – both Alastair Campbell and I were still at school – Stephen

Wagg was exiled by being *sent away* to school. The other deviant is Eugene Ring. Whereas most loyalists get hooked to a local team, Eugene picked his out of a newspaper and never saw them at home for his first 15 seasons.

But what *is* the 'local' team when there is more than one show in town? The next three chapters are from the conurbation of Manchester. Why should Harry Fletcher *choose* to follow Stockport County? He explains it in terms of parental anxieties about dangerous crowds. I must say I had no idea that this worry affected my generation until I read Eugene Ring's chapter.

'Divided cities'

The three Mancunian chapters, written from the perspective of exiles, are not explicitly concerned with divided local loyalties. While Phil Lee goes onto the defensive about supporting a club whose fans 'believed success was theirs by divine right', the same word – 'arrogant' – comes to mind for Rob Behrens and Harry Fletcher when they recall the Manchester United fans of their childhood. Rob has regrets, though, about 'this adversarial approach' which forced him to lose out on 'the genius of a football generation at Old Trafford'.

That certainly distinguishes him from two Bristolians, Jack House (City) and Cyril Gibson (Rovers), whom I explicitly invited to discuss loyalties in a divided city. At least their 'adversarial' approach has caused neither of them to forgo watching 'genius'.

The remaining third of the book explores constraints upon loyalties – or even upon watching live football at all.

Race and gender

The first three authors answer my question: what limits were imposed, if any, by gender or race? In grouping these three chapters thus, I risk being accused of devoting a minority of 'token' contributions to such major issues. If any reader seriously thinks that, then I invite him or her to read a few other chapters first.

It will thereby be seen that racism has been a worry to several of us, notably to Harry Fletcher and Rob Behrens at London grounds. But it is not only a London phenomenon: I have mentioned my taking it on in the Southampton programme; Phil Lee illustrates the 'intense racism' at Old Trafford; while Martin Lacey generally complains of its receiving less media attention than hooliganism.

I referred earlier to the work of Dave Hill, who found black over-representation on the pitch but under-representation on the terraces. This could be explained by experiences like those of black youngsters he interviewed in Liverpool. Having grown up with white friends, they accompanied them to games – only to be driven away by the terrace racists: witness the all-white Anfield crowd on the cover of this book. Having read Hill's book over Christmas 1989, I studied the Arsenal fans on Boxing Day at the Dell. I spotted only one Asian, and no Afro-Caribbean, faces. So I asked Syd Jeffers, a black Arsenal fan, to tell us more: were black Londoners being driven away like black Liverpudlians? He argues that the Highbury crowd *is* racially mixed and that anti-black prejudice has not been an issue for him. Like Rob Behrens, though, he is worried by the anti-Semitic behaviour at Stamford Bridge that has spread, he regrets, to Highbury.

The concern about the barriers erected against female fans likewise extends to other chapters. Fortunately, not all of the male contributors are as jaundiced as Alastair Campbell about 'mixing' football and romance: some of us have had partners interested, at least temporarily, in watching football. For a more enduring commitment to the game, see the chapter by Jean Thomasson. Note how little gender mattered to her: she was more interested than her brother in going, with their Dad, to Burnden Park; her daughters were initially keener than their brother; and her erstwhile husband failed to win wife or children over to Man Utd.

Jean has found women to be more surprised – shocked, even – by her football fanship than are men. So, too, have Tessa Davies and Cherry Rowlings: 'You don't look the type.' Tessa's rallying cry for England strikes an odd note in this book. It's as if we men – dating back to John Arlott – have been too immersed in our *clubs* to bother about internationals. This highlights the thrust of the discussion, by Williams and Woodhouse (in the Williams and Wagg collection), of the huge female audience for the World Cup on TV – with women outnumbering men for the 1990 Semi-Final against West Germany. I remember how my mother took an interest in 1966 and have felt guilty, with hindsight, that I made no move to take her to a live game.

But the guilt for erecting barriers to women's participation can be distributed much more widely – as it is in Tessa Davies's formidable catalogue of culprits. Cherry Rowlings's account of terrace harassment is disturbing. She had survived the playground hostility, but I've been especially worried about the role of junior schools. I was appalled when Rebecca, my step-daughter, was excluded not only from playing but even from *watching* on equal terms: when tickets for a Schoolboy international were being allocated, she was barred – although she was asked to organise (as the stereotypical secretary) the distribution of tickets to the lads.

Yet, it gets worse. As Tessa Davies shows, even with a staff determined to achieve equality, boys can still make the girls feel unwanted. No wonder she is pessimistic as she settles for being an armchair spectator.

Loyalties under pressure

The last five chapters concern two kinds of pull against initial loyalties. Pete Alcock and Geoff Fimister report different reactions to their children's interest in their home teams. Pete converted to his stepson's team. Geoff's son gave in to Dad, although his daughter seems to be of sterner stuff. Elsewhere, fathers of younger children wonder how they will decide: will Rory and Calum Campbell grow out of trekking from London to Turf Moor; and what will Benjamin Behrens make of his father's Maine Road affinities?

Finally, what of professionals whose jobs, over and above geographical separation, can put pressure on their loyalties? I have already considered John Hughes's dilemma. But what, I wondered, about Members of Parliament? Had no MP succumbed to pressures to switch? When I put that question to Bruce George, he not only confessed that he had but agreed to 'come out' publicly. On the other hand, John Major, representing what Rob Pugh describes as a 'football backwater', has felt no tugs from Chelsea.

Following football could, it seems, be part of the No. 10 job spec. Returning to the House of Commons after watching Manchester United win the European Cup at Wembley, Harold Wilson was disappointed that Richard Crossman had not even watched it on TV. The 'mark of a leader', Crossman reflected in his *Diaries*, 'is to be a man who sees football or at least watches it on television.'

Look back in anger – but forward in hope?

I put it to our present leader that he might wish to reply to some of the anti-Government anger expressed by other contributors. As it turns out, most of the anger is not aimed at Government – although I am not alone, I learn, in being outraged by compulsory all-seater stadia. Overall, the anger is outweighed by the constant statements of love and loyalty.

Yet I wish I could share John Major's optimism that 'within us all is a feeling that this season is the season for *our* team'. I might feel like that if I were following Wealdstone with Martin Lacey (*what* loyalty!). And I might feel like that if (with Mr Mellor's licence to stand) I were supporting a 'basement' team – if I were Eugene Ring anticipating a family duel between Blackpool and Stoke City; or Jean Thomasson, looking forward to life under Bolton's new manager; or Alan Plater, approaching every season with a 'reckless prediction' for Hull's revival; or Rob Pugh, with similar dreams about silencing the classroom ridicule of Brighton; or Roger Bullock, fancying 'fun and fellowship' at the Hawthorns; or Harry Fletcher, just because optimism is endemic, he assures us, at Stockport County.

But it's harder to be optimistic if your team is in the Super League but out of the super-elite, the Glamorous Gluttons who can afford the stakes. In truth, I don't know which prospect I dread more: the decline of Southampton, with two Chelsea pensioners as their post-Shearer strike-force; or having soon to sit down because two politically powerful Chelsea supporters have been taken in by the opinions that masquerade as argument in the Taylor Report.

And yet, even if I'm sadder and angrier than most, I don't suppose I'll stop going. Like Hunter Davies, I *know* that I have no choice. We're in this together: WE'LL SUPPORT YOU EVERMORE!

The cited work on the economics and geography of football can be found in the collection by Williams and Wagg. Fuller references to the 'literature for soccer' identified above are given at the end of this book.

1

Reminiscences of Reading

memories of a boy pilgrim to Elm Park

John Arlott

It was not until the question was posed to me that I realised that, by 1950, I had watched football in 10 countries and had seen the international elevens of six more. I could argue the case for Kubala, Nordahl and Doye being included in a European eleven and was probably following the progress of the major French clubs as closely as that of their English counterparts.

This may sound like the claim of a completely cosmopolitan football follower, but do you, I wonder, remember that cosmopolitan in the O. Henry short story? 'Just put me down as E. Rushmore Coglan, citizen of the terrestrial sphere,' he said, after a conversation which had roamed the world without bias; but he was thrown out of the café for fighting the man who dared to speak slightingly of the water supply of Mattawamkeag, Maine – the cosmopolitan's birthplace. Thus, while I am prepared to debate the respective merits of the post-war Scottish as opposed to those of the pre-war Hungarian defence, I must confess that I have never gone home happily from any game – not even from the Cup Final – until I have heard the result of Reading's match in the Third Division on that same day.

Getting the bug

They were a Third Division team when I first saw them, which was, I fancy, in 1923: I remember that the match was against Northampton Town and that is as far as my memory serves me. Reading, 18 miles away – in those days a one-and-sixpenny return rail fare – was the nearest club to my home, and a friend of my father's took me to the match: I was nine years old and, as I recall, I behaved abominably.

My next match I can pinpoint exactly: it was played on 2 October 1926. Reading had just been promoted to the Second Division – leaving behind them, in the Third, Charlton Athletic, Brentford, Queen's Park Rangers, Coventry City and Luton Town. Their opponents on thîs particular day were Portsmouth, who had been promoted from the Third (South) two years earlier and who were, that same season, to win their way to the First Division. They beat Reading – to my great hurt – by two goals to one. A penalty awarded to Portsmouth at a vital moment was taken by Billy Haines – the Portsmouth crowd used to greet him with 'To be a Farmer's Boy'. He bent down to place the ball, the referee blew his whistle and Haines, without even straightening up, toe-ended it into the corner of the net while the Reading goalkeeper was still adjusting his cap. I can see that goalkeeper – Duckworth, a Lancashireman – even now, running indignantly out to the referee to protest against the goal; but it stood; and Reading lost.

I remember, too, going after the match, with my autograph album, to the creosoted wooden hut which then housed the dressing-rooms at Elm Park before the present stand and offices were completed just a few weeks later. The first signature in that book, written in a somewhat laboured, boyish hand, was 'F. Cook' – Portsmouth's Welsh international outside-left. I later gave that book to a schoolboy; as I handed it to him, I lifted the cover with my thumb and there it was, all alone on the first page – 'F. Cook', my first autograph.

The bug had bitten. I was lucky: the Reading side of those days, although it never had a really good record during its five seasons in Division II, held some colourful players. Duckworth, in goal, was a stooping, eager player of incredible courage who would go down at the feet of advancing forwards with great daring. My own particular favourite was Billy McConnell, the Irish international left-back. Tall, rosy-faced, fast, utterly fearless and a terrific kicker, he was of the old school of backs. For four years he was a regular choice for Ireland, refusing one cap – against Scotland – to play for his club when they were in danger of relegation. A broken leg in 1928 ended the career of the man who was one of the deadliest tacklers of his day.

Dai Evans was a Welsh international left-half in Reading's promotion side. Evans was not a consistent player; nor, I now realise, was he particularly conscientious about his training; but he was a polished player who took the game of football with the natural ease with which it came to him. His transfer to Huddersfield, I always felt, coincided with the start of Reading's slide back to the Third Division.

Season of conquest

The 1926-27 season at Elm Park, however, held no thought of relegation. The small, quick, fiery Hugh Davey, Ireland's centre-forward, and Frank Richardson, the inside-left, a treasure for a Third Division side – his socks trailing, fair curls flopping over his face – were eager for goals. Behind

George Camsell, John Arlott's model centre-forward of the 1926-27 season.

Reading rise again. Just 60 years after John Arlott saw Reading reach the Second Division (only to be relegated in 1931), they went up again – to the joy of the Elm Park faithful – in 1985-86.

them, Alf Messer was a centre-half so dominating that, despite the contemporary Seddon, Hill and Kean, he came close indeed to English international honours. If Evans's transfer marked the beginning of the slide, Messer's move to Tottenham completed it. He was the coolest penalty-kicker I ever saw. He always put the ball about a foot inside the right-hand post at a height of about 18 inches off the ground: I never saw him fail with a penalty. When Messer left, Tommy Meads, Evans's successor, an immense worker and a fine long-shot, went with him to White Hart Lane and the half-back line, backbone of any side, was gone. But in 1926-27 Reading were not a selling side.

Their ground was about 18 miles from my home: it was a cycle ride – a hard one, but a cycle ride – and worth it. Eighteen miles there, 18 miles back. I can still remember every mile of the route and, given the same circumstances, I would cycle it the same 20 times a year again.

What a season that was – 1926-27. At every opportunity I would see football; I would bury my nose in the football papers which were then so numerous. Alas, that the young football enthusiast of today has no *Athletic News* which used to appear on Monday morning with a full account of every match in the four English Leagues *and* the Scottish First Division, with due attention to the amateurs and the Irish competitions, plus special articles as well. *Topical Times, Sports Budget, Football Favourite*, their names alone bring back their smell and look and feel.

Season 1926-27: Reading fought two replays against Manchester United before they beat them in the Third Round of the Cup: even Barson could not stop them. What new triumphs, we wondered, lay ahead of last year's Third Division Champions? To be sure, they were perilously near the bottom of the Second Division, but Manchester United were a pillar of the First Division: three matches should be enough to crystallise the difference between any two sides – and Reading won that third match. In the next round they reversed the League result and beat their old rivals, Portsmouth; then Brentford; then they went to Swansea and won there – and they were in the Semi-Final. Cardiff beat them – as they beat Arsenal in the Final – but the Semi-Final was a new conquest for Reading.

Season 1926-27. That was the year when Middlesbrough headed the Second Division and, in the process, set up a new goal-scoring record of 122 goals in a season, while George Camsell, their young centre-forward – he had only made three first-team appearances in the previous season – broke the individual goal-scoring record with 59 goals. The match, as I remember, was rearranged because of Reading's Cup-tie commitments and was played, I fancy – I have no means of checking – on a Tuesday evening, though why it should be a Tuesday, rather than a Wednesday – early closing day in Reading – baffles me. It was an awkward day and time, but, if I could raise tenpence – sixpence admission, twopence for a programme, a penny mineral on the way up and another on the return journey – I would be there. A rush through prep – always a household rule – and there was an hour on my ancient bicycle to cover those hills along the familiar route. Not one of my friends would come with me, or, rather, to do them justice, those who would have done so were stopped by their parents. I was there: I was in. From my reading, I knew this Middlesbrough side off by heart and here, now, in their red shirts with the white yokes, were those five goal-happy forwards – Billy Pease, Billy Birrell, George Camsell, Jackie Carr and Owen Williams – four English internationals in a row and the five of them worth 114 goals that season. But they did not beat Reading; and Camsell did not score. Their only goal came from Billy Birrell. It was a one-all draw when McConnell, way back in his own half, took a huge swing at a ball; it towered high down the middle of the field and dropped towards the Middlesbrough goal; someone went in and shaped to head it; missed; and the ball was in the net – McConnell the scorer of the longest-range goal I have ever seen.

It was a long wait after the game for the autographs but, at length, there they were, complete – and 18 miles lay ahead. Nor were the autographs my only profit from the match. Camsell was my main interest: he was obviously going to break all goal-scoring records that season; and I had gone to that match determined to find out how he was doing it. Five minutes was more than enough for me. The offside rule had just been changed and, with only one man other than the goalkeeper needed between himself and goal when the ball was last played, the centre-forward could lie right up on the deeper of the two backs, with only that one man to race for the through ball and the chance of a goal. As the flow of passes from Birrell and Carr – skilfully varied with long passes to the goal-scoring wingers – came down the middle, Camsell challenged for them: only McConnell's immense speed in recovery and some characteristic Duckworth dives prevented him from scoring.

Until then I had been an indifferent goalkeeper or full-back in school football. Now I had an idea – I was the only boy in the school who had seen the Middlesbrough match and football styles filter very slowly down to North Hampshire schools. I went to centre-forward. They might call me 'poacher', 'baby-liner' or anything else they liked: if it was good enough for George Camsell, it was good enough for me. I began to score goals – lots of them. I got into my form team, my house team, the school juniors and then the school team, all in a year and scoring all the time. It was my solitary spell of footballing glory. By the next season it was being done much better by better players, and I retired to full-back and obscurity.

Confirming the commitment

I was now interested not only in Reading's League matches, but in the reserve side too. Ask me the names of some of the members of our international sides in the 1930s and I shall be hard put to it to recall them; but about the Reading reserve sides of the same period I have no hesitation at all.

I remember them coming, those reserve players – signed during the close season to the accompaniment of flattering biographical notes in the local papers. There was an appearance in the pre-season trial match and then an obscure season in – and out of – the London Combination side; and they were gone.

One day, my father took me to see my great-aunt, who lived at Brimpton: at her house we met a satisfyingly grand gentleman who turned out to be a director of the Reading Football Club. I was tongue-tied, but it eventually emerged that I was a fervent supporter of the club. Would I care to have a stand ticket for next Saturday's match? As easily said as done: producing a piece of note-paper from his pocket, the director wrote on it an order for me to be provided with two – yes, two, so that I could take a friend – tickets for the stand at Elm Park on Saturday next. I could have wished, I seem to remember, that the fixture had been something more handsome than that with Kettering in the Southern League, but the stand was the stand. I cannot remember where we sat; my solitary recollection of the game is that a man named Bill Collier – a Scottish international, formerly with Raith Rovers, as I subsequently discovered – played a masterly if not over-strenuous game at right-half for Kettering.

No football season can ever be for me such a season as Reading's in 1926-27. The game came as a new impact: it was gladiatorial; yet, perhaps because I was always there so early as to be in the front of the terraces, close to the touch-line; or perhaps because of the shy remarks – and replies – over autograph books, it was also intimate. The Second Division of 1926-27 was not without its football greatness. Blackpool were there with Boy Browell; Manchester City with Jimmy McMullan behind Johnson and Hicks; Preston had Alex James, Morris, W.T. Roberts; Swansea had Fowler and the unique Lachlan McPherson; Chelsea, Andy Wilson, Miller and Law; and Jackie Bestall was at Grimsby, yet it was Portsmouth and Middlesbrough who went up.

For that season and all that has come from it, I have something of gratitude in my loyalty to Reading. The loyalty was there then, and an absorbing interest, a fierce anxiety that we should always have our best possible eleven on duty.

One of my great selection anxieties was Bill Johnstone – later to spend several seasons with Arsenal – who, in about 1928, came to Reading from Scotland. I now perceive that he was a skilful positional player, for he was eternally breaking through opposing defences, making or taking so many chances to run clear that he might have broken the goal-scoring record but that his final shots so often missed. Now the great local controversy – Johnstone or Bacon? – broke out. Bacon was a tall man from Derby County, with a shaving-brush tuft of hair growing out from a shallow forehead above a mighty jaw. His chest was like a drum, his thighs hugely tapering, and he had two shooting feet which he threw at footballs as if with intent to burst them. It was on 3 April 1931 – a Good Friday, as I recall, with Reading's relegation virtually certain – that A. Bacon, at centre-forward, realised all his dreams. The match was against Stoke City, at Elm Park, and Bacon proceeded to score six goals against them – six goals of immense excitement. He had a habit of hitting the ball well forward on his instep: not a toe-ender by any means, but from about the line of stitching joining the toecap to the instep – a point of impact possible only to a man of immensely strong legs and ankles. That day, everything he touched flew at the Stoke goal like a shell. But for some great saves he must have scored 20. His last goal was scored from an angle of about one degree to the goal-line on the right of the goal, and the ball, flying almost vertically into the goal, as I shall never forget, thrust the roof of the net high above the crossbar.

If Bacon is the hero of that story, Johnstone had his day in the 1928-29 Cup competition. In the Third Round, Reading beat Tottenham and then were drawn against Sheffield Wednesday, who were already strongly established at the top of the First Division – which they were to head for two consecutive seasons – while Reading were unhappily at about the bottom of the Second Division. Those fast Wednesday forwards bore down, prompted by Jimmy Seed, who was the inspiration of the side, and backed by the great half-back line of Strange, Leach and Marsden – all English internationals of the time. Somehow Reading kept them out: men went down like felled oaks and they did not score. Then – and the crammed crowd gasped with disbelief before it cheered – Johnstone scored and Reading were in the lead. We went on our knees to Johnstone, abjectly withdrew every unkind word we had ever uttered about him and thanked the stars of football that we had him. Did Reading ever come within shooting distance of the Wednesday goal again? If they did, I cannot recall it. I was behind the Reading goal in the second half and the ball seemed perpetually before my face. Why Wednesday did not score, only heaven and Joe Duckworth could tell you – and I suspect that Duckworth would not be too certain. Once Allen broke through and Duckworth dived forwards a full nine feet to push the ball off his shooting foot. It flew out to Hooper; and Duckworth, half-way up from his knees, pushed the winger's shot in the air, caught it as Allen charged him and miskicked it clear to Seed, whose header he turned over the bar. The penalty area seemed perpetually full of prone and muddy bodies; and Wednesday did not score.

Then it was Aston Villa – Smart and Mort, Walker and Dorrell, York, Moss – half a team of English internationals and the claret-and-blue jerseys. Nothing, now, was too great. I remember how it rained. There were ordinary chairs on the grass inside the barriers, so that the purchasers of special tickets could sit near the touchline. So heavy was the rain that the legs of the chairs sank into the mud: small boys were passed over the chair-sitters lest they should be crushed; I was aggrieved at being 'not small enough'. It was the end of Reading's Cup for that season and there has never been such another for them since.

Reading's manager in those days was a Scot named Andrew Wylie, who appeared to have a steady supply of players from his native district, for a vast number of Reading's two teams seem to have come from Falkirk or Bo'ness. In one of the pre-season practices – of 1928-29, I fancy – there appeared a left-wing pair from that area: Hunter inside and Oswald on the wing. Hunter was short, sandy, unhurried and a superb ball player. In the trial, he twice or thrice leaped into action, beat some three men and cracked the ball into the top of the net like a character from a story-book. Thereafter, he averaged something less than a goal per ten matches until he went to Sheffield United two years later, and thence disappeared, in a season. He was always, however, a masterly dribbler and a natural constructive player. He fed Oswald with perfect passes: perhaps it was a little unfortunate that the winger was so right-footed that, nine times out of ten, he doubled back and centred with his right foot, but that strong inside foot scored him – and Reading – some valuable goals.

Reading has always been a great club for centre-forwards – Davey, Johnstone, Bacon, MacPherson – who once put a free kick so fiercely over the bar as to send it out of the ground where it smashed the window of a house and the gas-bracket inside – Harston, Billy Lane, Palethorpe, Newton, Gregory, McPhee and, since the war, Blackman. If MacPherson and Bacon were the two most colourful, McPhee was probably the most dexterous. One of the best buys the club ever made, he was a steady scorer with his head and either foot over a period of 10 years. Palethorpe, however, was the most popular. A local lad from Maidenhead United, he had such a following that it was difficult to say whether the crowd at Elm Park were Palethorpe's supporters or Reading's. He was the centre-forward in the club's great season of 1932-33, when they totalled 103 goals and only some inexplicable weakness in an individually good defence prevented them from getting back to the Second Division. Tall, dark, good-looking and a cheerful trier, Palethorpe lacked just the extra touch of class. After Reading he played for Stoke City and Preston North End (he was the vital goal-scorer in their successful promotion bids), but once in the First Division – he went also to Sheffield Wednesday and Aston Villa – he was out of his class. His transfer was one of the saddest moves Reading ever made, for they sacrificed both support and opportunity of promotion by selling him.

War and after

Never, perhaps, did a side suffer such a tragedy – although one barely noticed it at the time – as Reading did on the outbreak of war. Manager Joe Edelston had at last brought together the side he wanted: cool backs, ball-playing halves, constructively-minded forwards with finishing power. Twice they ran to double figures within 10 days and were clear out at the top of the Third Division table when war came. That team went on to win wartime honours, but by the coming of peace it was irretrievably shattered and the chance was gone.

There is, I find, less open emotion in the directors' box and in the dressing-room than there was on the terraces when I was a boy. Yet there are still times when – like Ted Drake, old friend of obscure but happy days in Southampton – I cannot bear to look; times when I pray for the end 20 minutes from time, lest our one-goal lead should be taken from us. There have been times when, as a guest in the boardroom of some mighty First Division club, I found that the Third Division results were not read out – they stopped at the Second Division. Then it is that I have faced the superior smiles or the loud laughs and have asked, with my heart in my mouth, anxious as ever: 'How did Reading get on?'

Shortly before his death in December 1991, John Arlott kindly gave permission for the reproduction of this chapter, which originally appeared as 'Reading: A Supporter's Piece', in his book, *Concerning Soccer* (1952). His family subsequently agreed to a few minor modifications, principally to fit in with the format of this collection.

2

Return of the Wanderer

Jean Thomasson

It was October 1971 and I was sitting on top of a Bolton bus, on my way to visit Mum. After 12 years away, I had just come back to my home town. My husband had been appointed to a local headship and I was soon to return to teaching. As I looked down on people scurrying along side-streets, the scene reminded me of the famous Lowry, *Going to the Match.* But, then, that painting is based on Burnden Park which was, of course, the destination of all those figures below me: Bolton were playing Manchester City in the League Cup.

Back to my roots

I was no company for Mum that night; the floodlights could be seen from her bungalow and going outside – frequently – I could hear the shouts of the crowd. How the memories flooded back! Mum had never expressed any real interest in football but she tolerated Dad's fanaticism. He would return on match days, nose red, hands blue with the cold, either singing the praises of individual players or, after a particularly bad performance, declaring 'Never again!' Needless to say, he was always at the next game. He passed his passion on to me, relating vividly his experiences of the first Wembley Final, in 1923, when Wanderers beat West Ham 2-0. While Bolton fans will continue to recount that historic scoreline, the match has become generally more famous for the size of its crowd (capacity 127,000; attendance 200,000) and the performance of Billy, the white horse that helped to clear the pitch when the surplus spilled over.

My brother, eight years older, was more interested in cricket and played for a local team. So I was the one who, at the age of 12, started going regularly to Burnden Park. Having converted a schoolfriend, Margaret, I began to go with her, rather than Dad, to all the home games and some of the more local away games. When the away fixture was too distant, we would go to the reserve match, hoping to hear the first team score as quickly as possible. Standing behind the goal at the Lever End, we watched the likes of Nat Lofthouse, Tom Finney, Stanley Matthews and Jackie Milburn.

Our enthusiasm increased with every match. As the depths of pre-flood-light winter approached, kick-off times would be brought forward. I remember having to rush home from school netball matches on Saturday morning, with barely time to scoff my dinner before we set off. And then there were the Christmas fixtures: 30,000 at Burnden for the Christmas Day match against Manchester United and 53,000 at Old Trafford for the return game on Boxing Day. Those were the days! Margaret and I each had a favourite player. Hers was Nat Lofthouse, but I thought our goalie, Stan Hanson, was great. There was a popular song at the time, *Gal in Calico*, to the tune of which I made up my own words:

> Saw a man in a green polo
> Down at the Burnden Park.
> Now he lives in Springfield Road
> Grand place in the dark.
> Do I love him? Do I love him?
> Yes, on your life.
> Can I have him? Can I have him?
> No, he has a wife.
> Living down on Harper Green,
> Not far from his home
> At the end of every day,
> Round his place I roam.
> Who makes my heart sing
> 'Yippi Yi, Yippi Yo'?
> The goalie in the green polo.

Margaret couldn't go to the FA Cup-tie on 9 March 1946, so I went with Dad. Instead of standing in my usual place, we arrived early and found a good spot by the old scoreboard at the top of the railway embankment. The crowd was huge – 65,000 paid at the turnstiles; but thousands more climbed in, over walls and the railway line fence. I remember small children being passed over the heads of adults to the front. It was not until much later that we realised the scale of the tragedy that unfolded around us. Under the strain, barriers collapsed. People were lying on the ground to be stretchered away, having, we thought, merely fainted. The game was restarted after 15 minutes, so we were late back. Mum was waiting anxiously at the gate, having heard on the wireless that several spectators had been killed and many injured. After a five-day enquiry, it was decided that this was 'the first example in the history of football-following of serious casualties inflicted by a crowd upon itself'. At the spot where 33 lives were so tragically lost there now stands the Normid Superstore.

May 1953 saw Margaret and me at Wembley for the Bolton v Blackpool Cup Final. We had written numerous letters to the club, requesting tickets in the names of our numerous relations – the more we wrote, the better our chances. We managed three tickets, two of them, fortunately, for the same part of the ground. Margaret's father took the third, as Dad was by now quite seriously ill and, sadly, unable to travel. In those pre-motorway days, we had to leave at the crack of dawn, complete with scarves, rosettes and hats bedecked with blue and white ribbons. And what a noise the rattles made! They wouldn't be allowed inside the ground today.

The game, I shall never forget, went from triumph to tragedy in just 25 minutes. From the elation of being 3-1 up, despair set in: with two bad injuries and substitutes still more than a decade away, Bolton saw Blackpool pull a goal back and then equalise. I remember that, when Blackpool's fourth goal went in, there was some feeling of relief: we had been spared extra time and the inevitable heavier defeat it would have brought. When the final whistle went, we sat on the terraces, stunned, speechless and tearful, before starting the seemingly endless journey home.

After those fanatical years, things changed somewhat when I went to university and Margaret to college. We saw fewer games, but one that stands out in my mind was Burnley v Bolton in April 1954. And yet I remember absolutely nothing about the game itself. Having just recovered from hepatitis and gone against doctor's orders, I spent the match concentrating on not passing out from standing so long. It was the one and only time I wished that I could be at home.

By 1956 I had met my husband-to-be; now husband-that-was. A Manchester United fan, he began to take me to Old Trafford. Today, this would be considered a total and unforgivable betrayal – the team that Bolton fans especially loathe is captured in their regular chant, when nothing much is happening on the pitch, of 'We only hate Man Utd'. But it was different then, when opposing fans could stand alongside each other on the terraces and engage in friendly rivalry. Contrary to what Phil Lee claims in his chapter, I'd always assumed that it must be easy to support a successful team like United. And successful they certainly were. The atmosphere was indescribable – from queueing for the special buses in Manchester's Piccadilly, through the game itself, to being carried along at the end, in a sea of people, feet barely touching the ground.

Some games are clearly etched in the memory: United 10 Anderlecht 0 (played at Maine Road in September 1956, before the Old Trafford lights

The 'White Horse Final' of 1923, watched – once Billy had cleared the pitch –
by Jean Thomasson's father and (see next chapter) by Bob Holman's, too.

One of Jean Thomasson's 'Super Whites', Frank Worthington, later to become
a one-season hero at the Dell (see Chapter 5).

came into use); the home leg against Red Star Belgrade on 14 January 1958, which preceded, of course, the Munich disaster, as the team returned from the second leg the following month. Within 10 days of Munich, though, we were queueing round Old Trafford, on the Sunday morning, for FA Cup Fifth Round tickets – for a game against Sheffield Wednesday, which United won with a team that was almost unrecognisable after the tragic loss of so many players. And, before we knew where we were, United were in the Final against … Bolton Wanderers!

Money was short, so there was no trip to Wembley. But I was not disappointed: my loyalties, despite Munich, were not really with United and I was quietly pleased when Bolton won 2-0. We watched the game in a packed Manchester cinema, amid much controversy when Nat bundled goalie Gregg and ball into the net. But justice was done. We had lost in 1953 when Blackpool, with Stanley Matthews wanting his cup-winner's medal, had most of the uncommitted support. Now we had beaten the team which had the nation's sympathy.

We left the area in 1959, keeping contact through the local football paper, regularly sent from home. With three small children, going to matches was impossible and my husband, while still professing to be a supporter, never watched his team. I do remember, though, having the United scarf tied to our front porch in Whitehaven, as United beat Benfica in the 1968 European Cup Final, which Phil Lee vividly recalls.

Back to reality

After that October night in 1971, when Bolton won 3-0, I was well and truly re-hooked. In the next round of the League Cup, Bolton drew at Chelsea and I was at Burnden for the replay. We lost 6-0. But it didn't matter – I was back! Anna-Maria, my elder daughter, was by now 10 years old and more used to hearing about Manchester United from her armchair-supporter of a father. But, as my fellow-contributors repeatedly testify – see especially the cogent reasoning of Pete Alcock – there is nothing like the real thing. So Anna-Maria began to come with me, in all weathers. It wasn't the same, somehow, if we weren't wet through, and we would feel a certain sense of superiority as we jostled for places on the bus, afterwards, with those poor misguided souls who had had the misfortune to spend Saturday afternoon struggling round the shops.

The family's week revolved around football. The build-up to the week-end would begin in mid-week. There would be the local paper, radio and TV programme – not to mention our own discussions at home. We always had meat-and-potato pie before the match and plenty of 'chewies' during it. And we always picked up the local football special at the shop, so that we might read and argue about what we had seen. Reports from as many papers as we could find were a 'must' on Sunday morning and then we had the analysis in Monday's *Evening News*. Tuesday evening games were a bonus – the week was truly filled. One snag: that Manchester United fan! He would constantly deride our team. I particularly remember him criticising Peter Reid who was to make his name with Everton and England – this despite the fact that he had seen Peter play only on the odd occasion. Still, we didn't expect much else from a United fan; and when they were relegated to the Second Division in 1974, it shut him up for a while.

Present tensions

The armchair United fan has been given a free transfer to Torquay. BWFC reigns supreme! Anna-Maria is as fanatical as ever. Having qualified as a nurse, she is in Sheffield studying for her second degree. On the afternoon of the Hillsborough disaster, she was off duty; but, hearing the newsflash, she drove down to the hospital to see if she could help. She has described the shock of seeing, scattered about, the football scarves, programmes and bobble hats. To one familiar with the atmosphere normally associated with these accoutrements, the scene was unforgettably poignant.

She comes over whenever she can – Burnden on a winter's night, when the wind is right and the smell of the local tarworks drifts across the ground, is magic. Or we meet up, of a winter's evening, at football 'highspots' – Rotherham, Huddersfield, Chesterfield, Cambridge. The weather is often foul, the results often horrendous; but it's good fun. Her sister, Fiona, lives locally with her partner, Graeme. They have season tickets with me and we go to lots of away matches, too. Their brother, Erik, used to be less keen – much as *my* brother was. Now, living in Huddersfield, he has become as avid a fan as we are and drives over for many a home game.

Football occupies a large part of my life. In a stressful job like teaching, it is a valuable safety valve. You can shout, rant and rave and generally get carried away – although it can be a bit embarrassing when, the next morning, a lad in the Geography class says, 'Saw you last night, Miss, at Crewe – standing on the seat!' But then, if you've ever been in the stand at Gresty Road, you'll know that that's the only conceivable way of seeing the game from the back. You get to meet all sorts of people, which is refreshing. And even when the team is doing badly, a good moan with fellow-sufferers – usually about the referee – can be therapeutic. The dreaded withdrawal symptoms at the end of the season are eased, as ever, by monitoring comings and goings at the club and – a recent innovation – by watching match videos with a friend.

There is a lot of interest in football at the school, where I get some stick from those kids who wear their favourites' colours but who have never seen them play. That said, there are some keen Bolton fans in my GCSE class, who often make it difficult to get the lesson started on a Monday morning. I once overheard one of the lads say, 'She knows a lot about football.' He had no need to add 'for a woman'. I must admit, though, that I rarely come across that form of sexism these days. In fact, women seem to be more surprised – shocked, even – by my interest than men are.

Apart from two fellow Bolton fanatics, there are two other soccer enthusiasts in the staff room. One of them supports Blackburn Rovers. Even as his team strove for, and achieved, promotion last season – ultimately at the expense of Stephen Wagg and his daughter, as he explains in Chapter 10 – my colleague was very apprehensive about their aspirations to join the top flight, courtesy of a millionaire director. He fears that the game will be taken away from the man and woman in the street and shares my antipathy to new all-seater stadia. For him, Ewood Park is – like Burnden to me – the homely, north country ground, surrounded by little streets and full of vitality on a Saturday afternoon. The history teacher travels hundreds of miles to watch Barnsley. He and I endlessly discuss League positions, referees' decisions – and *managers*! Like me, he will continue to watch, however they play, always hoping to be there when the team turns the corner. With new manager, Bruce Rioch, maybe we are about to do just that.

Remember I said Mum wasn't interested in football? Now 96 years old, she told me last year how she used to go, when she was about 13, to a house next to Burnden. It seems a relative lived there, 'who had something to do with the team'. His wife made tea for the players and Mum helped to wash up. She could watch the game from an upstairs window. Checking out her story at the library, I discovered that the relative was groundsman for Bolton Wanderers at the turn of the century. I always knew I had football in my blood!

Come on you Super Whites!

The quotation concerning the Burnden Park disaster is taken from the Moelwyn Hughes Report, the full reference to which is given at the end of this book.

3

Forever Bubbling for West Ham

Bob Holman

The first FA Cup Final at Wembley in 1923 drew, as Jean Thomasson records in the previous chapter, an estimated crowd of 200,000. My father, like her father, was there – to see his beloved West Ham lose to her father's Bolton. He was to impart in me a love of football, both as a player and spectator.

As a removal man, Dad often had to work on Saturday afternoons, but he took every opportunity to get to the Hammers' ground at Upton Park. He took me to mid-week afternoon games – no floodlights then – to see the third team, and even to the pre-season trials of the Probables v the Possibles.

Soon I caught the football bug and every Saturday afternoon took the No. 25 bus from Ilford in order to watch all first team and reserve games. Arriving early, my mates and I would prevail upon a player – Ernie Devlin, I recall, was always especially helpful – to take our autograph books into the visitors' dressing room. During the match, we wriggled our way to the front and cheered balding Terry Woodgate with his ferocious free kicks; Norman Corbett, whose throw-ins reached the penalty spot; and the captain, Dick Walker, a skilful centre-half with the sleeked hair of a Denis Compton and the looks and cheek of a Max Miller. After the game, we had to wait until the players had showered and were leaving for their buses – few had cars then – in order to retrieve our autograph books.

At this time, in the 1940s and 1950s, West Ham were a lowly Second Division team. Years later, when the Hammers were in the First Division and had won the FA Cup in 1964, came Dad's proud moment when he moved the West Ham and England skipper, Bobby Moore, to a luxury home. Instead of giving him a tip, Bobby handed over a trophy engraved 'Bobby Moore, Hammer of the Year'.

Football and educational opportunity

Football was important in our household. I gradually perceived that it was also important as a means of social approval, even social advancement. During the war years, I missed much schooling while evacuated and, on return to junior school, I fared badly in class. I remember my shame at being unable to tell the time. However, football redeemed me. I played in goal for the school team that won both league and cup in 1947-48. The team photo shows my ears outdistancing the handles on the cup. Football had given me some standing at junior school.

I failed the 11+ examination, a failure which neither surprised nor bothered me for I possessed no grammar school aspirations. Then, presumably to compensate for all that missed schooling, I was kept back for a further year at junior school. Again I sat the 11+. Again I failed. However, at this juncture the education authorities upgraded Beal Secondary Modern to Grammar School status. Even with the increased intake, I still did not merit a place but was put on a reserve list and eventually interviewed. The headmaster started by asking what paper my parents read. My reply, 'The *Daily Herald*,' did not seem to impress him. He then asked the name of any book I had read recently. I was ready for that one and replied, '*Black Beauty.*' Unfortunately I could not reveal, under his probing, anything about its contents. Eventually, he noted that I played football and cricket for the school – subjects about which I could talk at length. He indicated that his new school wanted sportsplayers, and a few days later a letter came to say I was in.

Initially, I was miserable at grammar school. I had to make new friends, the discipline was harsh, my academic performance was poor. But sport – I eventually became captain of football and cricket – again ensured acceptance by both boys and teachers. After two years, for reasons I still fail to understand, I took off academically. Of course, football remained important and the only times I ever truanted were to watch big matches. In 1953, England, hitherto undefeated at Wembley, were due to play FIFA (which to us was the Rest of the World). The parents of my friend, Ken, possessed a TV, so we legged it over the wall to his home. However, the school team had a match starting at four o'clock so we had to return. We must have been the first truants caught climbing back in. At the end of my time at school, I won a state scholarship to university. Football had played some part in getting me onto, and keeping me on, the academic track that led there.

I did not proceed immediately to university, though. None of my relatives had received higher education and I was not sure it would suit me. Instead, I opted for National Service in the RAF. Here again, football had its uses. At the radar station of Bawdsey, it clearly rated above manning the national defences and I was excused duties to play left-back in the station team. In addition, there were many inter-camp competitions which were much more efficiently organised than the half-hearted attempts at fire drills or parades.

Forever blowing bubbles ... West Ham fans in Semi-Final mood in 1933 (above) and 1991 (below).

I failed, though, to distinguish myself as a radar operator. Weeks before I was due for discharge, I was told I could go. Unlike others, I was not placed on the forces' reserve list and I never heard from the RAF again.

Mobile supporter

After university I went on to jobs in social work and lecturing. After our marriage, Annette, a Glaswegian, and I lived in Hertfordshire, Birmingham, Glasgow, Bath and then Glasgow again. Geographical mobility is all very well, but it removes the football supporter from his or her roots. If I could not cheer West Ham every week, what was I to do? I adopted two ploys.

The first was to keep following West Ham's progress, while watching and supporting a local team. But which team? During our first stay in Glasgow, our children, Ruth and David, went out to play and were soon asked their religion. 'Christian,' they replied. 'No. Are you Protestant or Catholic?' These terms puzzled them for, although we are committed Christians, we have no strong sectarian or denominational leanings. However, Ruth and David established that they were Protestants and were duly informed that they were Rangers, not Celtic, supporters. Ruth, who has taken as much interest in football as Mrs Thatcher has in the poor, just ignored the matter. David, keen on the game, perceived the potential conflicts of being a Rangers' fan in an area where so many identified with Celtic. We resolved the issue by deciding to follow our nearest team, Partick Thistle. There, on Saturdays, the turnstile keeper invariably told me to 'lift the bairn over', a practice which, if taken in conjunction with the numbers who could watch from a hill overlooking the ground, may explain the Jags' low recorded attendances. We enjoyed the games for, like West Ham, the team was fast, erratic and exciting. They produced forwards who missed sitters and scored brilliant goals and goalkeepers who combined letting the ball slip through their legs with breathtaking saves.

The second ploy, as we moved around, was to visit as many different grounds as possible. Occasionally I managed to see a West Ham away fixture, but usually I watched two teams I did not support. I found great delight in attending Victorian grounds and recalling the part they had played in working-class culture. I grew to admire the small, but devoted, crowds at places like Crewe Alexandra, Rochdale and Hartlepool. In time, I approached the goal of visiting every ground in the four English Leagues. I completed it at Chesterfield on 15 April 1989. On the way back, I sat with stunned fans from a bigger game nearby: 95 spectators had been killed at Hillsborough.

West Ham in Easterhouse

Now we are back in Glasgow again. Having left the ivory tower of academic life, I spent ten years (1976-86) with the Southdown Community Project in Bath before moving to the vast estate of Easterhouse where I work for a small voluntary outfit.

I soon found that the Rangers/Celtic divide remained as strong as ever. I was helping a woman obtain a secondhand carpet. She insisted that 'There must be nothing green in it; there's no green in this house.' Initially, I thought she was joking; but, looking around, I could see the blue of Rangers yet not a scrap of Celtic's green. As before, I knew it was best not to identify with either team. However, you cannot avoid talking about football in Easterhouse. The question thus arose whether I should reveal my loyalty to West Ham in an area where English people are about as numerous as genuine socialists in Labour's shadow cabinet. I could not hide my background: as soon as I opened my mouth, youngsters decided I came from the Albert Square they saw on *EastEnders*. So I took to proclaiming, not hiding, West Ham. I boasted about their exploits and argued their supremacy over both Rangers and Celtic. The Scots replied in kind – and with a vengeance. In my five years here, West Ham have been relegated not once but twice. Celtic supporters crowed over me when their team made a million by selling Frank McAvennie to the Hammers where he promptly broke a leg.

Far from provoking ill-feeling, this public and private ribaldry and banter became a source of pleasure, even friendship. To my surprise, I discovered several Easterhouse residents who regarded West Ham as their English team. One woman asked me if I knew her uncle, John Dick. I didn't know him but, during the 1950s, I had watched the tall Scot score many a goal at Upton Park. I discovered that the then West Ham manager, John Lyall, had Scottish parents and that the attacking and passing game – which became the Lyall style – was much admired. Some youngsters began following the West Ham results and presented me with football cards and cuttings about the team.

Just as they have become more interested in the fortunes of West Ham, so I have closely followed the results of Celtic and Rangers. One afternoon, I was determined to ignore the frequent calls at our flat in order to watch a televised 'Old Firm' Cup-tie. After six minutes, the buzzer went. A neighbour was having her contractions. It was her first pregnancy; so would I take her to maternity? Having a minibus in an area where few people possess cars, I agreed. What did miff me was that her bloke thought it more important to stay and watch the football. Yes, football is everywhere in Glasgow – even in the dentist's chair. Our dentist turned out to be Jim Craig, now a football commentator and formerly a member of the famous Lisbon Lions, the Celtic team that was the first British winner of the European Cup in 1967. As I recline with open mouth, Jim provides an impromptu soccer quiz:

'Which Scottish ground is the highest above sea level?'
'Which pitch is completely surrounded by a hedge?'
'Name five Scottish teams whose first letter is the same as their last.'

Unable to respond – partly because I don't know the answers and partly because his drill is in my mouth – I later test him with some English questions:

'How many English teams play their home games in grounds outside their local boundaries?'

You can't be in Glasgow without talking football.

Football – the neighbourhood worker's friend

Football is useful to the neighbourhood worker because it is a means of making contacts, of laughing together, of forming relationships. While living and working on the Southdown council estate in Bath, as leader of the local Community Project, I captained the estate's football team. My legs slowing, I had by now retreated into the goal-keeping position, where I had started. I did not accept responsibility for the growing 'Goals Against' column until the day I overheard two opposing forwards confiding: 'Keep your shots low; the old guy can't get down.' I decided my playing days were over.

In my Easterhouse job, therefore, it has been my role to organise the youngsters' play. Most families on the estate live in tenements without gardens. There is thus a demand for youth activities. As a worker employed by local residents, I try to run clubs in which football plays a prominent part.

On Mondays and Fridays, clubs are held in the Salvation Army premises. All activities occur simultaneously in a single hall. Pool and table-tennis tables, a makeshift tuck shop and various board games stand cheek by jowl in one third of the space. At the far end is a platform on which toys are scattered, an area for darts and stacks of chairs. In between is the football 'pitch'. Players sit on two benches and are called out by numbers, with a maximum of three a side, to kick into goals which consist of sheets of wood. The game calls for the kind of tight ball control that even a Trevor Brooking might admire.

Tuesdays, my colleague and I run five-a-side football at the Easterhouse Project. This building arose from funds raised following Frankie Vaughan's initiative to pacify warring gangs. It consists of two nissen-style halls, one of which serves as the football pitch. Long and narrow, it takes a toll on an ageing referee like me.

Wednesdays, we may go to the Easterhouse Sports Centre. Spacious and with goal nets, this is our Hampden Park. What about football on a proper grass pitch? Hardly ever. Easterhouse possesses numerous outdoor pitches made up of gravel-like red sand. Scores of sociologists have so far failed to identify the reason for Glasgow's macho reputation for male hardness. It has little to do with gangs, razors or Jimmy Boyle. Rather it derives from Saturdays spent on pitches where a sliding tackle merits a skin graft and where a diving goalie deserves the military cross. If you've prepared on these pitches, games on grass become a luxury.

Football, football, football. My life-long love affair with the game has benefited me educationally and socially. Now I find it of use in my job. As a neighbourhood worker, I must not exaggerate its importance. Obviously skills in organising youth activities apart from football – particularly those which have more appeal for girls – advising on welfare rights; debt counselling; accompanying parents to children's hearings; and participating in food co-ops are just as, if not more, important. None the less, a knowledge of football does offer insight into a slice of working-class culture which, in turn, becomes a basis for communication in the neighbourhood. Further, the organisation of football gives youngsters in places like Easterhouse something they want and which often also involves their parents in community activities. Given its significance, it is surprising that vocational training courses which prepare social, community and neighbourhood workers pay so little attention to it.

Still spectating

I'm still spectating. I've been to the Ibrox super stadium. I've experienced the passion at Parkhead. Yet I most enjoy the small grounds which are even older and tattier than their English counterparts: Cowdenbeath amidst the disused coal pits; Albion Rovers, where the tiny crowd is confined to one stand; Montrose, where the stand has just three rows of seats; Stranraer, where the pitch is in a public park; and Arbroath, where a strong kick would land the ball in the sea. And, at all the grounds, the usual band of diehards who sell raffle tickets and chat with you over a cup of Bovril at half-time.

On a snowy January Saturday, I made my first visit to little East Stirling in Falkirk. As I handed over my £2.50, the turnstile keeper pushed back

50p: 'Only £2 for pensioners.' When I protested, he waved me through: 'Don't be embarrassed, dad; in you go.' And in I went. When I *am* a pensioner, I hope I will still be going to the game which has given me so much pleasure.

West Ham fans at the 1923 Cup Final – presumably on their way *in*.

4

Tigers, Tigers, Burning Bright-ish

Alan Plater

I was born in Jarrow, educated by the tribal elders of Tyneside and brought up in Hull. I therefore hold the following truths to be self-evident:

1. The finest footballers in the history of the game were born in County Durham.
2. And the greatest of these was Raich Carter.
3. Hull City Football Club is the natural centre of the sporting cosmos.

These principles are not universally accepted, especially the third. I have passed many happy hours debating it at places as diverse as the Den and Gigg Lane – even at Highbury and White Hart Lane where, by some clerical error, our lads have occasionally strayed.

They don't make Saturdays like that any more

The 1991-92 season saw the Tigers back in the Third Division after six years in the Second. Hand on heart, it was like going home. I started watching professional football on a full-time basis in 1946. City were then in the Third Division (North), as were Gateshead, Barrow, New Brighton, Southport and Accrington Stanley. Why did nobody put a preservation order on Accrington Stanley?

A kid of 11 is, to be sure, an impressionable creature, but I still remember, with crystal clarity, the giants of the period: Tom Callender, Gateshead's elegant centre-half; and Sid Bycroft, Doncaster's rugged equivalent, who was rumoured to offer opposing centre-forwards a choice of hospital.

In those days, a 'striker' was a tradesman in a blacksmith's shop or a man involved in a labour dispute. A 'centre-forward' was a bundle of courage like Wally Ardron of Rotherham or the lethal weapon, George 'Spud' Murphy of Bradford City, a designated villain until he joined City in 1948, whereupon he became an instant folk hero. If I close my eyes, I can see all of them in action. If I open my eyes, I read in the paper that a player I've never heard of has been transferred for a million pounds. It may be a funny old game, but it isn't that funny.

The wonder of life in the nether regions is that hardly anybody lusts for success; those who do are given directions to Leeds or Manchester. We have richer possibilities. Consider: on 14 May 1983, in Division IV, City won 3-1 at Rochdale, with goals by Brian Marwood, Les Mutrie and Garreth Roberts. The crowd was 2,730. All that is in the public record and my personal archive; but the true glory was the announcement on the PA at half-time. In a pure and lovely Rochdale accent the man said:

'For the benefit of the Hull City supporters who came on buses, your buses have now been moved. Now, I could tell you where they've been moved to, but you'll only forget. So your best plan's to ask a policeman.'

He went on to seek support for a forthcoming fund-raising effort in aid of the club: a sponsored walk to Wigan. Obviously, as a professional writer, I have a vested interest in material of that kind. Even so, I wouldn't trade the culture of the lower divisions for all the executive boxes in North London.

As a time-served Luddite, it follows that the shirts bother me too. In our days of innocence teams wore simple arrangements of red, blue, black, white or amber. We tolerated the eccentricity of Plymouth's green, Swansea's all-white and the bizarre blue-and-white quarters of the Rovers in Blackburn and Bristol; but the current vogue for designer logos, on a background of discontinued wallpaper lines in pastel shades, would have brought forth derision.

The sleeping giant

Creative derision has always been a speciality. During a period when City were struggling – twice a year, on average – a supporter stood on the popular side carrying a small banner: on it was painted the single word, BOO, but without an exclamation mark. Wasn't it Bob Paisley who said, 'If you want people to listen, speak quietly'?

There is no need to apologise for continuing to support Hull City: by their allegiances shall ye know them. Indeed, I have always thought that writers should list them with their credits: thus, Anthony Minghella (*Inspector Morse, Truly, Madly, Deeply* and Portsmouth); Neville Smith (*Gumshoe, The Manageress* and Everton); or Keith Dewhurst (*Z Cars, Black Snow* and Manchester United). It might help the critics with their insights, if that matters.

I first met Keith during *Z Cars* days and we perfected a form of tribal

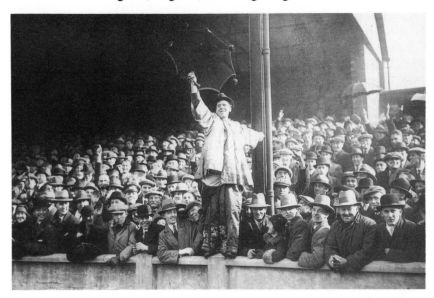

Umbrella stand at Boothferry Park.

Horatio Stratton 'Raich' Carter (right): 'He didn't *play* the game – he presided over it.'

greeting whereby he says, 'How's the sleeping giant?' and I tell him the latest Hull City jokes. These were (and are) routine stuff: e.g. our goal-keeper, in a fit of terminal depression, throws himself onto the railway line and the train goes *under* him; the birds fly upside-down over Boothferry Park because there's nothing worth crapping on; our manager has the players dribbling between rows of dustbins to improve their ball skills – and the dustbins win 3-2.

Hull is the largest city in the land never to have had a team in the First Division. By the same token, we have never won the FA Cup. Hence Keith's sleeping giant routine. Hence also, long ago, a song lyric I wrote, including the verse:

> I'll drink our kid beneath the table
> When The Tigers win the Cup
> And I think I'll marry Betty Grable
> When The Tigers win the Cup
> I will booze all through the night
> I will paint the Guildhall white
> And find a little man to fight
> When the Tigers win the Cup

A jazz piano player called Max wrote a nice tune to match the words, then moved to Copenhagen.

But the giant sometimes stirs and scratches. We scratched the great Manchester United back in the mists of memory – in 1952, to be precise – when we won 2-0 at Old Trafford in the Third Round. The match was dominated by the skill and charisma of Horatio Stratton 'Raich' Carter (Sunderland, Derby County, Hull City and England). These days he'd be called a left-sided midfield player but in truth he re-invented the game as he went along. He had silver hair and he didn't *play* the game – he presided over it. When we had two international inside-forwards – the elegant Scot, Willie Buchan, and the great Dane, Viggo Jensen – Raich wore the number 11 shirt, took all the corners and throw-ins either side of the field and also turned up on the goal-line when necessary, helping Billy Bly to defend a one-goal lead. He did all those Italian jobs – *libero* and *catenaccio* and such – years before the cute critics gave them names and without sweat. He might stroll or even jog a little, but he preferred others to do the running. He was the greatest of his kind; and he knew it. He still knows it. Ask him, and he'll tell you.

In November 1949, Raich, by now player-manager and sensing retirement, signed Don Revie from Leicester City for £20,000. He was to be groomed as the natural successor; but it didn't work. Carter and Revie drifted away and the giant dozed off again.

There was a re-awakening in the mid-1960s, mainly courtesy of ace goal-scorers, Chris Chilton and Ken Wagstaff, nicely timed to give Chelsea a nasty turn at Stamford Bridge in 1966. Tommy Docherty's team, including George Graham and Terry Venables, were sitting comfortably on a 2-0 lead, but Ken scored two in the last ten minutes to force a replay. We lost the replay 3-1 but it was a fair result and I prefer not to think about it.

Ken, incidentally, honed his skills under Raich Carter's tutelage at Mansfield. He now has a pub in Hull. I have no idea what became of Venables and Graham.

Oh look – the twin towers beckon

In 1972, twenty years on from that FA Cup win at Old Trafford, we put out West Ham United 1-0. And we have had glimpses of even greater Cup glory, only to be thwarted by short-sighted referees. When Manchester United beat us 1-0 in the Quarter-Final of 1949, when Stoke City beat us 3-2 in the 1971 Quarter-Final and when Arsenal beat us in the Semi-Final of 1930 – on all three occasions vital decisions went against us.

In 1930, Arsenal who, from all accounts, were both lucky and boring, went on to win the Cup. City, by way of consolation, were relegated to the Third Division (North). And, in 1949, the only goal, scored by Stan Pearson, was (and is) disputed – there's never a Russian linesman around when we need one – and our goalkeeper, the legendary Billy Bly, played almost the entire match with a broken nose. Billy was a sweet man and a superb keeper who fractured easily.

How do I know of these vile injustices, even those committed before I was born? To paraphrase Louis Armstrong: if you have to ask, you wouldn't understand anyway. You are never alone with a football club's mythology.

Oddly enough, local loyalty is a marginal issue. There wasn't a Hull-born player in the 1930 Semi-Final team. Then, as now, the glittering prizes usually went to the best assembly of Scots, Irish and Geordie exiles. Nothing has changed, apart from the token Scandinavian to add a touch of class; and we patented that, too, in the awesome form of Viggo Jensen, mentioned earlier. In 1948, he turned up on the Fish Dock, was introduced to Raich Carter and stayed on for 308 games and 50 goals.

I blame all our present ills on market forces and the 'trickle-down' effect. Before the 1991-92 season, Celtic found themselves with a pot of Paul Elliott gold and gave £1.5 million to Middlesbrough for Tony Mowbray.

Middlesbrough gave £750,000 to us for Andy Payton, our designated goal-scorer during the previous couple of seasons. Theoretically, we should have trickled down a few grand for a bright but cheapo Rover from Doncaster or even a Spartan from Blyth; but the word from the terraces was that the bank got to the money first with the message: the bucks stop here. The wolf has been at the door so long, they've probably given him his own executive box. The giant is asleep again but he isn't tired. He's hungry.

Heyup – it's August again

Yet each new season remains a time of rich promise and reckless prediction. Mine for 1992-93 is that Hull City will do the Double: a Division III play-off spot and the Autoglass Trophy. If we fail, we will fly a small banner bearing the word BOO, steam up the executive boxes with angry breathing and then go look for our buses. I realise Division III is now called Division II because of the Super League scam; but we know our place.

The Double will be some compensation for the disappointment of 1991-92. Given the giant-killing feats of 1952 and 1972, I had hoped that our FA Cup giant-killing was on a 20-year cycle. So, I looked forward in vain to the Euro-year of 1992 – only to see us go out to Chelsea.

Actually, I didn't *see* the Chelsea game, because I hadn't seen the previous rounds at Morecambe and Blackpool. This is a moral stance reaching back two decades. In 1972, 32,290 people showed up at Boothferry Park for the West Ham Cup-tie. Half of them hadn't been near the ground since Raich retired. A man in a suit and fancy overcoat, sitting near me, opened his programme and said, 'Now ... which one's Wagstaff?' I snarled inwardly. It was a double-edged snarl. If the guy didn't know Ken by sight, he shouldn't be there; and Ken wasn't playing anyway.

I took a vow. In the unlikely event of growing up, I would never turn into the sort of man who would behave like that. And I never have.

This chapter has been consolidated, by the author and with the permission of the *Sunday Times*, from two articles that originally appeared in that newspaper: 'It's great to be back ...', 11 August 1991; and 'Tigers, Tigers burning bright', 5 January 1992.

5

How the Saints Keep Marching In

David Bull

This love affair began on Boxing Day 1948, when my father first took me, aged nine, the 23 miles from my native Salisbury to the Dell, Southampton. The Saints not only won 2-1 against Nottingham Forest but also won over – for life – a new fan.

Nowadays, my 81-year-old father lives 45 miles north-east of the ground, while I'm 78 miles north-west. We meet up for two or three games a season, on the bench seats to which Dad retired in his seventies, after a lifetime of standing. For other home games, I share a terrace barrier with fellow-regulars, foregathered from various points west.

Life membership

One of them, Barrie Bedford, another Boxing Day débutant (1946 vintage), reckons that many a child must still be taken to his or her first game as a Christmas treat. If that's so, then the bumper-sticker industry should design a seasonal motto along the lines of the Christmas warning that 'A Dog is for Life'. Doting parents should be advised that the taste for football – at the venue of this initial bonding – may far exceed the lifespan of a puppy.

I say that on two assumptions: some parents won't want to get there early, so as to secure junior a precious place on the wall; and as Tessa Davies and Martin Lacey observe of different generations, taking the kids can interfere with Dad's drinking. Both have been overtaken by legislation: compulsory all-seater stadia and drink-and-drive laws, respectively.

Despite working on Saturday mornings, my father somehow managed always to get me wall-space – a spot in which I could remain for three hours, not worrying about a porous bladder (or was it, as my mother insisted, all in the mind?). The drainage channel running along the wall was ideal for small boys to pee in. Forty years on, while the channel remains, the practice seems hard to imagine – not least for reasons of sexual equality, so strongly championed in this book. Yet, as I recall, it was then the done thing.

I am conscious of having been sacrificed only once for the sake of pub-stops. My first real 'home' team, Salisbury City, were playing away to

Wimbledon in the FA Amateur Cup. Dad and a workmate had taken a rare Saturday morning away from the building site in order to make an early start. It was such an event that Mum and I stood in the road to wave them off. Only as the party receded over the horizon did she let out their secret: they were going to a football match without me. I hesitate to admit to my mortified reaction: whoever heard of anybody crying at not being allowed to watch Wimbledon?

Those were good days to be watching Salisbury City: tussles with Trowbridge Town, both in the Western League and FA Cup; and all those Amateur Cup-ties against fancy teams from London and beyond, with double-barrelled names like Walton & Hersham, Brentwood & Warley and Harwich & Parkestone.

Apart from the obstacle of Dad's long hours – he often worked Saturday *afternoons*, too – I encountered, in September 1950, a new threat to my appearances at the Dell: I started at the local grammar school, where Saturday morning attendance was a requirement and rugby the ethos. One teacher, 'Scruff' (such was the state of his beard), would regularly advise us to 'read any English book you've got', while he, William Golding, busied himself with other things, such as writing *Lord of the Flies*. He was obliged to participate, though, in those sessions where one of us had to address our classmates on a chosen topic. The class would then award marks, in the manner of ice-skating judges, for style, interest and so on. I'd obviously not understood the rules: when it came to my turn, I gave a goal-by-goal account of Salisbury 6 Winchester City 5, after extra time. I can still picture Scruff's barely-suppressed wince as he added his 'master's mark' to whatever total my classmates had accorded to my first, dismal exercise in football reporting.

No sooner had I reached an age when a few classmates and I could head straight from Saturday morning lessons to Southampton, than the family moved to Camberley – 47 miles from the Dell, but only seven from Aldershot. I saw more than my share of superstars at the Recreation Ground – thanks to the games against an 'All-Star XI' with which Aldershot launched its floodlights. What a privilege to see, in the same forward line, Peter Doherty, Raich Carter (Alan Plater's silver-haired hero) and Stanley Matthews (Bruce George's 'greatest living Englishman'). I don't suppose I'll ever again see a penalty like the one taken by Carter and Doherty. One of them (I forget which) stepped up and stabbed the ball a yard or two forward. The other followed up to score.

For more serious fare, I was now but a commuter-ride from London. Thus was I able, in the 1950s, to see Manchester City unfold its 'Revie Plan' at the Valley; to watch the Busby Babes in a classic at White Hart Lane; and to be locked into Stamford Bridge – with John Major and 75,000 others – for the 1955 Championship 'decider' against Wolves.

After 1958, I never again lived within 50 miles of the Dell. That was the year I went to university. Having applied, with pre-UCCA licence, all over the land – including Southampton (in vain) – I was accepted in three First Division cities, including Manchester. But, for academic reasons, I chose to become a soccer exile in Exeter. I was offered an escape, in 1961, to a research post in Edinburgh. The job interview included an exercise which invited me to reflect on the religious issues dividing Hearts and Hibs – although it emerged that I was the only candidate who thought so. I turned down this move to remain in the south-west until, in 1963, another First Division opportunity arose in Manchester. This time I grabbed it and stayed for seven years of memorable football. Then, early in the 1970-71 season – just two weeks after I'd witnessed the strange spectacle, at Elland Road, of Saints' Jimmy Gabriel being *sent* off on a stretcher for giving Allan Clarke no more than he deserved – I moved to Bristol, whence I've travelled to many a 'home' game, 78 tortuous miles down the A36.

Along all those roads, I continued mainly to watch the Saints: Manchester was an excellent hub from which to follow the promotion run of 1965-66, which took Southampton into Division I for the first time. True, there were lots of opportunities for less partisan experiences, not only at Maine Road and Old Trafford, but also during the 1966 World Cup, when I saw those two Goodison Park classics – Brazil v Hungary and Portugal v South Korea – and, in that one magical fortnight, Beckenbauer, Eusebio, Pélé and Yashin.

But I digress into dalliances, adventures away from my love for Southampton FC. If I am to avoid a chronological tale, I need to focus on half a dozen topics that will enable me, I hope, to illustrate my loyalties and passions: the role of the extended family; means of keeping in touch with one's 'home' team; getting tickets; grounds and games; competing loyalties; my heroes; and my occasional occupation of the 'inside-track'.

Keeping it in the family

For most contributors to this book, football loyalties embrace three generations: that of their parents; their own – and the prospects of following the game with a partner; and their children's.

During my second season, I completed my set of 11 pairs of aunts and uncles, when my father's youngest sister married into a family of South-

ampton supporters on the northern fringe of the Saints' hinterland. I was
next to meet them, in the week this book went to press, as we assembled
for Uncle Jack's funeral and glumly contemplated Life-after-Shearer.
Dad's side of the family was otherwise more barren, football-wise, than
Mum's. Her youngest brother introduced me to Salisbury City. Her sister
and brother-in-law, Else and George, have served innumerable teas for the
umpteen fellow-fans with whom I've called in for a 5.30 pm post mortem
on our way from the Dell to Bristol. And another brother, Fred, deserves a
medal, for reasons set out below, for his enduring nourishment of my
obsession.

I recalled, in this book's introduction, how, despite her interest in the
1966 World Cup, I failed to introduce my mother to the Dell. That break-
through for her generation was left to Uncle Fred, who courted and
converted for his third wife an anti-football partner. When he married Anne
in 1989, Dad and I treated them, as a wedding present, to seats for Saints v
Spurs. I paid a fiver to have the news of their wedding flashed across the
electronic scoreboard – surely one of the more customer-friendly features
of today's football-marketing.

My own generation's football-watching has been less male-dominated:
I have introduced three women – natives of Manchester, Birmingham and
Bristol – to the Saints. Two of them, and one of their daughters, became
keen – if not lasting – followers. Florence, a Mancunian, followed the Saints
all over the north, including Huddersfield on our honeymoon in September
1964. But her loyalties were suspect: she became such a fan of Ken
Wimshurst that when he transferred to Bristol City, in November 1967, so
did she. For the next few seasons, I accompanied Flo to several Bristol City
games in the north. Then, when we separated in 1970, I moved to Bristol
and stopped following the City – although I did keep in touch with Ken
Wimshurst, a lovely man and a source of Wembley tickets.

One of those tickets was for Margaret, a Bristolian whom I introduced
to the Saints on 3 March 1979, for a 2-0 win over Arsenal. She *loved* it and
demanded a ticket for the League Cup Final with Forest, just two weeks
away. I already had the two I needed, but was pleased to have an Ashton
Gate ticket transferred to one of the few locals with a *right* to be there –
even if it was only her second game. I subsequently formed a household
with Margaret and her three children. The two oldest, both boys, were
beyond conversion to live football; but, in March 1982, Rebecca (then aged
nine) made her debut on the Dell terraces.

Her thorough-going interest lasted into her teens, taking in the FA Cup
Semi-Finals of 1984 and 1986, until she and her mother drifted away from

Putting her Saints' foot forward
… for Mike Channon, David
Bull's super-hero.

live football. Rebecca acquired a good knowledge of the game and will often better my recall or recognition when we watch *A Question of Sport*. I have enjoyed assisting, then, in her triumph over the socialising forces at her junior school – my anger at which I vented in the introduction.

Keeping in touch

In its *Sports Echo*, Southampton is one of those towns still served by a 'Football Pink' each Saturday of the season. I am greatly indebted to Uncle Fred who, since 1954, has weekly sent me the *Echo*. It takes a special kind of dependability to remember, every weekend of the season, to wrap and post a newspaper for Tuesday morning arrival. We are talking of some 1,350 packings and postings to date. When the *Encyclopaedia of Football Loyalties* comes to be compiled, I shall book an entry on Uncle Fred.

Yet from 4.40 pm on Saturday until breakfast on Tuesday is a long time to wait for an in-depth analysis of your favourites' performance. I *used* to fill that gap with *Sport in the West* and its detailed on-the-spot accounts of games from the Severn to the Solent. The station's medium-wave proximity to Radio Luxembourg made reception difficult in Manchester – until I invested in a powerful second-hand radio. This huge toy became something of an overkill when I left Manchester, in 1970, for a flat in Bristol, about 200 yards from where this excellent entertainment was broadcast. And my box became even more redundant when the serious stuff of regional radio gave way to the tedious trivia (football coverage excepted) of local radio.

At the national end of the radio spectrum, we can rely on *Sports Report*, or its midweek companions, to which many a fan will continue to tune in from across the water – as I have, both in Galway and Brittany. In 1991-92, however, I began the season further south – out of medium-wave range and in need of the BBC's World Service on short-wave. One Saturday afternoon was virtually dedicated to a Manchester City fan awaiting City's score before getting married in Boston, Massachusetts. I inevitably recalled various efforts – mostly at weddings; on holiday; or on business abroad – to keep abreast of the Saints.

I guess we all have our wedding stories. On 2 January 1965, when I was best man at an Exeter wedding reception, a nicely timed exit to the allotted hotel changing room enabled me to hear a report of Terry Paine's two missed penalties in a 2-2 draw at Northampton. I had to run, though, on 17 September 1966, when, as *Sports Report* loomed, my holiday found me up a mountain path above Buttermere. Fortunately, it was downhill all the way and I reached the car radio just in time to hear how the Saints' keeper, Campbell Forsyth, had broken a leg in the home defeat by Liverpool.

In recent seasons I've often found myself working in Sweden or North America – usually in the early season or around Semi-Final time. Unlike the bridegroom from Maine Road, I tend to tune in to the World Service more by luck than judgment; so I've had to rely on finding the right newspaper. The Swedish Sundays carry the British results in very full detail. I was mystified, though, on 25 September 1989, to read that Saints had won 1-0 at Derby, thanks to a goal by 'självmål'. I could work out, from the League tables, that 'mål' was a goal, so I figured that an unnamed Derby player had conceded an own-goal. Naturally, confirmation of my translation was my immediate objective when I arrived at my Swedish hosts that evening. Yes, they assured me, I'd got it right; but, said my host's brother, 'I think you'll find it was a deflection from a shot by Rodney Wallace.' Marvelling at his dual command – of our language and of our football results – I learned that he was a football reporter, a keen follower of the British game who'd been briefed to expect a Southampton fan.

Such welcomes are, of course, harder to come by in the USA, a country singularly ill-equipped to host the next World Cup Finals. The Sunday edition of the *New York Times* does carry our Saturday scores; but for match reports, and for midweek coverage, you'll need the British papers. It was in 1977 that I first found an unofficial 'library' of them: the Ottawa branch of W.H. Smith took several tabloids, cleared them slowly and allowed you to browse. That's where I discovered that Mike Channon had moved to Maine Road. He was back at the Dell by the time of my next North American trip, when I tracked his progress with the help of a more official library – that of a Law School in Detroit. Its professors and students need the 'London *Times*' (as they call it) for the law reports; I needed it to study the start of the 1980-81 season, as Kevin Keegan and Charlie George teamed up with the born-again Channon.

Ticket tales

How does the geographically mobile fan get tickets for all-ticket games? Credit-card bookings will not totally eliminate the need for contacts and ruses when it comes to access to tickets for away games and admission to Wembley.

I think of the 1963 FA Cup Semi-Final, when Saints went out 1-0 to Manchester United at Villa Park. I did the obvious thing: I rang the only Villa fan I knew and asked him to get me four tickets. To say 'knew' is a wilful exaggeration. I'd met him only once and briefly at that; but that was more than sufficient to establish a shared passion that made my approach predictable and his willingness to queue a formality.

That 1960s fashion has been rendered more difficult, of course, by modern methods of crowd segregation. But who wants to be penned into the visitors' enclosure and to be imprisoned there, after the final whistle, for as long as the police fancy? My concern to avoid such ignominy, for a Fratton Park cup-derby in 1984, meant the usual phone call – to a Bristol Rovers fan in exile at Portsmouth Polytechnic. He duly got me tickets for the Pompey terraces, where we should not have courted hostility by wearing our Cup-tie favours. It was preferable to the standard prison sentence, but I'm now prepared to compromise: until the compulsory all-seater stadia abolish the freedom of choice that Conservative governments have deceitfully promised me, I shall probably *choose* to sit down at the bigger away games.

In fact, I long ago tried sitting away from home – having been introduced, at Gigg Lane one evening in 1964, to a whole cult, among away fans, of lingering outside the visitors' entrance to cadge complimentary seats. It seemed distasteful, but I became hooked during the promotion run of 1965-66 – especially after meeting, thereby, the son of Saints' trainer, Jimmy Gallagher. A student at Salford University, he became our car passenger and ticket-collector.

The promotion-clinching game was at Brisbane Road. Arriving too late for freebies, I was ready to pay at the turnstiles; but some of the players thought that an impossible indignity for the trainer's son and his Manchester minders. So Stuart Williams instructed me to tuck my red and white sombrero into my coat and to follow him. He led us to the dressing-room door, where Terry Paine took over. He shepherded us, with that inimitable swagger of his, up the players' tunnel, past the police sentry, over the wall and onto the terraces. As I say, I was more than willing to pay for admission to this historic match; but to follow Paine up the players' tunnel exceeded my most ludicrous fantasies.

Whatever the ticket arrangements, admission to League grounds is one thing; getting into a Wembley Final is another. As a longstanding objector to the outrageous system (subsequently tempered, albeit insufficiently) of allocating so many tickets to the unaffiliated, I was more than willing to trace tickets into such neutral hands and to buy them – at face-value, of course. Contacts at two non-participating clubs – Plymouth Argyle and Bristol City – proved our saviours in 1976. The Ashton Gate ticket came courtesy of Ken Wimshurst, a star of the Saints' 1963 Cup-run, whose transfer to Bristol City I mentioned earlier. By now on the City staff, he was likewise to come good, as I explained, for the League Cup Final in 1979. By then, I'd acquired quite a taste for this way of securing Wembley tickets for their rightful holders. Unfortunately, I've not since had occasion to engage in such self-righteous redistribution.

The 1992 ZDS Final presented no problem, for one very simple reason: I have no intention of watching games that are manifestations of hypocrisy by clubs who belly-ache about too many fixtures and who enter Noddy Cup Competitions. Leave me out!

Grounds and games

Counting Wembley and the Dell, I have seen the Saints play at 50 venues. Like a jittery batsman, I'd been stuck a while on 49 until it happened: on 3 December 1988 I reached my half-century – at Plough Lane, the very ground to which Dad had sneaked off without me almost 40 seasons earlier.

Brisbane Road is extra special – for three games, one seen as a neutral, two as a partisan. The first, on a Good Friday evening in the early 1960s, was a goalless draw v Luton and the third match that my pillion passenger, Ted Moffatt, and I had seen that day. We'd done West Ham v Cardiff in the morning and Spurs (his team) v Blackburn in the afternoon. That should have been more than enough. It was.

. The other two games at Brisbane Road were magic moments. By the oddest coincidence, the Saints virtually clinched promotion there, both in 1966 and 1978, with 1-1 draws. I've revealed how Terry Paine secured my access to the first climax. His equalising goal – a rare header – would give Southampton their first taste of Division I, always provided they avoid a 6-0 defeat in their remaining game. A goalless draw at Maine Road satisfied both teams: City went up as Champions; Saints as runners-up.

So I experienced a superstitious thrill of anticipation when, studying the fixtures for 1977-78, I noticed that the Saints' penultimate game would be at Brisbane Road. True to the script, they went into that game, needing a draw to be almost sure of promotion. As in 1966, the home team took the lead; Saints came back with a header (by Tony Funnell); and a subsequent 0-0 draw (with Spurs) took both teams up.

All those 0-0 draws! Actually, I've seen two or three entertaining goalless draws. On the other hand, I've yet to see a goal feast to match the 6-5 spectacular that I described to William Golding. I *have* witnessed a 10-goal treat – when the Saints beat Coventry 8-2 in 1983-84. But the strange date, in this regard, was 18 September 1965. I was at the Hawthorns for West Bromwich Albion 6 Stoke City 2, while Saints were beating

Wolves 9-3 at the Dell. Imagine being at an eight-goal display, but envying those who'd seen a dozen!

It's customary, of course, to blame goalkeepers who let in nine – especially if they're Scottish and you're Jimmy Greaves (or Bruce George: see below). So it was very fair-minded of Ted Bates to buy the Wolves keeper, Dave MacLaren, the following season. This former hero of Stephen Wagg's (see his chapter) was Scottish. And so was the man he came to replace: Campbell Forsyth had broken his leg, you will recall, while I was up a mountain. And so, too, was Eric Martin who arrived, in turn, to replace MacLaren later in that first season at the top. Whatever would Jimmy Greaves make of a side that fielded three Scottish goalkeepers in one season? He'd have to overlook the blinders I saw MacLaren and Martin play in 1-0 away wins – at Elland Road and Goodison Park, respectively.

Competing loyalties

It should by now be apparent that I was inescapably hooked on Boxing Day 1948.

My greatest chance of defection from the Saints came during my seven seasons in Manchester. I was able, there, to enjoy the skills of Best, Law, Charlton and their under-rated supply line called Crerand. And, as Rob Behrens reminds us below, things were happening at Maine Road, too, under Mercer and Allison. But during 1963-70, I was well-placed to watch the Saints on 24 grounds from Coventry to Carlisle – even if I did take, and use, a tent for the trip to Brunton Park.

Going to Old Trafford was problematic. Unable ever to be neutral, I invariably favour the underdog. In those vintage United years, that usually meant support for the visitors. But there was a contrary pull: savouring the prospect of European Cup-ties, I needed United to win. I even ran on to the pitch, in May 1967, to celebrate the League Championship (not realising that Phil Lee – see his chapter – was watching me from his perch in the Stretford End roof).

Heroes

When it comes to football heroes, I've never gone in for older men. I reserved my judgment, during my first eight seasons, until I could admire first a peer and then my juniors. The peer was Terry Paine, whom I first saw at Aldershot on 23 March 1957. It was his second game; he scored his first of 160 League goals for the club; and it was his 18th birthday (just four months before mine). I went home to tell Dad that I had seen a future

England international. I've since ventured such a prediction on five initial sightings: correctly for Martin Chivers, Steve Williams and Mark Wright; wrongly for Reuben Agboola; and – still hoping – for Matthew Le Tissier.

Terry Paine was the most remarkable floater of a cross I have ever seen. And what a goal-scoring record for a winger! I've already rejoiced in his goals at Orient and Aldershot and I enjoyed many others, especially the late winner against Charlton, late in the 1965-66 promotion run. That goal was laid on by Martin Chivers, whose deceptive speed, in a run from his own half, left Billy Bonds trailing. Without ever entering the hero class (partly because he eased out George O'Brien, another favourite), Chivers moved to Spurs, making way for a super-hero, a gangling young lad from my mother's native village of Shrewton, on the edge of Salisbury Plain.

Enter Mike Channon! When I saw his third game, at Deepdale in April 1966, he could barely stand up, let alone stand out. But his ability to leave opponents standing – or, very often, sitting – became beautiful to behold. With his combination of speed, cheek, close control and positional instinct, he made enough chances to re-write the record books. But his entertainer's urge to score brilliant goals seemingly helped him to miss far more goals than he converted. In that respect, he reminded me of Bobby Charlton. Compared, though, with that rather over-exposed commentator on the game, Channon must be one of the most 'natural' pundits that football has produced. Anyone who saw the Christmas special that he and Keegan fronted for LWT must wonder at ITV's decision ever to use the services of St John reading straight-lines from his autocue to set up another over-rehearsed scoring chance for the once-spontaneous Greaves.

My esteem for Paine and Channon – with 1,216 League appearances and 345 goals between them – may never be equalled. The premium on player mobility, from the lure of the lira to the new northern millionaires, makes it unlikely that Southampton FC can ever again retain two such brilliant long-running servants: witness the departure, in successive close seasons, of Rodney Wallace and Alan Shearer.

Three other homespun talents merit a mention here. I have a special affinity for the late Steve Mills. I saw his Saints debut (v Notts County in the League Cup, 3 October 1972); his League debut, later that season at Stamford Bridge; and his England Under-23 debut in 1974. Like many of his admirers, I looked forward to his full England debut, but a car accident put a premature end to his career. Next came Steve Williams, a playmaker of so much talent. But too much fouling and mouthing stupidly blotted his copybook. And now Le Tissier. Despite a Williams temperament, he ought surely to have gone all the way; but Graham Taylor could maintain the longstanding tradition, whereby languid genius – of the likes of Bowles, Currie, Marsh, George and Osgood – is squandered by England managers in search of wearisome workhorses.

Charlie George and Peter Osgood are readily excluded from my heroes' gallery, along with Keegan and the other 'Golden Oldies' whom Lawrie McMenemy brought to the Dell: qualification for my gallery depends upon being homegrown. I'd contemplate a few exceptions. Ron Davies almost made it; but, within his generation, he was overshadowed by Wimshurst and Paine. The Yugoslav, Ivan Golac, was very special. His volley, against West Brom in February 1981, was as good a goal as you would want to see (and as the Albion keeper, Tony Ogden, might have liked to see). And then there was another languid No. 9, under-used, like George and Osgood, by England. I refer to Frank Worthington, who made, in one season (1983-84), the kind of impact that made you wish you'd watched him for the previous 15 or so.

Inside track

I have never aspired to be one of football's 'insiders': on the contrary, I've had occasion to decline invitations to step inside. By and large, Danny Baker would be proud of my attempts to remain independent.

I have confessed, though, to my temporary membership of the complimentary ticket-cadgers. Apart from enabling me to follow Terry Paine up the players' tunnel at Brisbane Road and to pursue Ken Wimshurst for Wembley tickets, this inside track afforded several treasured moments – like being able to re-live, with Martin Chivers, the run, described earlier, that made the vital goal against Charlton. Some 20 seasons later, as I explained in the introduction, I enjoyed more inside moments as I fulfilled some of my aspirations to *participate* by writing in the club programme. These included admission to the directors' tea-room, when the club won the programme-of-the-year award in 1986.

Finally, a most memorable evening on the inside – the club's centenary dinner in February 1986. I was seated with two managers of yesteryear: Bill Dodgin and George Roughton, neither of whom needed prompting to reminisce. And then there was the autograph-hunting. Between courses, grown men (several older than I) plagued the tables, collecting the signatures of Saints' players spanning more than 50 years. My menu has 70 autographs on it, including that of Ted Drake (1931-34), the legend who goes back to John Arlott's days. He wasn't taking too much notice of me as he autographed yet another menu – until I ventured to mention that this one was 'for my Dad', who had seen him play. Mr Drake turned, beamed and enquired, as if he'd known my father from schooldays, 'How's he keeping?'

I could assure Ted Drake that my father keeps going. He still keeps going to the Dell, with the fan he introduced to the ground, and its unpredictable entertainers, 44 seasons ago.

So now you're going to believe us: we've won the Cup (1976).

6

Baggies They're Mine

Roger Bullock

West Bromwich Albion were in my blood. Nurture and nature fused to produce that 'love that will not let me go'. That was the favourite hymn of the Reverend Fred Sutton, who came to know the Albion well as many a baptism, wedding and funeral at Trinity Church was interrupted by roars from the nearby terraces – much as the Reverend Jack House has experienced (see Chapter 15) when officiating hard by Ashton Gate.

Victorian beginnings

It all began with my Grandad. He'd followed the Baggies since the 1890s. He had the programme for the first-ever game at the Hawthorns in 1900 and could recall walking through cornfields to get there. He'd seen the 1912 Cup Final replay, when Barnsley robbed Albion with a late goal, and he knew personally many of the pre-war stars. Jesse Pennington, W. G. Richardson and Jimmy Murphy – to whose later role at Old Trafford Phil Lee pays tribute in his chapter – were all pals of his. And special among his friends were the remarkable father-and-son goalkeeping duo of Hubert and Harold Pearson, who jointly served Albion continuously for 28 years.

Like many wartime babies, I had a much older brother. His Albion interests were well-established by the time I was dimly aware of a wider environment. And when I was on my mother's lap beside the roaring fire for a bed-time Rupert story, he would be sitting at the table looking at annuals and writing out the fixtures for his imaginary league, an activity which my Grandma called 'a-footballin', and whose secrecy and privacy were universally respected.

So, I was well socialised before my first match, a Division I game: Albion v Derby on 24 February 1951. Despite costing me ninepence to get in and threepence for a programme (I soon learned that this expenditure could be recouped by collecting beer bottles for a halfpenny each or by selling my programme for fourpence to supporters anxious to interpret the half-times on the score-board) and despite Jackie Stamps's late winner for County, I still cannot adequately describe the thrill of that afternoon and the instant love of the Albion it engendered. What a cluster of contests then ensued, each one seared into my memory: Albion 1 Blackpool 3 – with their forward line of Matthews, Mudie, Mortensen, Brown and Perry; Albion v Charlton, with the great Sam Bartram beaten three times.

Each of these games recalls a childhood. Their memory invokes all the smells and sounds of Lower Trinity Street. The opening day of the 1952-53 season began with us eating pikelets in my Grandma's house and listening to *Sports Report*. We waited as the announcer went down the First Division and heard Tottenham Hotspur 3 ... oh! wailing and gnashing of teeth; then – wait for it – ... West Bromwich Albion 4! To read this scoreline today is to recall Grandma's unique custard pie, her mysterious outside loo and the wild lupins that flourished in her back-yard.

To a child in a happy home, everything seemed permanent and sunny. Sunny in that I recall a 3-2 win over Newcastle, during Albion's Cup-winning run of 1953-54, when 60,330 people packed the ground with another 20,000 locked out. Pressed since noon against the perimeter wall, we junior fans were not allowed to put our legs over the rim. The bodies of unconscious fans were passed over our heads to the first-aid men on the red gravel that surrounded the pitch. Dozens passed out in what I recall were tropical conditions; yet the date was 20 February, a time of year when now, in spite of the 'greenhouse effect', I will watch football only if protected from the chill by long coms and a padded anorak.

It seemed eternal, too, in that players' names hardly changed. Jimmy Sanders, Ronnie Allen, Len Millard, Ray Barlow and Gordon Lee were permanent fixtures. Indeed, they did stay longer in those days, the average for those five being 14 years; but a later scrutiny of club records shows that Jackie Vernon had gone by 1952 and Stan Rickaby by 1955. Even the adverts on the stand – Loo Bloom the tailor and Johnnie Walker – displayed names as fixed as any patron saint.

To a child, an interest in football and the local club seemed inextricably linked with the community. You saw players on the bus; Johnnie Nicholls once passed by our park game and shouted 'Good save, Ginger' as our goalie crashed into the pile of coats; Ted Sandford kept a café next to the ground; Jack Sankey drank in the Royal Oak and was allegedly a scout; while David Burnside, the amazing ball juggler from Bristol, lodged with Mrs Maybury, who recently celebrated 68 years as an Albion fan.

Matches also impinged on family and school life, so that, even 40 years on, I can picture the exact scene. On 5 September 1951, I skipped my piano lesson to see Albion 3 Newcastle 3 and got smacked. Two years later, as a scholarship boy recently admitted to the famous King Edward's School, I committed an even graver crime: I skipped the Bromsgrove Match, a rugby game played for the Siviter-Smith cup, to go and see Bolton and Nat Lofthouse. My delinquency obviously peaked early.

Something to cry about

But the highlight of my early life was May Day 1954 when Albion beat Preston in the Cup Final after being 2-1 down. Charlie Wayman's second goal for North End seemed grossly offside as we watched it on our television, purchased for the occasion along with a distorting magnifying glass and specially-designed TV lamp. I naturally cried at the referee's indifference to our appeals, only to be told off, by the less sentimental members of my family, for being so silly.

Of course, there were many high-spots to follow: the 1968 Cup win, the reign of Ron Atkinson and the Regis-Cunningham combination. Each is clearly associated with various episodes and events in my life. I remember hearing in 1973, on a crackling radio in Algeria, news that Crystal Palace had lost and were to be relegated; could this save Albion, I wondered? Alas, on my return to Heathrow ten days later, a desperately-purchased newspaper revealed a terrible truth: Albion were not only down but bottom of the League.

Occasional blips of success apart, Albion's subsequent history has been one of slow decline. There were many warning shots: the earlier demise of the great northern town clubs; the collapse of former League Champions and near neighbours, Wolves; losing to lowly Brighton in the League Cup in 1977; and the terrible season of 1985-86, when every negative club record was broken. It all culminated in 1991, with the ignominious 4-2 Cup defeat by Woking and relegation to Division III for the first time in Albion's 112-year history.

So the fixture list which once billed Arsenal, Spurs and Manchester United among its forthcoming attractions now advertises Hartlepool, Torquay and the Autoglass Cup. *The A-Z of Albion*, published in the still hopeful times of 1979, says, of Darlington, 'Their long but low key history has involved Albion only once' – blissfully unaware that the Baggies would be very grateful to snatch a late winner at Feethams some 12 years later.

Why the passion?

So what is it about Albion that still arouses such passion? Why at the age of 49, working 200 miles away from the Hawthorns, do I still hope that my travels will fit in with Albion's matches? Why did I slope away from the

THE FOOTBALL ASSOCIATION
CHALLENGE CUP

SEMI-FINAL TIE

Photograph by A. Wilkes & Son, West Bromwich.

WEST BROMWICH ALBION
v.
PORT VALE

At VILLA PARK, BIRMINGHAM
SATURDAY, MARCH 27th 1954
KICK-OFF 3 p.m.

OFFICIAL PROGRAMME ISSUED BY ASTON VILLA F.C.
SIXPENCE

J. Goodman & Sons (Printers) Ltd., Birmingham, 4.

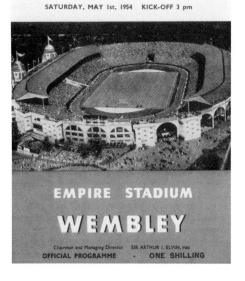

THE FOOTBALL ASSOCIATION CHALLENGE CUP COMPE

FINAL TIE

PRESTON NORTH END
V
WEST BROMWICH ALBION

SATURDAY, MAY 1st, 1954   KICK-OFF 3 pm

EMPIRE STADIUM
WEMBLEY

Chairman and Managing Director   SIR ARTHUR J. ELVIN, MBE
OFFICIAL PROGRAMME   ·   ONE SHILLING

most prestigious dinner to which I have ever been invited to hear the Albion result on my car radio?

There are obviously personal reasons: connections with one's roots; the need for continuity; the memories of happier times; and so on. A Freudian analyst would have a field-day with such fixations and dependencies. But is it any more regressive than other infantile pursuits? Is my following the Albion another man's model railway or rugby club brawl?

There is a sociological view, too. The pains of upward social mobility, and the guilt associated with it, have to be overcome and, like some latter-day Richard Hoggart, following the Albion is my way, spurious and pretentious as it might be. Certainly, it makes for a life of contrasts. A Saturday in 1968 saw a tea party in the Fellows' Garden at King's College, Cambridge, followed by Albion v West Ham at 7.30; and you would be surprised how many Fellows wanted to come. In 1976, I had no sooner cheered Albion's third goal against Carlisle than I had to rush with my cello to play in a 6 pm kick-off St Matthew Passion. Such schizoid cultural experiences seem to enrich my life-style rather than shatter it.

George Mikes, a shrewd observer of British society, once remarked that the middle classes do nothing that is not to their advantage; so what is in all this for me? As a social researcher, I am paid to chart social change and explore its effects. Football may be said to reflect the state of the nation, so it seems as good a place as any to start. But while the insights gleaned are certainly useful, they do not explain why it has to be Albion.

Naturally, over a 40-year period, a great many social changes have been observed. People no longer come to the match on bikes and gone are the entries where you could park them for threepence. Flat caps, rattles and bugles have also disappeared. Bingo came and went, singing began in 1966, reaching a climax of obscenity in the mid-70s. Hooliganism, the bane of the last 15 years, has declined to the point that a riot at Albion v Bury now seems inconceivable. Cigarettes and oranges, the fragrance of the crowd in the 1950s, have been replaced by burgers and Brut.

Baggies' Black Country home

But some changes reflect much wider social trends. The Black Country has seen terrible industrial decline with most of the iron and engineering plants gone. Men no longer carry that foundry smell and the sacrifice of pre-flood-light days, when workers had to go back to late shifts after watching afternoon games, is no longer required.

The Black Country also has a very different population from the 1950s. Immigration from New Commonwealth countries has changed the character of the younger age groups, although not very many black people go to matches. Support from the Handsworth side of the ground has, therefore, declined, reinforcing that frontier between Sandwell and Birmingham that is so important to locals but so invisible to outsiders. There is also little doubt that the crowds have become more yobbish, and the *Family Favourites*, middle-brow, pre-match music I enjoyed as a boy has long been replaced by the latest popular din. Again, the presence of the Shirley Silver Prize Band, playing *Zampa* before big matches, and the mass stamping to Jimmy Shand records at half-time on cold days seem to belong to a bygone age.

The team, too, has become remote and mercenary. I do not know where any of them live any more and one catches only an occasional glimpse of flashy sponsored cars. Players come and go, sometimes on loan, with bewildering frequency. Do 11-year-olds today see them as permanent as I saw that 1954 Cup-winning side? They were real Albion players, I thought, even though only two of them actually came from anywhere near West Bromwich.

But my enduring feeling, as an ageing, middle-class fan living 200 miles away, is one of ambivalence. The ambience of the Hawthorns is full of contradictions. At one level, there are executive boxes with mobile phones and satellite coverage of sporting events across the world; at another, the same wooden shed is selling the same beef drink that I supped 40 years ago.

To one who enjoys the benefits of middle-class life, there is much that I personally dislike about the fans: the litter; the aggression; the sheer lack of urbanity. But, having seen how good a service industry can be and having known 'value for money', I have also overwhelming feelings of sadness. Supporters seem to be 'ripped off' at every turn. The services for spectators are atrocious, the style of buying a ticket is 'take it or leave it' – no one has time to discuss your seat preference – and, although it grieves me to say it, Third Division football is poor stuff for £8. Indeed, as the ball is in the air for most of the time, there is a danger that, if you sit too far back in the stand, you miss most of the match.

And yet the fans still have great qualities that I cherish. Although some still look poor in terms of dress and physical condition – 'uncared for', as a Dutch visitor once put it – there is much to admire. Of course, they all hate the Villa – an attitude to which I whole-heartedly subscribe and which makes me wonder how the country has avoided permanent civil war – but they are still very fair: witness their clapping in of the visiting goalie. And they still appreciate skill, they still mock pretentiousness and they still give generously to those in need. Indeed, their lack of envy for players earning big money tells us more about class attitudes than a dozen sociological surveys. While they appear bemused and frustrated that Albion were not in the running for Gazza, they know full well that Albion are not much of a side and winning a major trophy can be only a dream. The Black Country wit is also as sharp as ever and does much to relieve the gloom of seeing Albion struggle for a draw on a January afternoon.

So that is how a self-indulgent Albion fan feels in 1992. I never expected a drop to Division III and, with the advent of a Super League, I suspect that the Albion I first knew is gone forever. But not all is lost and the Black Country resilience never ceases to amaze me. How many times has the earth around the Hawthorns been ravished – by farmers, coal owners, iron masters and, lately, the M5 motorway?

Indeed, some things have turned out better than expected. Hooliganism is in decline and racial abuse has not set in despite the forecasts of the former local MP, Enoch Powell. As a cog in the local community, Albion have played their part in this, being a club with little history of spectator trouble and one of the first to field a multi-racial side. So that is why the Albion are still important to me. They give focus, fun and fellowship to the many thousands for whom the Black Country is 'home'.

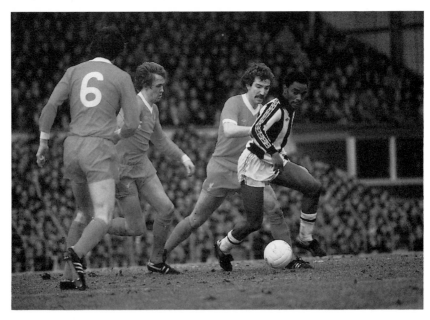

Albion were one of the first clubs to field a multi-racial side. Laurie Cunningham leaves Liverpool standing.

7

Bonkers about Burnley

Alastair Campbell

It was at 4 am on 2 April 1975, as I settled down to sleep in a rowing boat in the West Yorkshire village of Micklethwaite, that I realised I was probably mad.

The journey had started at my home in Leicester almost 24 hours earlier, from where I'd hitched to Burnley to join a supporters' bus to Carlisle, where we lost 4-2, before we got back on the bus which broke down, meaning by the time we got to Burnley I'd lost all hope of getting home to Leicester so I tried to thumb it to Micklethwaite where I would prevail upon a family friend from the days when we lived in Keighley, my birthplace, to put me up, but no cars ever came and I walked and I walked and I walked until I got there at 4 am and decided it was too late to wake them up so I went to sleep in the boat in the garage. Complicated? Following Burnley always has been.

Friends in high places

I was 18 and, if not mad, certainly mad about Burnley. I still am. I was at school in Leicester, where we'd moved seven years earlier, and which I hated, not least because people in Leicester supported Leicester and didn't take Burnley seriously enough for my liking. Any money I had that didn't go on fags for the bike sheds went on trips to Burnley games home and away. Once or twice my German teacher took me because he supported Burnley too.

Nowadays, reporting politics for the *Daily Mirror*, I travel round the world – meeting Burnley fans wherever I go. I was at the Earth Summit in Rio earlier this year and stayed at the Copacabana Palace Hotel. The manager, Philip Carruthers from Accrington, was a Burnley fan. There we were at Prime Minister John Major's reception for the press, diplomats and eco-freaks, arguing about whether to include Willie Morgan in our 'all-time-great' Burnley XI, while all around us they were pretending to save the world. When I went to the Gulf with Major, just before the troops were ordered into battle, the first tattoo I saw was on the arm of a young Squaddie: SUPER CLARETS.

The Prime Minister is aware of my passion. We flew to the Gulf on 6 January 1991. I'd complained, in my *Sunday Mirror* column that morning, that he was forcing me to leave the country on the day Burnley were at home to Man City in the FA Cup Third Round. I stayed tuned in to Clubcall right up to take-off time but at half-time, with the score 0-0, we had to get on board. Major got the GCHQ boys on the plane to get the result beamed up to us. One-nil to City. Vote Labour, I say. Burnley would have won if I'd been there. There was a lot of Burnley talk when Margaret Thatcher was PM, too, as her press secretary, Bernard Ingham, is a Clarets supporter.

It was living in Leicester that turned my passion into madness. I became so obsessed that I refused ever to remove my claret and blue scarf. The headmaster, fearing this would encourage others to break from uniformity, tried to persuade me to leave it at home, or at least on a peg in the cloakroom. I refused. Persuasion gave way to a direct order from my French teacher. I refused and told him he'd have to expel me. So he did and I went home. I went back the next day, scarf still on, and they never said another word. Even the presence of Gary Lineker, who was a few years below me in school, could not persuade me to dump the Clarets for the Blues or the Foxes, whatever they called themselves.

I made a rare exception to my scarf rule, when travelling on a Leicester special train to Burnley, at the height of the hooligan problem. The risk of being caught as an impostor taking advantage of City's subsidised travel meant I had to go incognito and even, on spotting the odd familiar face from school, to pretend I supported Leicester. It was the same sort of impossible lie I had to live at Hillsborough, for the FA Cup Semi-Final against Newcastle in 1974. I was, as ever, dependent for a ticket on an older friend, Peter Loughlin from Keighley, who ranks as the most loyal football fan I've ever met. On this occasion, the tickets were for the Newcastle end of the ground, where Peter and I found we were the only Burnley fans. Ho'way the Lads my foot.

So why Burnley? Because they were the best. I was born, as I say, in Keighley. I was nearing my third birthday, and beginning to take an interest in the things my older brothers were doing and saying, when Burnley won the League Championship in 1960. In the next three years they finished fourth, second and third. So why waste your time on Leeds or Bradford City, my Dad thought, when the best in the land are playing just over the county border?

He'd take me and my brothers right down to the front of the terracing that existed in front of the stand in the days before Bob Lord's ego got the better of him and he built a new stand to name after himself. One of my earlier and most shattering memories is of Gordon Harris coming over to take a throw-in and standing so close we could touch him. He shaped up to take the throw and let out a really loud fart. I was devastated. I'd heard my Dad fart, I'd even farted myself but I couldn't believe that Bomber Harris farted. Did all heroes, I wondered, have bowels of clay?

But it didn't stop me. If Dad couldn't take us because he was working, Peter would drive us over, or we'd pile into the back of a van with a friend called Jane Davis whose Dad, Eric, a mill owner, would take us to Turf Moor. I'm not sure my Dad realised just how deep a relationship he was starting when he introduced me to Burnley. He still goes to see them and I felt I was saying thanks for the memories when, in 1988, I took him and my Mum to Wembley to see Burnley play Wolves in the Sherpa Van Trophy Final. Both clubs were in the Fourth Division, yet they attracted a crowd of 80,841.

It was after we moved from Keighley to Leicester that Burnley started the slow and painful slide to near oblivion. They had fallen from being first in the Football League, during 1962, to lying 92nd on 9 May 1987. When they kicked-off that day, they were just one game from demotion from the League and had to beat Orient to stay alive. That was the day when Orient manager, Frank Clark, was allegedly approached by a Burnley bobby who told him: 'Do yourself a favour, mate. Don't win.' Burnley won 2-1. Grown men and women wept. Men and women who'd stuck with them from top to bottom. Through thick and thin I'd seen them whenever I could. I'd promoted their cause. I'd tolerated ridicule at school and later at university, by which time we were deep in Division II and slipping fast.

Running in the family

It was at Cambridge University that I learned that football and romance don't mix. In the winter of 1976-77, I persuaded my girlfriend, Maxine, to travel to Notts County. The nearer to Nottingham we got the snowier it got. We arrived just as the ref was inspecting the pitch, watched by players as anxious as I was that their journey wasn't in vain. But the ref turned and shook his head and I could feel a beautiful relationship was coming to an end. Then Mike Summerbee came to the rescue. He saw us, took pity on us and invited us into the players' bar. The time we should have spent freezing on the terraces was spent getting sozzled with marvellous men like Ray Hankin and Paul Fletcher. The romance was kept alive. Summerbee's help was all the more remarkable because I generally hated anyone who'd ever been connected with Man City – ever since I had a bobble hat snatched from my head as, nine years old, I walked into Maine Road. (The Notts County match was finally played in March, by the way. We lost 5-1 and Summerbee had already moved on to Blackpool.)

Though we went out together for several years, Maxine never did see much football. In 1978, the year Burnley won the Anglo-Scottish Cup, I took her to the Quarter-Final first leg at home to Celtic. Steve Kindon scored the only goal of the game, prompting Celtic fans to mount a demolition job on the entire stadium and prompting Maxine and me to flee.

Since then I've settled down with Fiona, who loathes football but who has given birth to two boys who love it. Aged five and three, one is a Burnley fanatic, the other coming along nicely. The only time their mother went to Turf Moor was in 1983, when Burnley – trailing 3-0 from the first leg and just about to drop to the Third Division – beat high-flying Liverpool 1-0 in the second leg of the League Cup Semi-Final. So excellence is in the boys' blood. It was on the day we beat Liverpool that I was offered a job on the *Daily Mirror*. The news editor couldn't understand why I wasn't more excited, but a man can take in only so much in a single day.

I took my elder son, Rory – at his insistence – to see Burnley (by now in the Fourth Division) at Aldershot last year. He was rewarded with an unforgettable goal by Steve Harper. Although the points won were later lost when Aldershot went into liquidation, that goal was as good as any Rory will see as long as he lives. His second match was a Cup replay at Derby where, despite losing 2-0, thousands of Burnley fans chanted 'Jimmy Mullen's Claret and Blue Army' for 40 minutes, prompting the players to come out half-naked from the dressing room in salute and inspiring John Sadler of the *Sun* to write a marvellous page-long article about what he called 'the most heartening, stimulating and optimistic football occasion I have experienced for many years'. I hate much of what the *Sun* stands for but Sadler's article was one of the best pieces about football fans I have ever read. He described the 'deafening bedlam, the colourful spectacle' and added:

> I wanted others to see and hear it. Big men, important men who are making decisions that could alienate the game from ordinary working folk.
>
>   I wanted Graham Kelly to be there to prove to him that those who talk of Super Leagues should not underestimate the passion of the so-called little clubs.
>
>   I wanted Sir John Quinton to be there so that the bank chairman

Young love, true love? Will young recruits – like Rory and Calum Campbell – grow up to follow their father's team or their local lads?

chosen to preside over the elite could learn something of life at the other end of the scale.

I wanted officials of Manchester United and Arsenal, Liverpool and the other fat cats behind the move to change the face of football to hear the voices of the people.

The bedlam of Burnley was not simply a cry of support for another of the FA Cup's beaten teams. It was a roar of defiance.

He quoted manager Jimmy Mullen: 'In all my 23 years I have never witnessed anything like that. It left my players prepared to die for those people.'

What with Harper's 30-yard shot at Aldershot and the fans' chanting at Derby, Rory had quite an introduction to the game. Since then he and I have regularly joined the fanatics who make up the Burnley FC London Supporters Club to traipse around the country on the excellent deals secured with British Rail. Calum will be joining us this season.

All three of us sponsor a player's strip, and while I suspect one day they may decide they actually want to support Arsenal, who are three miles from where we live, rather than trek up to Turf Moor, the fun we get from Burnley is as fulfilling as any other pastime. What pride I felt at Cardiff last year as Rory stood on his seat, put his hands above his head and started fellow fans in the chant of 'Jimmy Mullen's Claret and Blue Army'! I was proud, too, that he had the good sense to fall asleep during a pretty tedious 0-0 draw at Barnet. The pleasure I get at witnessing the pleasure he gets every time he stops a player for his autograph, or every time his favourite player, Ian Measham, recognises him on the way in and ruffles his hair, makes the journeys worthwhile. And to think that in the first year he followed Burnley, they won the Fourth Division Championsip.

The only other team I support is the Labour Party. When Labour lost the election, on 9 April 1992, life was grim. Burnley had no game on the Saturday. It was one of the worst weekends the Campbell household has ever known. But the following Tuesday, Rory and I trekked up to Turf Moor for a night match against Cardiff. Robbie Painter scored after 14 seconds. Life was worth living again.

8

And Smith Must Be Forgiven

Rob Pugh

State education and Brighton and Hove Albion have both been dismissed, often enough, as lost causes. Both have cried out for greater resources, more support and better leadership; both continually promise the earth yet rarely deliver; and both require the patience and the tolerance of a striker marked by Doug Rougvie. Yet following the Albion and being in state schools – latterly as a History teacher – have been important, often overlapping, features of my life.

Brighton were my first love, before the education system took me from home and school in Tunbridge Wells to read History at Hull University (1979-82); then to Brighton Polytechnic (a year at 'home' for teacher-training); and so to teaching posts in Cambridgeshire and, since 1987, Kent.

First love

For a spotty-faced youth in Tunbridge Wells, the choice of 'home' club was not immediately obvious: the Goldstone Ground, Priestfield Stadium, The Valley (long before Charlton Athletic began their tour of south-east London) and Selhurst Park (before Palace began to take in lodgers) were within similar striking distance. The Goldstone won my allegiance by virtue of a direct bus link. Direct or not, I find it difficult, today, to comprehend how I ever tolerated the four-hour round trip. In those days, though, only the football mattered.

What's more, I soon had a hero. He had the energy of a hibernating tortoise, the pace of an injured snail and the ball control of an overweight hippopotamus. Yet Fred Binney knew how to hit the back of the net – so long as he was playing at the Goldstone. Alas, his metabolism was oddly affected upon visiting such outposts as Mansfield, Chester and Rotherham; and medical science could do nothing to help Fred score away from home. Yet for me, as a 'butterfly' home supporter in that 1975-76 season, Fred could do no wrong.

My world temporarily fell apart at the start of the following season, when the new manager, Alan Mullery, got rid of Fred; but, then, little was I to know that even the great man could be replaced. My new hero had pace, skill and vision – if Peter Ward had possessed strength and courage, he would have been a famous hero, like a Greaves or a Lineker. He was good enough for me, though, as the 70-mile round trip from Tunbridge Wells to Brighton became, over the next three seasons, a regular victory procession. I can even recall the odd away win – at the likes of Gillingham, Orient and Charlton.

My schoolfriends – so many of them supporters of Spurs, Chelsea and Liverpool – could no longer mock the famous name of Brighton and Hove Albion, as, for the first time ever, we climbed into the First Division.

To Hull and backwaters

Things changed, alas, as I headed north. Trips to the meccas of northern football – Elland Road, Roker Park, and Maine Road – were valuable cultural experiences, but sites of heavy Brighton defeats. Albion's away wins in the top flight were as rare as spectators watching Wimbledon at Selhurst Park. Indeed, my happiest footballing memory of those years came when I travelled down from Hull, on the final Saturday of the 1980-81 season, to see a 2-0 home win over Leeds, which ensured another season at the top. Yet, just like my schoolmates, my university friends were less than impressed: during 1981-82, Brighton still meant nothing more to them than a welcome double for their teams. Not even Armstrong on the moon could have felt as lonely as an Albion supporter in East Yorkshire.

It was in the following season that I trained at Brighton Poly – but a stone's throw from the Goldstone – while the Albion reached the FA Cup Final. Bliss was it in that run to be alive – as Wordsworth almost commented. But Hell was it for the League games – as Wordsworth would have agreed, had he been a spectator not of revolution, French-style, in 1792 but of relegation, Brighton-style, in 1983.

Being able to *share*, close to home, the misery of relegation was little better than the isolated grief, when living over 300 miles away. But, as the euphoria of Wembley receded, I was migrating again – this time to the quiet market town of Ramsey, deep in the football backwater of Cambridgeshire – to experience a phenomenon not covered in my teacher training syllabus: the cruelty of children. Never mind their inattention in class or their failure to hand in homework: these were as nothing compared with the vicious jibes on the Monday morning after the Saturday defeat before – at Huddersfield, Stoke or Grimsby. Yet my missionary zeal rarely wavered as I set out to convert the young natives of Ramsey to the true cause. The legendary

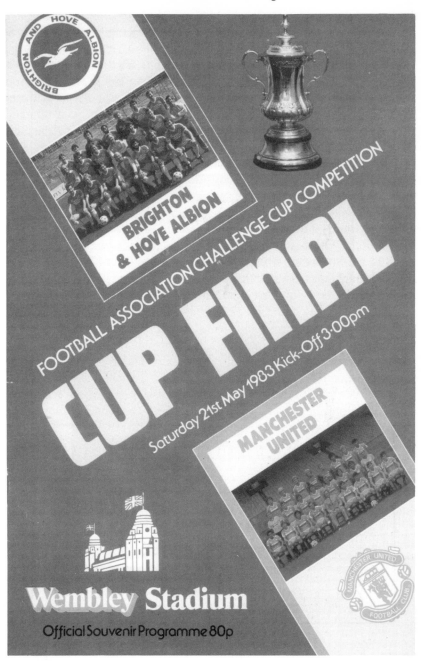

exploits of Ward, Horton, Lawrenson and Moseley held no fascination, however, for those brought up on a TV diet of Stapleton, Rush and Hoddle.

I did gain some credibility in that first year of teaching when the club got rid of a clown and appointed a manager: Chris Cattlin took over from Jimmy-Disco-Dancing-Put-On-Your-White-Shoes-Melia. And there was sweet revenge over the hordes of Liverpool fans at school when, for the second season running, we knocked them out of the FA Cup. Such moments were rare interludes, though, during my four years in Ramsey. Teaching became easier; supporting the Albion more stressful.

Probably my worst (though ultimately satisfying) experience in the Fens came in February 1986 when the best Albion side in a few years progressed to the FA Cup Fifth Round, following surprise away wins at Newcastle (then in Division I) and Hull (then a reasonable Second Division side). Even more amazingly, the local side, Peterborough, had also made it to the Fifth Round. John Wile's side made Coppell's Palace look like choirboys. But this mid-Fourth Division outfit had enjoyed the smile of Lady Luck, in the shape of four home draws. Bath City, Bishops Stortford, Carlisle and Leeds had been seen off. Now I'm quite sure that Otto von Bismarck knew no more about the magic of the FA Cup than William Wordsworth. Yet his maxim, 'Nothing succeeds like success', struck me, on that Monday lunch-time (before TV hi-jacked the draw), as more than 50 new 'supporters' of Peterborough United awaited, with one very anxious Brighton fan, the Fifth Round draw on Radio 2.

So confident were these converts of dismissing any of the remaining clubs that I prayed for an away trip to Anfield or Goodison: *anywhere*, please, but Peterborough! Then it happened:

'Number Eight – *Peterborough United* – will play ... Number Two – *Brighton and Hove Albion.*'

Cheers echoed around the room, as I slumped in my chair, moaning quietly. But that was only the beginning: Cup fever *gripped* the school as the big game approached. I tried, of course, to play it cool: your teacher refuses to give a prediction. The kids were less inhibited: few could foresee anything other than a Posh victory. The cautious among them predicted 1-0; but the forecasts ranged to 5-0.

My Friday night was sleepless; the Saturday weather foreshadowed disaster. Snow and ice carpeted the ground: how could *artists* like Dean Saunders and Denis Mortimer perform in such conditions? I must have been the sole Brighton fan on the packed East Terrace. Worse, three or four kids from school were standing close behind me, while my three adult companions were solidly anti-Seagull. Not since Custer at the Little Bighorn could the victim have felt more surrounded. Conditions were farcical: players could hardly stand, let alone run; and none could find the net. Half-time score: 0-0.

Then, early in the second half, disaster: Brighton went 1-0 down. Thank goodness, they soon equalised. But then, with 10 minutes left, the world caved in: Peterborough's only skilful player, Errington Kelly, scored. Excuses to be off school on Monday – and for at least a month thereafter – were racing through my mind, when indescribable joy returned to erase them: the much-maligned Steve Jacobs had bundled in a second equaliser. I jumped and screamed with delight, forgetting, for the only time in my life, the golden rule – Jasper Carrott gold, no less – of the terraces: when surrounded, as an away supporter, by the home fans, don't shout about it!

The replay was safely negotiated, 1-0, and Southampton loomed in the Quarter-Finals. The handicap of having Mick Ferguson at No. 9 was too much and we lost 2-0. But my deep gloom was lifted somewhat by the knowledge that no one at school supported David Bull's favourites.

The New Kent Road

And so, in 1987, to Broadstairs – 'home' to Kent, albeit at the 'wrong end' for Brighton. That said, the journey to home games is a lot easier than travelling from Ramsey. But the stick from the kids – none of whom supports Gillingham, the county's only remaining Football League team – is just the same. Reaching the play-off final in 1991 was an unexpected triumph. No matter that we lost 3-1 to Notts County: Brighton's appearance at Wembley was sufficient to silence my classroom cynics.

Not for long, though! Byrne and Small, the heroes of that hour, having departed, the kids were soon back on form in 1991-92, parading their wit at my expense, as Albion reverted to the other end of Division II and were ultimately relegated. To make matters worse, I had a Notts County supporter in my A-level set. Making no concession for the way in which County's power, pace and brute force had triumphed, at Wembley, over the artistry, flair and imagination that Division I deserved, he continually gloated at his team's victory – secure in the knowledge that there is no teacher-assessed coursework in our A-level History syllabus. And I was desperately running out of excuses for Albion's results. No longer could I point the finger at rank bad luck, biased refereeing – like that of Kelvin Morton, who awarded the arch-enemy, Palace, four penalties against Brighton on Easter Monday 1989 – or injuries to star players: at least the kids don't laugh when I reel off names like John Crumplin, Mark Barham and Clive Walker, as they've never heard of them.

My days as a Brighton supporter have now gone full circle, as we are back in Division III (or, to be exact, Division II, as a consequence of the Premier League 'scam' to which Alan Plater alludes). Trips to Fulham, Orient and Reading again beckon. Somehow, after the disasters of last season, Barry Lloyd remains as manager. As I write, with the 1992-93 season almost upon us, no new players have been signed and the few remaining quality players are all looking to leave. The club is £3 million in debt and the pessimism is overwhelming. The only optimism being voiced is on the club's phone-line.

I often lie awake at night, wondering how all this could have happened: how could a club with drive, ambition, support, money and decent players, only a decade or so ago, end up like this? And yet still, in my dreams, I shall one day walk into school, after a week's half-term, during which Brighton have walloped their Super League rivals, Arsenal, 4-0 at Highbury; have beaten Man Utd 3-0 at the Goldstone in midweek; and have then tanked Liverpool 4-1 at Anfield.

That'll be the day when the kids *want* to concentrate on History: never mind Brighton; let's talk about Bismarck, sir!

And Smith must score! If this caption doesn't make sense to you, please turn to the 'Riddles' on p. 223.

9

The End of Something Small and the Start of Something Big

Martin Lacey

Shortly after 4.40 pm on 27 April 1991, I waved goodbye and watched my childhood vanish over the horizon.

Lower Mead was the perfect ground, a fact widely acknowledged by connoisseurs of such matters. Watching non-League football can be an experience akin to standing in a muddy field with all the atmosphere of outer space, but not at Lower Mead. Lower Mead, the erstwhile home of Wealdstone FC, was the real thing – albeit in miniature.

A corrugated shack of a main stand (bought secondhand in 1920-something) and steep terracing on the remaining three-and-a-half sides, with both ends covered. No matter where you stood the view was superb; and you were so close to the action you could reach out and touch the players. The best bit was the Elmslie End, a cavernous long shed with a downward sloping roof that seemed to overhang the very goalmouth. It was raised a couple of feet above pitch level. And it was so close to the goalposts that you rarely saw the ball hit the back of the net, certainly not if it went in below head height. The only way you knew Wealdstone had scored was from the ripple of jubilant arms waving. It started with the kids hanging over the railings at the front and, in a fraction of a second, was transmitted to the lads at the back, who would surge forward in a huge celebratory ruck. There were no crush barriers in the Elmslie End; there was nowhere to put them since the floor was made of railway sleepers. Over the years, I must have lost at least a fiver in loose change through the cracks and I'm told that, when the stand was demolished, the money found underneath would have gone a long way towards paying the club's debts.

Lower Mead uppermost

It was Lower Mead that made me passionate about Wealdstone, me and hundreds like me. I'd been reading about Wealdstone in the *Harrow Observer* for about a year before, at the age of 11, I attended my first game.

It was an evening fixture, Wealdstone v Woking in the Isthmian League, at the tail end of 1970-71. Wealdstone won 3-0. I recall reading with disbelief that the attendance that night was 300. It felt like 3,000 – 30,000 even. To this day, I wonder if it wasn't a misprint. 1,300 perhaps?

Before my introduction to Wealdstone, I'd already been to most of London's Football League grounds but Lower Mead was the best ground of all. As Wealdstone attacked the Elmslie End in the second half, the crowd kept up a non-stop barrage of singing, chanting and abuse. It had become Wealdstone's trademark. For years the passion and noise of a Lower Mead crowd was unrivalled anywhere in non-League; and, although it declined sharply in the ground's last years, there were still occasions – perhaps on a wet Tuesday night, when nothing much was at stake but something intangible gelled and the crowd fired up the team – when 500 Wealdstone supporters became more of a passionate, ferocious, emotive whole than twenty times their number would be on any Football League ground in the country. A generation of goalkeepers will testify to it.

Most of my teenage memories relate in some way to Wealdstone FC. Indeed, most of the formative experiences of my teens – drunkenness, drug-taking, Syd Barrett albums, occasional violence – related either to Lower Mead or the crew I hung out with there. It was a place of escape, from the discipline (and rugby) of grammar school and from the polite conventions of home. In retrospect I think I had an idyllic childhood, suburban and secure, the type I would like to provide for my own children; but it didn't seem like that at the time. I have a feeling I was always on the run from something. And Lower Mead was the refuge.

God in those days was George Duck. It was the era of Best, Bowles, Marsh, Currie – and Duck. George Duck was the most complete centre-forward ever. He could score equally unerringly from three yards or thirty; with head or feet; after taking on three defenders and running from the centre circle or snapping up a half chance from a corner. He never, ever, missed a penalty (well, not that I remember). He also kicked Stan Bowles's backside behind the referee's back during a Cup-tie with QPR. The supporting cast around 1975 were pretty damn good, too. Goalkeeper John Morton, Chris Kinnear, John Watson, Bill Byrne, Bobby Moss, John Henderson (where are you now?) – but Duck was the man. Eventually he left the club under an acrimonious cloud and went on to play for rivals, Harrow Borough and Dagenham, which has caused many supporters to attempt a *Nineteen Eighty-Four*-style rewriting of history: 'He wasn't *that* good.' 'Henderson did all the work.' To most Wealdstone supporters, God is Alan Cordice, a one-club man who was forced to retire through repeated injury, a perfect gentleman and a player who brought significant silverware to Lower Mead. But honestly, Duck *was* that good, the only player who ever fired me with inspiration for the game itself, the only player I ever wanted to *be*.

By the time I was 17, I was showing alarming signs of maturity. Saturday night was no longer all right for fighting. I joined the Supporters Club committee and was active in a campaign to get the most notorious hooligans banned. This had something to do with the fact that the most serious incident of violence I'd been involved in was not with the notorious Barnet mob or our deadly enemies from Wimbledon but a fight between rival Wealdstone gangs seeking ascendancy in the Elmslie End. I also reported matches for the *Harrow and Ealing Post*, a local freesheet, and contributed, a few times, to *Long Ball Down The Middle*, one of the earliest football fanzines (first published 1975 and still appearing once every three years or so). My involvement with fanzines has become a story of its own. More of this later; meanwhile, I was learning to love Wealdstone from afar.

The exile

In a partly conscious reaction to the stultifying normality and high expectations of my childhood, I moved, upon leaving school, to Sheffield. I initially lived there with my brother in a flat over his junk shop without indoor sanitation or the other comforts I was used to in Pinner; I worked as a labourer, gravedigger, machine-operating zombie and temporary warehouseman, between long periods on the dole; played punk rock; starved and behaved in as irresponsible and hedonistic a fashion as I could manage. For six months, I continued to watch Wealdstone, often hitch-hiking to matches, this being 1977-78, the season of their best-ever FA Cup run, when they disposed of Hereford and Reading, *en route* to a Third Round exit at QPR. Then I gave up.

I don't know why: there were simply other things to do. I lived in different parts of the country, and the world. I never quite lost interest: in Banff, Alberta you can buy the *Sunday Express* on Tuesday night. I would always look up Wealdstone's result, scorers, attendance and, for five seconds, picture myself there. But essentially it was part of my past and I didn't envisage going back.

That five-year phase of self-discovery taught me more of real use than fifteen years of formal education had; but then I discovered purpose, ambition and materialism, found myself back in London and was drawn, inevitably, to Lower Mead. The faces had changed, both on the field (Stuart Pearce, Vince Jones) and off. Not one of the old gang was there, nor hardly any of the twenty or so, from my year alone at school, who were regulars

in the 1970s. But the emotion was the same, the escape as efficient. It was
no longer teachers or parents I wanted to forget but the boss, customers,
bank managers, the building society. For 90 minutes on Saturday – not to
mention a couple of hours' hard drinking beforehand – I could believe that
nothing in the world mattered except which team of 11 idiots was more
adept at kicking a ball around. That, I guess, is a universal attraction.

There were successful years – most notably the non-League double, of
Gola League Champions and FA Trophy Winners, in 1985 – and bad years.
In 1988, Wealdstone were relegated and, driven by house prices and career
plans, I moved back to Sheffield, my wife's home town and a place for
which I've always had an illogical affection. I was, by now, a homeowner,
employer and soon-to-be father. People expected me to lose interest or to
become – in the way that Pete Alcock describes – a follower of Sheffield
Wednesday. I didn't. I seemed to spend half my waking hours on the 11.15
Sheffield to St Pancras. Sheffield to Lower Mead was a relatively simple
journey, certainly compared to Dover (7.30 start; change trains; home after
midnight) or Dorchester (8.00; tortuous, cross-country drive). The cost?
Worth every penny.

Wealdstone were by now playing abysmally but my enthusiasm was
undimmed. 'But they're only a non-League team', people would say to me
– as if my obsession would be understandable if I supported Liverpool.

Those people may like football but they're not *fans*. I've always been a
fan, not a *football* fan. By that I mean I don't appreciate the game for itself,
as sporting achievement, as an aesthetic thing. Football to me is not
beautiful and it is certainly more than a game. Oh yes, I can appreciate the
stunning moment of skill from a Hoddle or Gascoigne doing something I
won't see at Wealdstone in a hundred years. But how often do those things
happen, even in the Premier League? Maybe 5 per cent of top matches leave
the spectator exhilarated; maybe 5 per cent of Wealdstone matches are so
inept, I might as well be watching a kick-about in the park. For the other 95
per cent of the time, there's honestly not much difference. Sure, if you pit
the Super League team against the Southern League team, you'll soon see
the difference in speed, fitness and skill; but at their own level they're pretty
much indistinguishable. The competitiveness is the same, the tactics are the
same, the joy of winning and despair of losing are the same. To me, football
is a compulsion like gambling, except with emotions instead of money. I
care who wins. I must care who wins. A game in which I'm neutral is a dull
game. I have been to watch Wednesday and local non-League football; and
I always go away disappointed. The only team I care about is Wealdstone.

I could be logical and attempt to explain this loyalty: while everything else in my life has changed, I cling onto this one connection with my home town, my accent, my childhood. But it defies logic. A fan understands. Someone who merely likes football never will.

27 April 1991. You could fill a whole book with the sorry series of events which brought Wealdstone FC to death's door. Maybe one day someone will, though for now the few people in possession of the full facts are less than forthcoming. Suffice it to say that a decade or more of poor financial management, compounded by the apathy of the local populace, had left the club having to sell its home for a supermarket development in order to survive. For the last Southern League fixture at Lower Mead – v Cambridge City – it was a glorious day, not at all apt for a funeral. And the Wealdstone supporters, by now used to making mountainous events out of molehill-sized occasions, were not in funeral mood. Symptomatic of the club's decline, only 820 turned up for that last game. But that 820 consumed enough alcohol and made enough noise to compensate for the absent hordes – and started demolishing the ground into the bargain. There was huge anger, frustration and sadness. Having failed to locate an alternative site in these crowded London suburbs, Wealdstone were devoting £2.5 million of the sale proceeds to buying a 50 per cent share in Watford's ground at Vicarage Road and were promising there would be enough left over to build a team which would take us to the Football League. We were not interested. If we'd wanted to watch League football or spend our Saturdays at Vicarage Road, we'd have supported Watford in the first place. It was also inaccurate. The deal was comprehensively bungled, leaving the club effectively penniless, at least pending the outcome of complex legal actions.

Like most of the supporters, I continued to watch Wealdstone at Watford. What else could we do? But the soul had been ripped out of the club. With 400 spectators in a 26,000-capacity ground, the atmosphere was often morgue-like and the once highly-rated players responded by getting relegated. Sheffield to Watford by public transport is a nightmare journey. By the mid-point of the season, I'd abandoned British Rail for the delights of the M1. The biggest disadvantage was having to watch Wealdstone painfully sober, though there was the positive aspect of being able to take my children, aged three and one, to matches when the weather was clement. They enjoyed it more than I did! At the time of writing, it seems likely that Wealdstone could soon be in the hands of administrators, leaving little prospect of an upturn in results. The board continues to make confident-sounding public pronouncements on the future. Yes, the creditors may be put off, legal actions won and debts paid. Common'sense tells you it will not work out this way and the end really is near.

Oddly enough, I am almost indifferent. To me, Wealdstone was Lower Mead and Lower Mead was Wealdstone. The club I loved is dead.

Something stirs

I mentioned earlier my occasional involvement in one of the first fanzines, dating from 1975. Considering the woeful quality of football coverage in the mainstream media, it's amazing that football fans didn't take matters into their own hands much sooner.

By 1985 the mass violence, which in the 1970s had been so common-place that it went unreported, was fast becoming a bad memory. But Heysel brought it all sharply back into focus: every incident was seen through a magnifying glass, every minor brawl exaggerated into a riot. It seemed that the press was intent on driving the final nail into football's coffin.

Fans were under attack from all sides. The media had us typecast as hooligans. The average club programme credited us with the intelligence of six-year-olds. The clubs believed we should pay up and shut up – if they wanted to move, merge, change colours, up prices or build executive boxes on a favourite terrace, it was nothing to do with us. The police, who I was brought up to believe existed to help and protect the law-abiding public, enacted an arbitrary suspension of civil liberties when it came to football and seemed to think attending a football match, especially as an away supporter, was tantamount to a criminal offence in itself. There have been many matches where the only hooliganism on view was from the yobs in uniform. And to cap it all, the Government was about to come up with a scheme so ludicrous, impracticable, ill-thought-out and downright dangerous, it seemed as if their intention must be, more or less, to abolish football. This was the compulsory membership scheme – ID cards for football fans. Finally, there was the enemy within: the rump of the hooligan problem who could still cause trouble disproportionate to their numbers; and the terrace racists who, though potentially far more dangerous to society, went largely unopposed by the authorities and unmentioned by the media.

It's possible that someone foresaw the demand for football fanzines before 1985 but assumed the media were a closed shop and DIY was simply not an option. In fact, music fans had been doing it themselves since 1977, starting with *Sniffin' Glue*, the bible of punk, and progressing through literally hundreds of successors, including my own *NMX* (25 issues, 1979-82) and *Overground* (three issues, 1983-85). It took a renegade from this scene to prove that it was possible and to set the wheels in motion. *When*

Saturday Comes was not quite the first of the modern breed but it was certainly the most successful and influential. The first issue, however, was a free gift with a music fanzine called *Snipe*. I was *Snipe*'s printer. *When Saturday Comes* was mentioned in the *Guardian* Football Diary; Mike Ticher's office copier could not keep up with demand; and my involvement with football fanzines was revived – now on a full-time, national scale.

Fanzines instantly struck a chord. Fans wanted coverage of their team that was intelligent and knowledgeable but also biased, committed, out-spoken and irreverent. It reflected themselves.

The pioneers such as *Leyton Orientear, Chelsea Independent, The Pie* (Notts. Co.) and *City Gent* (Bradford) had a lot in common. They were loosely left in outlook, campaigned vigorously and had a firm idea of the line between making fun of other clubs and pointless abuse. Indeed, for the first couple of years, as each club in turn got its 'own' fanzine, the growth was entirely positive; but as growth turned to explosion – from a dozen titles at the end of 1986-87 to around 350 by the end of 1991-92 – there were inevitable setbacks.

First, since the whole philosophy of fanzines was that 'anyone can do it', anyone did; and, as a result, some of the new fanzines were rubbish. Worse, some were racist rubbish and some used the platform to provoke rivals with crude abuse. Fanzines started as an *alternative*: if you simply wanted your prejudices confirmed, there were plenty of options already.

Then came 'professional' fanzines. It's not hard to see how running a fanzine can become a full-time occupation, nor even that there is scope for a viable business if the club it covers has enough supporters. But the biggest asset a fanzine has is its outspokenness, recklessness and an ability to say what needs saying when it needs saying. Can that be reconciled with the need to make a living, meet deadlines and provide a product that is palatable to consumers, distributors and – heaven forbid – advertisers? One or two, notably *Through the Wind and Rain* (Liverpool), have met the paradox head-on and survived with integrity intact. Others have fallen gratifyingly flat on their faces. There are fanzines run by people who don't even support the team they're writing about – or didn't until the fanzine opportunity came along. At least twice, people who admitted they knew nothing whatsoever about football have sought my advice about starting a fanzine.

Yes, but these are the exceptions. During the season, I print up to a dozen football fanzines every week and, almost invariably, they are excellent. In seven years, I can count on the fingers of one hand the times I've had cause to take issue with the content of any of them; and on the fingers of one finger the times I've actually refused, on principle, to print something.

The fanzine achievement

In terms of circulation and reputation, fanzines are a success. But what of the original aims? The ID scheme is dead – though not, sadly, as a result of the Government's discovering common sense or listening to the voice of reason in the form of fanzines and the Football Supporters Association. The ID scheme is dead because 95 people died to prove grounds were unsafe. At least its architect, Colin Moynihan, paid the ultimate electoral price. Surely there was not a Labour-voting football supporter anywhere whose election-night depression wasn't momentarily lifted upon hearing that he'd lost his seat – nor, for that matter, any Tory-voting fans who didn't allow themselves a secret whoop of joy at the news (even John Major – oh, surely? He seems to know a liability when he sees one).

The media have also toned down their act. A dozen yobs wrecking a bar somewhere in Europe, where there happens to be a football match involving an English team, is no longer considered news on a par with a royal divorce. Racism on the terraces has been reduced, if not entirely eliminated, and that's entirely due to pressure from within rather than to new laws, which the police lack the will or the means to implement.

It is at the clubs themselves that the inroads have been smallest. Most clubs are still run as the ego-extensions of rich businessmen who regard them as their personal playthings and see constructive criticism as arrogant interference. Their attitude is still 'If you don't like it, you can go else-where,' which takes no account of the fact that football is not just a product and not just 90 minutes' entertainment. The football fan has an illogical brand loyalty which means he may get a bad product or poor value for money, but it takes a lot to make him go elsewhere. Chairmen and directors depend on this loyalty but they neither possess it nor understand it.

There have been small success stories: fanzines influencing decision making, cooperation and consultation. I was recently invited into the boardroom at Wealdstone to discuss my ideas for promoting the club. This was a full five years after I'd first offered my assistance. During most of those five years our fanzine, *The Elmslie Ender*, has been banned from sale on the ground as a result of some utterly trivial – and demonstrably true – comments about a rival club. Not that we could have saved the club or anything; but it's ironic that, while the board was losing millions, the directors could turn their backs on our offers of sponsorship and treat us with, at various times, suspicion, indifference or outright hostility. That's fairly typical of the fanzines' experience. At least two have paid a heavy

A 'biased, committed, outspoken and irreverent' response to 'the woeful quality of football coverage in the mainstream medium'.

financial price for getting the wrong side of the boardroom and ending up in court for libel.

These people only understand power. They fail to understand that fanzine editors do not want power; they want their team to be successful and they are willing to contribute whatever they can. Perhaps the directors don't and aren't?

Closing ceremony: last day at Lower Mead.

10

Going Down, Going Down, Going Down

Leicester City and Me

Stephen Wagg

> People like us
> Gonna make it because
> We don't want freedom
> We don't want justice
> We just want
> Someone to love.
>
> Talking Heads, *People Like Us*

I was born in December 1947, into the very middle of Middle England. My birthplace was the prosperous East Midland town of Loughborough, known then for its unfashionably competitive athletes (based at the local PE college) and for the Brush engineering works that stood next to the railway station.

My mother, an attractive young war widow, had married my father the previous January and they had settled initially in the nearby village of Shepshed. My father, the son of a clerk at Derby Crown Court, by then long dead, had recently been demobilised as a major in the Royal Engineers. He determined now to make his way, similarly, in the civilian world; and so, while I lay gurgling contentedly in one corner of the family flat, he sat in another, studying to become a chartered surveyor. In time, suitably chartered and established in a business partnership, he was helping to sell some of the many new houses which sprang up on the edges of Loughborough in the affluent 1950s.

Finding my feet

Around 1950, we moved to a new home at the end of a suburban road in Loughborough: to one side of us lay a variety of well-kept detached and semi-detached houses; to the other were farmed fields and, in the distance,

97

the beautiful Charnwood Forest. For a sociable child like me, this was not the most convivial of environments and the main friends that I recall from those days were men whom twenty years later I would begin to describe, to my father's considerable disgust, as 'working-class'. There was Michael, the sphinx-like farm worker, in his black beret and round, National Health spectacles, who let me ride his tractor but, as I remember, never uttered a single word to me. And there were the builders who came inevitably to colonise the adjacent fields for housing and who welcomed me, a four-year-old boy, as second long-stop in their lunch-break cricket games. (My mother, anxious that I should not impose, sent me over to the site with my own tea, milk and sugar for brewing-up time). From these raucous, friendly men, I gained my first experience of a sense of belonging, outside the family, and my first taste of the camaraderie that can be had through sport.

When I was eight years old, it was decided that I should go to boarding school. Sadly, the boarding school tradition with its peculiarly English combination of extreme cruelty, excellent facilities and favourable pupil-teacher ratios remains the source of much national pride. For me, a sensitive young soul, stranded miles from anywhere with no tractors to ride on and no builders to brew tea with, the experience was emotionally devastating. But football saved me – in two ways.

First, football was prescribed for Wednesday and Saturday afternoons in both the autumn and spring terms. This was truly a godsend, because, as I later discovered, most schools of comparable status had long since convinced themselves that 'soccer' was a game only for the uncouth and switched to rugby. I had a middling aptitude for association football and it soon became, to me, the only fully comprehensible part of the school curriculum.

Secondly, my father, noting this new enthusiasm, took me, in a school holiday, to see my first match at Filbert Street, the home of Leicester City. If my memory serves me correctly, this was the spring of 1958. I was 10 years old. Leicester played Burnley and won, I think, 5-3. We sat high in the stand, with me straining to see over a forest of caps (like those affected by male members of the Royal Family at gymkhanas) and trilby hats. The excitement was unspeakable. A goal for Leicester and I, along with an assortment of heating engineers, hosiers, typewriter salesmen and manufacturers of sweets, was on my feet, arms aloft, and – to my mild surprise – with no embarrassment. I returned to school and described the whole experience in an English essay, the rambling and generally inchoate style of which was not unlike that of the local Saturday evening sports paper, the *Sports Mercury*, or 'Buff'.

Within weeks, the Buff had become emotionally indispensable to me, linking me to somewhere I knew I belonged. It arrived at the school by post every Monday morning in winter time, carefully folded and bound by my mother. I studied the match reports carefully and slowly mastered the style and code in which they were written. The Leicester defence, I noted, were frequently 'at sixes and sevens'. Similarly, a run of defeats could land the club 'in the doldrums'. If Leicester managed momentarily to get the ball from the opposition, the Buff correspondent would grab his telephone and carefully enunciate into it the words, 'It-was-all-City-at-this-point.' Day and night, I longed to be there, while such deadweights were being dropped on the English language.

When I was home, football, to the growing impatience of my father, became my sole topic of conversation. Moreover, the phrase, 'When Saturday Comes' (now, of course, the title of a popular football fanzine; but see Martin Lacey, above, on this development) evokes perfectly the feeling which I first knew in the late 1950s and which, fortunately, I have never quite lost. In the school holidays, Saturday meant, first and foremost, the *match*.

Excitement mounted during the morning, which was mostly given over to listening to *Saturday Club* on the BBC Light Programme. As Brian Matthew, whom I visualised immaculate in his V-neck pullover, pressed some perky young men from the north about when they were next going into the recording studio or on what they thought of their young fans, my mind ranged feverishly over the afternoon's prospects against West Ham, Newcastle or Nottingham Forest. If Leicester were playing away, then I faced an anxious afternoon of waiting for news to filter through on BBC TV's *Grandstand* where it would emerge miraculously via David Coleman's earpiece. At twenty to five, I would stare gravely at the screen as the BBC's chattering teleprinter disgorged the final scores, one by one, with the omniscient Coleman gabbling, 'Now, Division One. West Bromwich Albion, fifth from bottom this morning, *Two*. Leicester City, two places and three points below them, but with a game in hand ...'

On the other hand, if Leicester were at home, I began to experience a tightening across the chest at midday, just around the time that Brian Matthew was extracting final tour details from the Swinging Blue Jeans. Lunch would perhaps be spent fretting over whether a favourite player would pass his late fitness test – although injuries seemed more rare in those far-off, less frenetic days. Or, when glamorous big-city opposition – Tottenham Hotspur, say, or Manchester United – were due at Filbert Street, I might wonder, in my timid provincial way, how we (the City and, by extension, I) might survive at least with our dignity. But mostly I just ached to be part of it all: the crowd, jocular and expectant; the Salvation Army band, puffing piously toward kick-off time; and the *Post Horn Gallop* announcing the presence of the Leicester players in the tunnel below, clad, in the improbable words of the programme, in 'White Knickers' embellished by 'Blue Stripe'.

All this unbearable excitement was but a brief car-ride across Charnwood Forest but it was also, of course, a world away. The life of my home, when I lived in it, was clean and tidy and restrained. Filbert Street was none of these things. To get there, we entered Leicester from the north-west and passed through a district called Frog Island, which encompassed the usual lattice work of terraced two-up-two-downs; a biscuit factory; a disused railway station; and a canal, chock-full of stagnant greenery. Frog Island and the more immediate environs of Filbert Street remain much as they were. A comparatively recent red brick tower (containing, I think, flats for nurses at the nearby Royal Infirmary) now looks down on the same terraced streets and hosiery factories that have enclosed the football ground for most of this century. There are brief glimpses of social change: some of the factories are now derelict; one or two houses have sprouted a satellite dish; and a row of Penguin psychology books or Virago novels is occasionally visible through someone's front window. To me, such places have always seemed less congenial, but more real, than other places that I know.

The ground itself (I still can't bring myself to use the word 'stadium' here) evokes the same feelings. It's that familiar, Football League confection of bricks, mortar, corrugated iron, wooden benches and concrete slabs. A row of luxury boxes and a comfortable suite for 'Vice Presidents' have been added but cut little ice with the likes of me. I grew up in an ascetic environment where socks were darned endlessly and money was not for spending, but for depositing in the Leicester Temperance Building Society. It was always pointless trying to tempt me to a football match with the promise of a cushioned seat: I would be there anyway and, besides, we had plenty of cushions at home. Filbert Street was, as I say, somewhere else. It was, as it remains, dingy and irresistible. I still smile when I recall how my mother wouldn't let me go there before I'd washed my face and hands.

Strong, silent types

In my time of 'going down the City', the period that most endures for me is the first one, spanning the late 1950s and early 1960s. My clearest and warmest memories are of those drab, pre-hedonistic years. I remember, for example, going with my father and two of his friends to see an evening

Leicester City 'in "White Knickers" embellished by "Blue Stripe" '.

Gary Lineker to the fore for Leicester City, having recovered from being behind Alastair Campbell at school (see Chapter 7).

match around 1959. I was seriously concerned about the fitness of the Leicester goalkeeper, Dave Maclaren – then my hero, despite an acknowledged tendency to let in the odd 'soft one'. There was to be an early-evening check on Maclaren, and a young man called Gordon Banks, of whom none of us had heard, was standing by to take over. Would he be up to it? Well, Maclaren's wrist (or whatever it was) had not mended and my question was soon answered in the affirmative.

Gordon Banks was probably the nearest that I, a repressed, suburban Philistine, ever came to the appreciation of art. To me, he was the personification of physical grace. This grace was expressed through an unlikely physical frame: a shock of jet-black hair crowning a friendly and vaguely oriental face and a physique that the *Daily Express* once described as 'roly-poly'. Gordon ran lazily, in a jogging mode, kicking his heels quite high behind him and leaning his head slightly to the right. He caught a football almost always without apparent effort, reaching casually behind his head or swooping long and low to clasp a ball he'd seemed, until the last moment, not to have noticed. He took over as my hero.

I virtually met him once when out shopping with my mother in Leicester, one Saturday morning. He drove his Standard 8 into the car park that we were just leaving and I, almost asphyxiating with embarrassment, persuaded my mother to get his autograph. He signed cheerily enough and then turned to me and asked 'Going down this afternoon?' (Leicester were at home to Everton). I opened my mouth to say 'Yes', a simple enough undertaking in retrospect, but no meaningful sound came out. Come to think of it, boys like me didn't make a whole lot of noise in those days, unless we were shouting for our *Crackerjack* propelling pencils. That's why the football crowd was so liberating.

Gordon Banks was a member of my favourite team. It remained together for several years in the early 1960s and it has survived better in my memory than many more recent formations. Most of them, as was customary in that era – were from Scotland or the north of England. The Scots were Frank McLintock, a young, combative Glaswegian later to become famous playing for Arsenal; Ian King, a dapper, crew-cutted and distinctly laconic centre-half; and Jimmy Walsh, also from Glasgow, a full-hearted attacking player with curly hair of a vivid red, who now runs a local newsagent. In 1962, the City took on another Scot, called David Gibson.

Gibson was small, frail-looking and, as people seldom seem to be nowadays, bandy-legged: as Leicestershire people would say, 'He couldn't stop a pig in an entry.' He was one of those players of enormous skill whom the popular press persisted in calling 'canny little schemers'. He and his ilk began to disappear in the late 1960s, when coaches and market forces took over and it became so much harder to play than to stop others playing. Clubs now wanted players only of a certain physique. I remember listening to a Leicester match on the radio, one winter evening around 1969, and hearing that Gibson had been brought on as a substitute against the brawny Liverpool side (Yeats, Smith, Hunt …) at Anfield and wondering if he'd be all right. He's in his fifties now, and a postman. But, in my mind's eye, he's still 24, running out of the players' tunnel, immediately flicking the ball up with his feet and catching it on his neck. How do they do that?

Then there was Richie Norman, a rather elegant left-back I always thought, who came from the north east; Ken Keyworth, a large impassive man with a lot of skill for a large impassive man; and Howard Riley, the only local boy, small, stocky and very fast – he seemed to run on tip-toe – and with a ferocious shot. I still see Howard around, occasionally on the terraces or maybe on a Saturday morning in the supermarket, tossing a packet of *Mother's Pride* into the trolley, while Mrs Riley checks out the vegetables. He was impassive, too. To tell the truth, they nearly all were. One or two – Banks, perhaps, and McLintock – might occasionally have words with the referee but mostly, and they weren't unusual in this, they kept it all in. And, to me, this impassivity was part of their appeal. To many people nowadays, especially those who've had the social science training that I've had, my admiration will seem depressing and retrograde: surely these were deferential workers accepting their place; men blighted by a masculinity that imprisons emotions. But, for me, the point was that they had dignity, and decency; and, on a Saturday afternoon, they let their feet do the talking. Again, they were everything that I was not. I was always arguing the toss (with teachers and parents); they just got on with it.

My greatest football hero was the captain of this team, a Yorkshireman from Scarborough called Colin Appleton. Colin Appleton was a completely unglamorous figure. He had the face of a deep-sea fisherman, the skin creased and the eyes narrowed as if by a piercing north wind – the sort of face that had somehow never been young. His hair was Brylcreemed back over his head in the 1950s mode and this gave full prominence to his large ears. You couldn't, in all honesty, imagine his face on many bedroom walls. But it was on mine. He was a lovely footballer, who cantered effortlessly through a match, tackling with guile and spreading passes almost unfailingly to teammates. He escaped most people's notice, although an *Observer* correspondent, reporting one of Leicester's strangely frequent wins at Liverpool, did note that Colin had made his first bad pass with around 10 minutes to go. Colin Appleton was one of the hundreds of uncelebrated

master craftsmen of the Football League who played in a time before the
publicists took over.

Recently, to my considerable surprise, my daughter (then 14) came home
with a video of the FA Cup Final of 1961, between Leicester City and
Tottenham Hotspur. She'd borrowed it from a friend at school who supported Tottenham. We watched it together, she with quiet curiosity, I
finding, with some embarrassment, that tears were trickling down my
cheeks. Here, in grainy black and white, modestly comporting themselves
at the Empire Stadium, were most of the men who had filled my own head
when I was 14. As older supporters of each team will remember, the game
was scarred – like several finals of the pre-substitute era; see, likewise, Jean
Thomasson's memories of 1953 – by an injury, early on, to the Leicester
right-full-back, Len Chalmers, who hobbled doggedly around the field
thereafter, but took no real part. Leicester played the ball around nicely, did
their best, lost the match and walked off rather sheepishly with a tentative
wave. Nobody on either side, so far as I could discern, had raised either a
foot or a voice in anger in the entire 90 minutes. Occasional glimpses of the
crowd revealed thousands of grinning young men, in glasses and belted
raincoats, their already short hair brilliantined ruthlessly into their scalps.
A vanished world indeed.

Into the family enclosure

> Did I see you walking with the boys
> Though it was not hand in hand?

> Neil Young, *Harvest*

I think that I always saw supporting a football club as a symptom of male
inadequacy. The players, the transfer talk, the incessant debating of managerial policies all, it seemed to me, filled an emotional space that should,
more properly, have been filled by something else. For some of us, though,
the transience of life (marriages fail, redundancy looms, friends move away
…) is too much to handle without the reassurance that, every winter
Saturday, at ten to three, those shirts of whatever colour will be running out,
somewhere or other. To my great consternation and amusement, however,
this preoccupation is now shared by one of the sanest and most self-
possessed people I know: my daughter, Cassie.

Cass was born in 1977, by which time for people like me issues of gender
and sexism had become inescapable. Being libertarian by inclination, I was
glad therefore to have a female child, for this promised fewer interventions:

girls tend not to want toy flamethrowers or to watch *Terminator II* – the sort of thing that might have had me reaching, however tentatively, for the word 'No'. She was seven when her mother and I parted and has since divided her time happily and equally between two homes.

Through me, she was already familiar with the very male-dominated world of sport: from the age of four she came with me while I played cricket for a village team. Here, a succession of rather withdrawn women, usually busy assembling 24 spam salads, told her to mind her language and to stay away from the changing rooms. Notwithstanding these rebuffs, she grew to like cricket, developed an informed appreciation of the game and sometimes accompanied me to watch county matches. She also came, once or twice, to Leicester City. We sat in the 'family enclosure' where, once again and this time with a nice irony, her language caused some disquiet: one Saturday, several members of the row in front momentarily diverted their gaze from Leicester 1 Watford 1, to give her an admonitory stare. I took these trips to be no more than reciprocal gestures on her part. I'd taken her swimming, to the cinema, round the shops; so why not keep me company on one of my strange Saturday afternoon pilgrimages? After all, I'd often given up football to look after her; when she was of age, I thought, I would go back to it and she would get on with something sensible.

This indeed looked to be the case until one Saturday afternoon in May 1991. Leicester City, following an especially miserable season, stood on the brink of relegation to the Third Division. I had an inflexible commitment to play cricket. Cass, I expected, would as usual be going down town with her friend, Zelda, to discuss life, buy cheap earrings off a market stall and enjoy getting turned out of shops. Instead, to my mild surprise, she announced that she was going alone to see if Leicester City could beat Oxford United and thus remain in Division II.

It was close but they did and she returned in a state of euphoria, from which she shows no sign of emerging. Filbert Street, a fractious and disgruntled place in recent times, had been a carnival. She had, she said, been chanting and participating in innumerable Mexican waves. She had run onto the pitch at the end of the game. She had somebody's autograph. She was now a fan. We must go at once to the club shop where, she believed (mistakenly, as it turned out), a Leicester City duvet cover could be obtained.

This strange dream in which, against all expectation, I was confronted with my own adolescence and its single devotional theme, was only just beginning. Football, now, was all we spoke of. Did I think X was a good player? And how did I rate Y? Whom did I fancy for promotion? Did I realise that Leicester were now in the Quarter-Finals of the Zenith Data Systems Cup? How far away was Grimsby; and could we go there in a fortnight's time to see Leicester at Blundell Park? She began, when staying with her mother, to telephone, seeking, or volunteering, football news. One night, Leicester are at Highbury in the Rumbelows Cup but there's no mention of this on Radio 5. Have I heard anything? No matter – she'll ring the club.

A few weeks into the 1991-92 season, she pronounced herself in love with an expressionless waif called Paul Kitson, newly prominent in the Leicester team and, by now, on her pencil case. She began spending time at the City's training ground, where she befriended two similarly devoted young women and discussed with them how Kitson's fiancée might not be right for him. There was talk that Kitson would be the next £1 million transfer out of Filbert Street and she demanded constant reassurance that he would stay. When, in the spring of 1992, he moved to Derby County, she was mortified, becoming one of nearly a thousand people to telephone their disapproval to the local paper and forbidding all mention of Derby in the house. The terms of this ban were extended in May 1992 to include the words 'George' and 'Courtney', when a referee of that name awarded a penalty against Leicester in the Second Division Play-Off Final at Wembley and a tearful Cassie threatened to inflict severe genital damage upon him.

I don't really worry about this obsession because it's leavened by irony, which comes, I think, more readily to Cassie's generation than any previous one, and because it goes with genuine love for, and knowledge of, the game. Cass, for example, often plays football in the lunch hour and once demonstrated to me how she drew a tackle, played a pass and ran for the return, all in what seemed to me to be a prohibitively tight skirt. Likewise, she volunteers to babysit for parents with Sky TV, so that she can watch football from foreign leagues.

Besides which, she is growing up in a world where there is much sex and little love. Young women of 14 or 15 are already accustomed to being treated as sex objects and to the intolerance that peers, male or female, can show towards the sexually uncompliant. Maybe, therefore, football offers a chance to change the subject: 'No, actually, I don't want to go out with you; ... but what did you think of Leeds v Manchester City on Sunday?'

More importantly, at the moment, Leicester City draw from my daughter a love for which there is no satisfactory alternative expression. Her commitment is unconditional and, although in a sense it's never requited, it's never rejected either. Like the fanzine writers, she offers devotion mingled with dignity and humour. Moreover, she searches the players' behaviour for evidence of a comparable tenderness, endlessly replaying video snatches wherein team-mate A embraces goalscorer B, more in affection than in exultation. This draws the highest compliment she can bestow: 'Really sweet.'

Whether all this oppresses Cass, I don't know. But it certainly beats *Terminator II*. I think my daughter is a feminist. For her, at the moment, a woman's place is on the terraces.

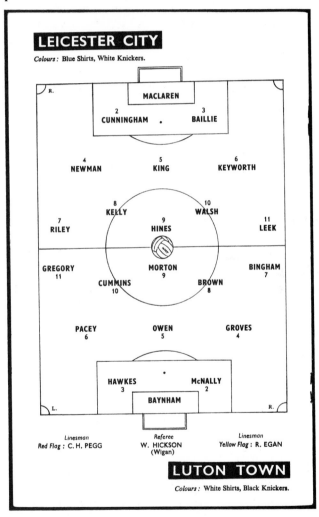

'Strong, silent types' – a line-up of Stephen Wagg's early heroes: Leicester City v Luton Town, 24 January 1959.

11

Blackpool: Illuminations of a Distant Fan

Eugene Ring

Saturday 28 February 1953: I am on the top deck of a No. 73 bus on its way to Hammersmith Broadway. The weather is dull but dry and the anticipation great. The booking hall of the station; and my best mate from school, Tony, is already there. Piccadilly Line: sixteen stops and we emerge at Arsenal – surely the only soccer club with a rail station named after it. We climb through the station's subterranean passage – a passage that has always filled me with a kind of sickly anticipation for what was to come: it matters so much. Reaching the street above, we find that the crowd is already forming in Gillespie Road. It is only midday. We queue at the turnstiles for the North Bank. Eventually we are let in and take a position near the front, just behind and to the left of the goal. There are still two hours to go before kick-off. We eat our sandwiches; somehow I don't enjoy them. The body's adaptation to the excitement, anticipation and uncertainty doesn't allow for the extra demand of digesting food. At last, the waiting is over and the teams emerge from beneath the East Stand which – with its matching counterpart – is still, to me, the most refined and elegant stand, with its 1930s modernism, of any in the country.

I don't remember a great deal about most of the game except that it was tense and tactical. Arsenal were to be First Division Champions that season and their visitors, Blackpool, would finish seventh, some seven points behind. League form counted for little in this game, however: this was the Sixth Round of the FA Cup.

It was only in the last quarter that the stalemate was broken. For much of the game the Arsenal defence had been preoccupied with Stanley Matthews, who had wandered very little. Eventually, his hugging of the right touch-line created the space in the middle that, first, Taylor and then – after an Arsenal equaliser – Brown were able to exploit. The winner came in the 88th minute. Ernie Taylor, diminutive but deadly, pushed the ball into space just inside the Arsenal penalty area. Allan Brown, leading the

Blackpool attack, accelerated into the area. Only Jack Kelsey, the Arsenal keeper, could possibly beat Brown to it. It was the classic 50:50; and, like many movements in sport, the instant appears to be timeless. In some way, the brain freezes the moment before its fulfilment; and all the possible outcomes are processed. The outcome that matters, that is willed for, occasionally – just occasionally – happens. I didn't really see the impact of Kelsey with Brown. I didn't see the shot either. The post was obscuring both. What I did see was the ball nestling in the back of the net. The aftermath was less joyous: Kelsey was up; Brown was prone, his left leg held up behind him at an unusual angle. It was broken in two places. He was to miss the historic Final of 1953 – of which more below.

I have tried to present, in recounting this match and this incident, what I recall rather than what I read then or have seen written since. This is very difficult and I find it very odd to have to go back 40 years to recapture my most vivid live memory of following Blackpool. That moment, that match, encapsulate all that is pleasurable about supporting one's team and the game of soccer. The moment is the microcosm of the whole: anything can happen; and it sometimes does.

For the record, Blackpool went on to the Semi-Final where they beat Spurs 2-1 at Villa Park, thanks to a faulty, last minute back-pass by Alf Ramsey. I heard the second half on the radio. And so to Wembley, where they beat Bolton 4-3. Jean Thomasson describes, in her chapter, how she travelled from Bolton, in support of the losers. I ventured no further than a neighbour's house to watch this 'Matthews Final' on TV: black and white; minuscule screen. How had all this come about? I was 13 and lived in London.

Football supporter – a career

There are as many supporters' careers as there are football supporters, but if there is a pattern for the majority it centres on some kind of introduction by another fan, most probably – as several of my fellow-contributors testify – one's father. This was not my experience. I was the eldest male child in a family of five. We lived in a road of 30 terraced houses, mainly inhabited by retired or elderly people. There was only one other child in the road of my age and she wasn't interested in soccer: tennis yes; but not soccer. My father was a musician, classically trained, whose livelihood had been disrupted by the war and who had never been to a match in his life. My mother had had no involvement either and we had no close family in the locality. I indulge myself in recording these facts because I have spent a great deal of time trying to understand how I became so interested –

obsessed even. My family were, in the context of our location, extremely isolated. My understanding and appreciation of the game had to be self-taught, not from the primary experience of going to a match but from the only other readily available source: the newspaper.

For an example of the effects of isolation on learning, we have the case of Bohuslav Martinu, the Czech composer, who was born and brought up in a watch-tower, from which his father had to alert the town to fires in the surrounding forests. Martinu records the astonishment he felt when he realised that the people in the streets below were the same size as his parents: other people had always appeared as ant-like creatures from his vantage point in the tower. Impaired learning has a number of consequences, two of which were very important in my case: you are prone to fantasising to compensate for a lack of experience; and you are liable to get things wrong.

Thus it was with my selection of Blackpool. The morning of Sunday 8 February 1948 was decision-time. My method was respectable enough: I would choose the club who had scored the most goals the day before. This process of selection was not complicated by any reference to geography or by loyalty to locality. On 7 February 1948 the Fifth Round of the FA Cup had been played. Looking down the scores, I noted that Blackpool had run up five goals – the highest score of the round. Not only was my approach uncomplicated as to geography; it was also free of any considerations as to the quality of the opposition. Blackpool's opponents that day were Colchester United of the Southern League, who had gallantly disposed of three League clubs – Wrexham, Huddersfield and Bradford Park Avenue – in the previous rounds. The decision was made; the die was cast. I would support Blackpool.

It was two years almost to the day – 18 February 1950 – before I managed to get to my first Football League match. Craven Cottage was the venue and Blackpool, naturally, the opposition. My father, after much pressing and persuasion, agreed to take me – *his* first League match. I was not allowed to go alone. Football grounds were dangerous places and crowds could be dangerous, too. Whether or not his fears were based on reports of crowd disasters – the Burnden tragedy experienced by Jean Thomasson was still, of course, a vivid memory – he certainly instilled in me a healthy respect for the potential dangers. Amusingly, he always drew attention to the major role of music in pacifying the crowd.

My father accompanied me for three successive home games, and to a game at Stamford Bridge, before boredom got the better of him and he let me go on my own. At this time I was still at primary school where the football interest centred on Fulham and Chelsea. I have no comprehension

The 'Stanley Matthews Final' of 1953. Hat-trick hero Mortensen (right) takes
the supporting role that history has accorded him.

Eugene Ring

of why I rejected conformity in this matter. Part of the explanation may have been that the local football support came from the rougher, bullying element. What I do know was that I was no closet supporter. The Monday morning after Blackpool's Cup Final defeat by Newcastle United in 1951, a press cutting alluding to the magnificent skills of 'Wor Jackie' Milburn lay across my desk. I remember no bullying, though, for my eccentric support of Blackpool.

In 1951, I finished at primary school and – thanks to a combination of factors, such as the 11+ and the availability of places in Catholic Schools at secondary level – I found myself at a rugby-playing school, where soccer, even in break-time with a tennis ball, was actively discouraged. However, my passion for soccer was sustained by meeting a kindred spirit on my daily journey to Ealing. Tony Brunning, unlike myself an excellent sporting practitioner, was nevertheless an avid fan of Wolves. So our journeys were a wonderful opportunity to sustain our distant interest. To this day I have no idea why he supported Wolves. I must have asked him but have no recollection of his reply – I must ask him again.

For the next seven years, we toured the First Division grounds – watching our teams. London didn't have the pre-eminence then, in terms of First Division representation, that it has now. My recollection is that, for most of the 1950s, Blackpool and Wolves would visit only Highbury, White Hart Lane, Stamford Bridge and the Valley. Charlton were relegated in 1957, but West Ham and Fulham came up in the next two seasons. We saw some great players, for we did more than just follow our clubs. I am grateful to have 'caught', in the latter part of their careers, such greats as Wilf Mannion, Len Shackleton, John Charles and Neil Franklin. We saw some great games, too. A wonderfully exciting FA Cup-tie, which Newcastle won 5-3 at Craven Cottage; and a game at the Valley, one late summer evening, when Charlton and Blackpool drew 3-3, Blackpool coming back from 1-3 down in the closing minutes.

Leaving school, we went our separate ways. Tony became a seminarian. I didn't know what I wanted to do. I tried a number of jobs, one of which was with the Medical Research Council at Hammersmith Hospital, next door to St Clement Danes School, which had a considerable footballing reputation. My laboratory afforded a view of its playing fields and I could occasionally watch a match or their first team in training. I was always impressed by a young goalkeeper, who turned out to be John Jackson, latterly of Crystal Palace and one of the best keepers never to have played for his country.

After this protracted interlude, I went up to Liverpool University in 1962.

At last, I was in a geographical location to explore the heartland of English League soccer: Lancashire! After all, six of the 12 original members of the Football League were from Lancashire (or what was then Lancashire). Liverpool was an exciting place to be in 1962 – for reasons lovingly demonstrated by Geoff Fimister in his chapter. With Liverpool newly arrived back in the First Division after eight seasons in the Second, the omens were good – especially when, on my very first day registering at the Students Union, I recognised the official administering the registration. It was none other than Billy Liddell, his hair still parted centrally in that characteristic way. A more versatile and effective forward no other club possessed; it was a pity that his career had ended just before Liverpool's return to the top flight, for he had carried their forward-line, season in and season out.

Bloomfield Road – at last but rather too late

It was not long before I had made my first visits to Anfield and Goodison. And then, on Monday 13 May 1963 – more than 15 years since that fateful Sunday when I decided to support Blackpool – I paid my first visit to Bloomfield Road. I stood on the Kop as Blackpool contested a goalless, First Division, draw with West Ham. Both clubs finished on 40 points that season, with Blackpool in 13th place. I didn't appreciate it then but there was an air of decline about Blackpool FC at that time. I had never known, or contemplated the prospect of, my club playing outside the First Division. That is not to say there had been no relegation battles: even in the Golden Era, Blackpool had finished 19th in 1954-55 and 20th in 1960-61.

H. Ellis Tomlinson, in his excellent history commemorating the first 100 years of the club – a history to which I am greatly indebted for bolstering a failing memory – dates the decline from 1962. I think this interpretation is correct for, thereafter, Blackpool were not to finish in the top half of the table again. Relegation came in 1967 but in no ordinary way. It is a great consolation to the fan of a failing club that they 'go with a bang' and Blackpool FC certainly did that. Blackpool won only one home game that season and that by 6-0 against Newcastle United. I was there. Quixotically, they contrived to win five away games and not against fellow-strugglers either. They beat Everton at Goodison 1-0 when an Alan Skirton free kick rocketed in minutes from time. They defeated Southampton 5-1 at the Dell on New Year's Eve. Hugh Fisher scored his only goal for the club, impressed Ted Bates and was transferred to the Saints before the season was out. The final irony came on the last day of the season: already doomed,

Blackpool won 3-1 at Anfield. I stood on the famous Kop that day and, as you can guess, Shankly's Liverpool *were* trying.

My life was now radically changing. I was working in Liverpool and had just got married, so there was much to distract. The first season in Division II taught me one important lesson as a fan. No matter what division your club is playing in, excitement never leaves the game. Blackpool nearly made it back to the First at the first time of asking, being pipped by QPR by a fraction of a goal on goal average. To be fair, had it been calculated by the current method of goal *difference*, Rangers would have been home and dry by three goals. Two more seasons passed before promotion was obtained. It proved to be a false dawn: Blackpool were relegated from the First Division in 1971 and have never been back since.

As Alan Plater demonstrates in his chapter, life out of the top sphere has its compensations. For me, these have been twofold: an opportunity to visit all parts of the country, experiencing our rich panoply of grounds; and the pleasure of introducing my children to the game. My work took me from Liverpool to the Potteries and then on to Birmingham. For the last 15 years, I have resided in Bristol. This mobility, allied to Blackpool's mobility between the lower divisions, has enabled me to visit, to date, some 82 of the current Football League and Premier League grounds. The architecture of grounds has always intrigued and fascinated me. Simon Inglis's excellent volumes have put substance to this interest. Just as appreciation of our grounds is increasing and awareness of football's heritage is taking hold, we are seeing its destruction. It appalls me that Craven Cottage – my first ground and undeniably one of the most attractive, with its Leitch Stand and the unique Cottage – is almost certainly doomed. How I mourn those two distinctive stands at Molineux and the Valley – to take just two examples – which gave character to their locations. There was no denying where you were watching. Contrast those edifices with the anonymous DIY-kit grounds recently erected at Walsall and Scunthorpe – it could just as well be Weymouth. The experience of travelling and 'doing' the grounds, at first in supporting 'my team' but now very much for the sake of emulating Bob Holman (see his chapter), has been enhanced by the company of my children, mainly my son.

A new fan in the family

Daniel was born in 1971 in Stoke-on-Trent about a mile from the Victoria Ground. I took him to his first match – Bristol Rovers v Sunderland – when he was six and he accompanied me to the occasional game from then on –

at first locally; then on my Blackpool travels. For some time, the realisation that he was a 'Stokie' didn't quite dawn. Going to the match, any match, was enough.

He learned to become a 'fan' in, of all places, Melbourne, Australia. He was 13 and I was working there for five months. On one of my earlier visits, I'd brought back a pennant of Richmond VFL club, given to me by Leonie Sandercock, who happened to be the author of the definitive history of Australian Rules. After one or two family trips to 'the game', Daniel became an avid fan and travelled alone, all over Melbourne, to his team's matches.

When we returned to the UK, he became a serious Stoke City fan and has now contrived, by enrolling at Staffordshire Polytechnic (becoming Staffordshire University), to be a season-ticket-holder on the Boothen End. Our greatest pleasure is the 'multiple game day' when we try to take in at least two new grounds on the same day. We once managed three: Tranmere 11.30 am; Burnley 3 pm; and Stockport 7.30 pm. And we once managed to see both Blackpool and Stoke City on the same day. Over recent years, our teams and their fixtures have taken us to, if not opposite, then distant, parts of the country.

But now 1992-93 sees Blackpool and Stoke in the same division. Let battle commence, son.

Fuller references to the books mentioned in this chapter, by Inglis, Sandercock and Tomlinson, are given at the end of this book.

Stoke City v Blackpool in headier days: a duel resumed, in 1992-93, for Daniel and Eugene Ring.

12

A Strange Kind of Love

Manchester United, Sir Matt Busby and Europe

Phil Lee

I have never found being a Manchester United fan particularly comfortable. Maybe that is why I am still so fiercely loyal. Sheer bloodymindedness, carrying on despite the obstacles it places in the way of friendships and other calls on time.

It also seems to me that many football enthusiasts practise a strange kind of inverted snobbery. A good friend of mine who died tragically last year was born into Manchester City support, but spent the last ten years of his life living near Stoke as an avid Port Vale supporter. His group of friends claimed they didn't want Vale to go up to the Second Division as it would spoil the romance and mystery of supporting a small team run on a shoe-string budget.

Football romantics?

Much the same points are made by other supporters, including a few of my fellow-contributors, who proudly describe their teams as non-glamorous. The new *Six-o-Six* programme on Radio 5 celebrates such beliefs every Saturday evening.

Support here thrives mainly on the idea of the one-off victory over the bigger teams in Cup competitions and occasionally, perhaps, on a good run in the League when all is carried before 'The Team'. A team that cost little or nothing and is one in the eye for the big swanky clubs, forever spending money on so-called quality players and destroying football's true values. One of the best laughs of all is when a Big Club spends very big money on a player who does not deliver the goods.

This commonly voiced position is not just born of support for the underdog. People who put it strongly seem to feel that commercial values have undermined the once great game of football and that the presently constituted Big Clubs have in some way contaminated the game. They cite much contradictory evidence to confirm these prejudices. The countless northern working-class towns with proud teams that have gone downhill. The constant parade of old players who talk about earning only two bob and being left with nothing from the game. The extremely well-paid present-day players with their agents and greater commitment to their bank balances than to the club. The ever-rising prices and all-seater stadia are all thrown into this irrational hotch-potch and complained about bitterly over endless pints of half-remembered trivia.

At root these people are stuck in some sort of dream world, sometimes a sort of socialist utopia, where people play for the place where they were born and have no desire to earn a professional's crust. They are just proud to play for the local Lads. A bit like playing cricket for Yorkshire and rugby union for England. This is just one reason why it has never been that easy supporting Manchester United, or any other Big Club. The average football fan seems passionately irrational in the face of the massive commercial values that dominate the rest of their lives but which are somehow expected to leave their beloved football untouched.

'Real' football

There are further layers to anti-Manchester United feelings, though. The Busby Babes team that crashed at Munich in 1958 was already surrounded by an aura of youthful, all-conquering romance before tragedy added legend and heroism. Matt Busby's struggle for life and then his efforts to rebuild the club took United beyond the confines of the sports pages and onto a national stage. The fact that only ten years later United were to become the first English club to win the European Cup, with the best three footballers in Europe playing for them – Law, Best and Charlton – alongside other 'greats' such as Crerand and Stiles, merely fuelled this romance and helped establish United as the best-supported team in Britain, with club supporters' branches all over the country. This is a common enough feature of most European countries but one which at that time, before mass television coverage, was unusual in England. The association of United with Catholicism also bred particularly strong attachments in Eire and parts of Northern Ireland and Scotland.

Born in Manchester, I have spent much of my adult life away from it. The invariable reaction to my declaration of allegiance is 'Oh, no! Not another one!' People usually calm down a little upon clarification of my birth-place. This irritation with attachment based on tragedy, success or whim of choice is something I can identify with. Young kids in Leicester or Camborne wearing Liverpool and Arsenal shirts get up *my* nose, too. Yet my four-year-old son understands only too well that the best team in the

League is called Manchester United. Of course, he hasn't got a clue as to why. He's been a couple of times to Old Trafford and cheers when they score on the telly. But he was born in Sheffield and now lives in Leicester. What of his own eventual attachments? Pete Alcock and Geoff Fimister have set out, in their chapters, the alternative tugs for inter-generational loyalties. How will it work out for my son and me?

My son and I can, and occasionally do, walk to Filbert Street in less than ten minutes. On match days we could tell when Leicester score by just opening the window. They really are our local team. It is the first time I have lived so close to any professional football ground. When I first came to Leicester in 1989, I flirted with the idea of being a regular, and attached, supporter. Moreover, my dad had contracted Alzheimer's Disease and had forgotten to renew our United season tickets. So it was going to be hard – from over a hundred miles away and with a young child – to watch United regularly, particularly given all the talk of membership schemes and bans on away fans. I even tried going to Filbert Street with committed fans but it didn't work. The football that first season was very poor, but even when it got better it simply wasn't the same.

I have watched United play poor football innumerable times without ever questioning my support. What is it that has forged such fierce and apparently unbreakable loyalty? Success? Presumably that is why young kids in Camborne and Carlisle wear Liverpool and Arsenal shirts. I am not sure whether my support was reared by success alone. The first time I went to Old Trafford my Dad and I had actually set off to watch Stockport County. Our new next-door neighbour drew up to us in a car as we got off the bus in Stockport and urged us to go and watch some *real* football.

It was *real* all right. I was, as they say, gob-smacked. First, by the size of the place and the sheer volume of people. It was 1957 and the height of the Busby Babes era. United were top of the League and playing second-placed Wolves. But second, and most importantly, I was won over by the football. I was young and inexperienced and had little to judge it by. Stockport County it was not, nor the countless amateur teams my Dad had taken me to ever since I could remember. This was the team of Duncan Edwards, Tommy Taylor, David Byrne, Johnny Berry – who was magical that afternoon – and Denis Viollet, effortlessly scoring four as United walloped their nearest rivals 7-2.

Something more than success

I was hooked. Was it by success? Maybe. Certainly there can have been few better introductions for any eight-year-old to the arts of the game. I was privileged and I wanted to go every week.

To be fair, my Dad is a true football romantic. He had always gone to watch whichever of the two Manchester teams was doing less well. If they were both having a run, he'd be off to Oldham or Stockport. I guess that is why he'd never taken me to United. He knew what a hassle it would be. There was no chance of a season ticket, even if you could afford it, and we certainly couldn't. For me to see properly we had to be at Old Trafford at twelve noon. Yet, once he realised my commitment, he got me there – on time – week in week out, whatever the weather. We went to the reserves and the A team, as well as the all-conquering youth teams.

I first saw Bobby Charlton play for the youth team – against Bridgwater in the FA Youth Cup. They won by a cricket score. Charlton scored, and I do not exaggerate, something like 15 goals. Some from as far out as 30 to 40 yards; how hard and accurately he could shoot! All the adults were saying, 'He's going to be a good 'un, that lad.' How true! My dad took me to the European Cup Semi-Final against the famous Real Madrid team of Puskas and Di Stefano. I was sitting next to an old woman in rollers who merely yelled, 'Get back to yer bloody bull ring,' every time Real touched the ball. United drew 2-2 and the common reaction around me seemed to be that it had been 'men against boys'. United were too young and naive but in a few years they would be unstoppable. Everybody said so; even Manchester City supporters!

What stopped them, of course, was Munich. Eight players dead and many others desperately wounded in an air crash that could easily have been avoided. I can still remember returning from school that fateful day. Two neighbours were leaving our house and I heard one say, 'Mary says best not tell him.' 'Tell him what?' I demanded of my Mum as soon as I got in. She couldn't say; just kept crying and crying. She had taken me to games and had personal connections with two of the players who had died – David Pegg's fiancée did her hair each week and Billy Whelan, who knew my Dad, had been to tea at our house. Eventually she got it out. I just didn't believe her. When my Dad got home from work, he said the city centre was just full of people crying all over the place. He was crying too. I wanted to go, somehow, to be part of it. So he took me on the bus into Manchester – way past my bedtime – and it was true, there were hundreds of people just crying spontaneously all over town. In an odd sort of way participating in this mass demonstration of grief helped.

It was something more than success, then, that shored up my loyalty. The few years after Munich were lean ones for United. Tragedy blended with the fact that I just loved playing and watching the game and went to a school where everybody – girls as well as boys – was committed to City, Stockport or United. It certainly wasn't male bonding or anything like that that led me into being a strong supporter. I more often than not travelled to games with one or more of the three Jackson sisters, who lived opposite. I still remember climbing up into the Stretford End roof, in 1967, so that the smallest sister could get a better view of United collecting the Championship Trophy. They were, and one still is, every bit as fanatical as I am. Strange, as I do not think of myself as a fanatical person; and possibly, if I had been brought up in Plymouth or Leeds, I might never have developed such a fierce passion for one team. But I did.

Sir Matt Busby

Eamon Dunphy, in his 1991 book, *Sir Matt Busby and Manchester United: a Strange Kind of Glory*, comes close to hinting at why. There was something special about the teams that Busby built; and I feel that those of us privileged to watch them knew it.

Manchester United were not a particularly successful side prior to Busby's management – First Division Champions twice and FA Cup-winners once. They were not a Big Club and had spent most of their playing days in the shadows of Manchester City. Busby made United a successful club and did so in a manner that had many of the qualities of a fictional romance. It is worth remembering that a fair number of Big Clubs have become so relatively recently and were not born with silver spoons in their mouths. Others have failed to become so through crass commercial and managerial decisions.

Busby came to United with a vision and was given the opportunity to realise it. He had been offended as a player by the way that directors and managers had patronised the players and was determined to resist what he saw as the worst elements in the old amateurism and the new commercialism. To combat the former, he became the first man to train players by playing with them every day. He introduced club blazers and regular perks such as seaside trips and days off to play golf. He understood people-management and was able to build a solid, happy club. Contrary to much contemporary opinion, he hated some aspects of commercialism and very

Life after Munich: the United side of March 1958.

'A strange kind of love' … locked out of United's 1976 Cup Final defeat.

rarely ventured into the transfer market. He believed in a strong youth policy and the Busby Babes were the brilliant products of it.

He took United into Europe despite opposition from the Football League and Football Association. Indeed, the former threatened to remove United from the First Division if they entered the European Cup. Other League Champions before United had been faint-hearted. Busby successfully called the authorities' bluff.

Bobby Charlton describes Busby, in Dunphy's book, as being like a God. And Georgie Best told Dunphy that if he 'walked past [Busby] and he smiled I felt I was in the presence of a superhuman being, which he was, still is to me'. This is powerful stuff. When I was about 10, I got Busby's autograph outside Old Trafford and felt the sheer charisma of the man. I was most certainly in awe of him. But it was only with time that I could appreciate what he had done to transform United from a club with a bombed-out ground and with hardly any good players into one of the most · famous and respected clubs in the world. Not a lot of fans have the privilege to live through something like that during their own lifetime; and it is a vital component in my commitment to United. Bill Shankly did similar things at Liverpool, probably with even greater lasting effect; for, prior to his stewardship, Liverpool too were a mediocre club.

I believe that all true fans would like someone similarly to transform the fortunes of their club. For their team suddenly to be managed by a person with vision who, through sheer effort and will, makes it the best in the country, Europe and – arguably, a couple of times – the world.

The fact that it happened to United should have made supporting them easy. Yet, as I say, it often wasn't, particularly if the only measure used is success and/or brilliant teams out on the park. The immediate period after Munich was lean for United. Dunphy implies that being so close to death and losing so many close colleagues and friends affected Busby's judgment. It should be no surprise that such trauma could have such an effect. The club was determined to carry on and be great again; and this inevitably meant serious entry into the transfer market, with often unsuitable players being purchased to fill this or that gap. It is at this time that United begin to attract the 'moneybags' label; and Busby starts to be credited, wrongly, with believing that success could be bought.

Like all myths it was fuelled by partial truth. Busby did buy some members of the successful side that went on, in 1968, to win his most coveted prize, the European Cup. He bought the often under-estimated David Herd for £38,000. In 1962, he broke the British transfer record to buy Denis Law from Torino for £115,000 and Paddy Crerand followed from

Celtic for £55,000. Alex Stepney was a late addition from Millwall, in 1967, at a cost of £52,000. United were most certainly big spenders now, but for the first time. Many other great players came the more usual Busby-inspired route. Bobby Charlton had been on the books prior to Munich. George Best came free in 1963, as had the extremely talented Johnny Giles a little earlier. Nobby Stiles, a United supporter all his life, signed as an apprentice and would – in his own words – have paid the club to play for them. Bill Foulkes, Johnny Aston and Shay Brennan also cost nothing. Tony Dunne came from Shelbourne in the League of Ireland for the bargain price of £6,000 and David Sadler cost £750 from non-League Maidstone. United were spending but the majority of the team was still home-grown.

There were other significant indications that United were not a club stupefied by, or stupid about, money. In the summer of 1961, the ceiling of £20 a week for footballers was removed. Little was known about the wages top players would now be able to command. I remember the comedian, Tommy Trinder, chairman of Fulham, boasting that his star inside-forward, Johnny Haynes, would earn £100 a week. Busby paid all his players £25 a week. It is widely known that, during the 1960s, Manchester United and Shankly's Liverpool were the two poorest payers of wages in the First Division, if not the Second as well. Later in the decade, Busby was to do some strange dealings, promising each of his top players that he was the best paid. It is a good example of the accuracy of the main theme of Dunphy's book that, because of the way professional soccer is run and because of the values within it, whoever goes into the game is in the end tarnished by it.

The pinnacle of success

I shall always remember that warm night in May 1968 when United won the European Cup. It was the eve of my part one examinations at Bradford University, but I wouldn't have missed being at Wembley for the world. The game itself was, in all honesty, a bit of an anti-climax and – but for a magnificent save by Stepney from Eusebio with minutes of normal time remaining – United could easily have lost. As it was, extra time brought three excellent United goals and an emotional 4-1 victory.

The Cup run had, as usual, been much more exciting than the Final. I had seen all the home legs, including Best's brilliant goal that beat Gornik and the incredibly tense win over Real Madrid in the first leg of the Semi-Final. None of us expected realistically that a one-goal lead would be sufficient to see us through to the Final. But we had hope; very large amounts of it.

British media football coverage was unbelievably insular and provincial in those days. That away leg in Madrid was covered live by neither television nor radio. My Mancunian friends and I gathered in the university bar with a very large transistor radio, borrowed from the Electrical Engineering Department, and with a friend's girlfriend who spoke fluent Spanish. We drank and drank and tried and tried to find Spanish radio coverage. This we achieved at half-time. We were in such suspense as we asked Christine, our translator, to tell us the score. She calmly informed us United were 3-1 down and apparently well and truly out of it. All euphoria extinguished, we sat stupefied, gazing down at our beers and fearing the worst.

After about 15 minutes, the deafening radio background noise went suddenly quiet. Christine explained that David Sadler had scored a rather scrambled goal. Mass euphoria was back on the agenda. We were insisting on a running commentary by now. And, by all accounts, Real were panicking. With 12 minutes to go, the Spanish commentator suddenly sounded as if his family had all been shot in front of him. Christine informed us that Bill Foulkes had scored a third for United. This I could not believe. I celebrated and all. But Foulkes as a scorer: this simply was not possible. In all the years I had watched him he rarely ventured into the opponents' half. And he had never scored from open play.

The exceptional spirit shown in that second half was the result of all the hard work that Busby – and, in particular, his assistant, Jimmy Murphy – had put in during 23 years. It was on that night, even more than in the Wembley Final to follow, that Matt's players truly honoured him and Jimmy and all they stood for. Yet it was the European Cup victory that effectively brought the Busby era to an end – even if the scale of United's demise did not become apparent until after Busby's retirement a year later. Many of the top players – notably Law, Crerand and Charlton – were near the end of their careers. George Best was eventually to succumb for different reasons. It is interesting to note, though, that his most productive playing days for United were in this declining team. Under the managements of Wilf McGuinness and Frank O'Farrell (1969-72), Best scored 57 goals for United and, contrary to popular belief, missed only six games.

It is also now almost conventional wisdom to suggest that Busby held onto the reins of power for too long and was over-indulgent in his selection and treatment of favourite players. Certainly McGuinness and O'Farrell suffered terribly from his interference and reputation. Two facts are less well appreciated: Busby's long-term fight against the almost feudal way the game was run; and how, by becoming powerful within that system, he was in the end corrupted by it.

Busby stepped down correctly when he was 60. In a properly run commercial sport or business, he would have been able to have become a director of the club. At that time, however, the football regulations, still soaked in a 'shamateurism' designed to keep all power away from professionals, decreed that no director could receive a salary. Busby therefore had to be made managing director. Once in that position he should have walked away from team management affairs. His failure to do so had disastrous consequences for the club, team, players, future managers and himself.

True love

It was very difficult over the next few years to be proud of Manchester United. So many things went wrong; too many to mention. George Best was not given sufficient credit for his professionalism. He was never respected properly. A younger Busby would have made him captain and secured his commitment and the other players' respect. As it was, the greatest talent I ever saw play was lost to the game. An endless series of players who should never have been allowed to wear the famous red shirt came to Old Trafford, stifling the strong tradition of building the club from its youth team upwards. In 1974, United were relegated to the Second Division, albeit for one season only.

Those were bad years. And the United fans, with their expectations of immediate success and the flair associated with the Busby Babes or the Law/Best/Charlton era, did not help. Every defeat, every team selection that did not work and every failure to win something was greeted with complaints along the lines of 'United are the best club in Britain; why can we not find a manager/players to show that?' I had constant arguments with grown, and usually articulate, men and women around that recurrent theme.

Busby's reputation as a manager, and the three successful sides he built, had created a Frankenstein's monster for any subsequent manager or player: a fiercely loyal crowd that believed success was theirs by divine right.

I used to hate some of United's bigoted fans. I still do. My love of United and my tender age blinkered me, up until 1968 or so, to much that was generally ugly about the game and, more particularly, about United. The over-easy assumption of supremacy and the intense racism were always as strong among season-ticket-holders as on the terraces, but tended to be expressed in slightly less strident tones: 'He's quite good for a Blacky'; 'They're so thick, they can't follow team instructions.' It seemed to get much worse in the early 1970s, when the game began to appear more cynical and less dependent on skilful players. All of this could have buried my loyalty to a club created so arbitrarily by the whim of a neighbour's kind offer of a lift in his car.

My loyalty wasn't dimmed, though. As in any case of real desire, the fact that the love object reveals weaknesses and vulnerabilities can tend to make the love stronger. I was every bit as fanatical with United in the Second Division. In fact, they remained, that season, the best-supported team in England. As I constantly informed the carping critics who had expected their support to drop, I would have supported United even in the Fourth Division.

As I hinted at the outset, envy can be a problem for those of us who follow a successful team. Other supporters certainly seem envious of United even when they are not particularly successful. To beat United, widely regarded as the country's most glamorous team, appears often to be a measure of progress, regardless of respective League positions. I still find this one of the most difficult things about supporting them, particularly at those times when a new manager has been trying desperately to rebuild in the face of intense hostility from both sets of fans. Just how many times have I watched away defeats of fairly poor United teams greeted by the home fans as if their team had just won the Cup or League title? Too many times to remember. Almost as many times as I have watched perfectly good home victories dismissed as not spectacular enough by supposedly loyal fans.

Such occurrences simply reinforce my commitment and provoke empathy for the managers and team. I used to write letters to the managers with constructive arguments and advice on team selection and players to buy. I still do this occasionally. I am convinced that Paul Ince owes his transfer to a nice letter I wrote Alex Ferguson. I even applied twice to manage the club. The *Daily Express* claimed that United had received five applications when Tommy Docherty got the post: four serious and one joke one. I wonder who the other two serious ones were apart from Tommy and me?

Perhaps my earlier criticisms of the romantic football fan were misguided. For I am every bit as romantic about United. To be a committed football fan almost requires you to enter into a type of relationship that is romance-driven. Supporters of different teams merely romanticise different things. The feelings that lower division supporters get when their team knocks a Liverpool, Arsenal or Manchester United out of the FA Cup must be unbelievable. One can see, then, how powerful the attraction of supporting such teams must be. In some senses, it is almost as easy to romanticise failure or a glorious past as it is a successful present. And, inevitably, successful presents turn sour. The path of true love never runs smooth; it is the difficulties that make it real and lasting.

Looking back, I suppose it was inevitable that I would fall for Manchester United. That first visit to the ground still lives with me every time I go. The feeling of being so small in such a large and glamorous place. I no longer dream of playing for the club, but everything else lives on.

The period in which I saw two of the greatest British teams ever, and many of the world's best players, was all before my twentieth birthday. Until then players had never been fully rewarded; nor did they train properly. And the worst excesses of professionalism had still not started to squeeze the goodness out of the game. It was, I feel, soccer's true Golden Age. And I was lucky enough, for much of that time, to watch one of the best British representatives of it, home and away.

Europe and the future

What makes it still so exciting is the prospect that Alex Ferguson might have begun to lead the club into another period of greatness. Over five years, he has built up a fine squad which has succeeded, during 1989-92, in winning both the FA Cup and the European Cup Winners' Cup and in challenging seriously for United's first League Championship since 1967.

The critics will claim that those have been the successes of what is now, most certainly, a 'moneybags' club. I would respond to that in two ways. First, Ferguson is the first manager since the waning of Busby's influence to be allowed to realise his own vision for the club. Proper youth policies are now in place again – United won the FA Youth Cup in 1992 – and there is strength, much of it home-developed, throughout the club. Secondly, it is now inevitable that clubs wanting to maintain their success and support will have to buy quality players. Liverpool have consistently bought their success. Competition for good players between ambitious clubs is now an integral part of football.

To win European competitions, clubs have to compete with the likes of Barcelona, Juventus, AC Milan, Real Madrid and Marseilles, each of whom has vast amounts to spend on quality players from around the world. It will not be long before there will be a European Super League. Ambitious English clubs are investing heavily to guarantee that they can become a part of that. Implicit in the romantic view of football is an inbuilt suspicion of, and resistance to, such developments. That is what I object to. The romanticising of smallness, the past and a game free of commercialism. Football in the old days was run by the equivalent of feudal tyrants, hiding behind amateurism. It was corrupt and exploited the players. There is no distant romantic past; and we can only be realistic about the future.

A Golden Age (1962-72) may be past. British football may now be played by the super-fit at a hundred miles an hour, but there is still room for skill. There are still players who can take spectators' breath away – Paul Merson, Ryan Giggs, Gary Lineker, Des Walker, to name but a few – and to do that in the modern game, with its tight-marking, packed midfields and constant closing-down, is no mean achievement.

I look forward to the day when English clubs have grounds and facilities like those we saw in Italy during the last World Cup. Competition is no longer on the parochial basis it was when football first became an organised game. I want to see Manchester United regularly competing in a league with the best of Europe's teams. Such a league need not be a self-perpetuating hierarchy. There would still be national leagues and the national champions could compete for promotion places.

If United do not make it, then I wish good luck to those teams that do. I will still take some pride from the role that my team has played in creating European-wide football and will remain a United supporter, whatever league they are in.

This chapter has drawn upon two histories of the club – by Percy M. Young (1960) and Eamon Dunphy (1991) – and on an interview with Dunphy published in the December 1991 issue of *When Saturday Comes*. Full references to the two books are given at the end of this book.

13

Keeping to the Maine Road

Rob Behrens

The post-war history of Manchester City is one of under-achievement, incompetence, unpredictability, outrageous transfer extravagance, persistent meanness to loyal servants and occasional, dizzy, triumph. This history is also the secret history of my feelings: a tale of loyalty, pride, and unpardonable narrow-mindedness and naivety. As such it is not an easy story to tell.

Born to be Blue

I was born on the day that City played and drew with Manchester United in 1952. In *Midnight's Children*, Salman Rushdie wrote of the magical powers possessed by Saleem Sinai when he was born on the stroke of midnight at the moment of India's independence in 1947. Saleem had the magical power of being able to listen to the inner voices and conversations of other people. For me, derby day 1952 brought no such luck. All I got was an extended 30-year lesson in endurance. And there was nothing magical about that. My father was mildly irritated at having to miss the game, but my grandfather expressed his delight in a congratulatory telegram, heralding the arrival of a third-generation Manchester City supporter. The deed was done. In so far as one can be, therefore, I was born into a tradition. Allegiance was assumed, not chosen.

After incessant nagging, I was taken to my first match (a boring derby) in 1957 and nagged to be taken home at half-time. By 1958 I had been forgiven and had a regular ring-side view of a long and fairly miserable decline. For each home game my mum would win permission from the special constables on duty to drive the Ford Anglia up to the front of Maine Road and drop my grandfather (severely disabled from a stroke), my father and me directly outside the season-ticket entrance. The challenge each year was to avoid relegation and City's fate was usually in doubt until the very end of the season. My dad encouraged me to believe that this at least retained our interest until May.

It is not so much the particular games but the sounds and aromas of the ritual visits that I remember. At the terraced, uncovered, Scoreboard End – with its crude, manually operated, half-time scoreboard – the wooden rattles crackled and whirred (it was not until later on that the Kippax Street stand became a focal point for chanting and singing). At half-time, the watery Bovril revived and warmed us as we listened to the Beswick Prize Brass Band; while, throughout the game, the main stand supporters grumbled continually and I received my schooling in gallows humour. When City made an unexpectedly good start to the season in the early 1960s, I vividly recall a season-ticket-holder near us turning the match programme upside down so that the First Division table would look more familiar.

Despite having poor teams, during this period Manchester City had some special players. A number of false dawns were heralded with the arrival of big money signings like Denis Law, Alex Harley (who scored two goals on his Maine Road debut) and Peter Dobing. Law blotted his copybook somewhat by saying the unsayable – he wouldn't want to play for City if they were relegated. He was soon on his way to Italy. Redoubtable survivors from the 1956 Cup Final included Ken Barnes, an elegant wing-half; Dave Ewing, an uncomplicated centre-half; Bill Leivers, a stout full-back; and Joe Hayes, a nimble forward. Bert Trautmann regularly performed heroics in goal – sufficient to make a mediocre side look plausible.

A former German prisoner of war, Trautmann joined City in 1949 to replace the legendary Frank Swift. Surviving initial opposition from a number of chauvinist City supporters, years of insidious hate-mail from a variety of cranks and racist abuse from opposition terraces, Trautmann played more than 600 times for City until he retired in 1964. He won god-like status when he broke his neck during the 1956 Cup Final, diving at the feet of Birmingham's Murphy. Despite excruciating pain, Trautmann played on until the game was won and even collected his winner's medal. His physical presence and immense bravery, his stunning flexibility and superb positional sense, made him a goalkeeper in a thousand. His capacity to save penalties was prodigious. And so was his temper. Towards the end of his career, in 1963, he furiously disputed a goal scored by West Ham United at Maine Road. When the referee took no notice, Trautmann picked the ball out of the net and kicked it with force – and remarkable accuracy – so that, from 25-30 yards, it hit the unsuspecting official from behind. The great man was instantly dismissed, tore off his jersey and strode from the pitch. It took me weeks to recover from the shock of witnessing this; and it cost Trautmann seven days' suspension and a £10 fine. More than 50,000 people showed up to pay tribute to Trautmann at his Testimonial in 1964.

Days later, offers of a 'job for life' from the board proved to be worthless and Trautmann was sent packing.

Because City struggled to keep their First Division status, and finally lost it in 1963, they lived constantly in the shadow of near neighbours, Manchester United. Resurgent under Matt Busby, and transformed into a national institution by the horror of the Munich aircrash, United were nevertheless the great rivals. Although only five at the time, I remember vividly the news of the Munich disaster. Shamefully, neither then, nor until much later, did I find it easy to associate myself with the tragedy. Certainly, my father went into the city centre, in the way that Phil Lee recounts, to participate in the communal grief. For me, however, a five-year-old with limited understanding, it was United's mourning and not something that had a great impact. Perhaps this was a reflection of my own callousness or of what the United v City divide then meant in south Manchester primary schools.

United supporters certainly outnumbered City supporters at my school. And in the parks there were always more red shirts than blue ones. United fans were not slow to press home their advantage in what we instinctively felt to be arrogant behaviour. My friends and I shared a common passion for football, but we were friends in spite of our allegiances to rival teams. In this sense there was no common football tradition in Manchester, but rather two competing traditions. In hindsight, of course, I think this adversarial approach diminished the experience of being a supporter. There may have been a certain spirit in the observation that 'I wouldn't say I hated Manchester United, but let's put it this way: if they played in my back garden, I'd draw the curtains.' But that kind of attitude blinded some of us to the genius of a football generation at Old Trafford – a genius lauded in this book not only by a partisan Phil Lee but also by Jean Thomasson and David Bull who experienced it as neutrals.

Two years in the Second Division left City directionless. One home fixture, against Swindon Town, saw the crowd plummet to below 9,000. I was not among them and still feel guilty about it. However, I seem to know about 12,000 who say they were there. The appointment of Joe Mercer as manager in 1965 changed everything. Mercer's arrival marked the beginning of the greatest period in the club's history. For me, it was a brief enchantment, though not without acute physical dangers.

Enchantment and danger

Mercer, a peerless player, a shrewd judge of talent and perhaps the most decent man in the history of football, brought along Malcolm Allison as his coach and assistant. Allison, a fine coach and motivator, soon began to wipe away the supporters' sense of inferiority. Together, Mercer and Allison were unbeatable. They brought to Maine Road a rich vein of talent and at knock-down prices. Mike Summerbee ('Buzzer'), Colin Bell ('Ding-Dong'), Francis Lee ('Frannie') and Tony Book were bought for a total of £157,000. Along with the home-grown talent of Mike Doyle, Neil ('Nellie') Young, Glyn Pardoe and Alan Oakes, they formed the core of an all-out attacking team which won, in three successive seasons, the League Championship (1968); the FA Cup (1969); and both the League Cup and European Cup-Winners' Cup in 1970.

Throughout this period, Bell, Lee and Summerbee were rampant, never more so than during the epic 3-1 win at Old Trafford in 1968, a night every City supporter present will long remember. Bell had just about everything: an angular grace, wonderful balance, amazing stamina, terrific acceleration and a capacity to score goals with either foot. He was one of the finest players in Europe; and, for many City fans at the time, it was irritating that he was long in the shadow of Bobby Charlton. Bell's career was cut short by crippling injury. His comeback game against Newcastle United on Boxing Day 1975 was a moving, exhilarating and unforgettable occasion. Lee and Summerbee had less talent but more 'chutzpah'. Unlike any other forward I have watched, Lee seemed to run at players before swerving to pass them. He had one of the fiercest shots in football and scored goals of awesome power. He also had a unique capacity for winning and converting penalties (United fans alleged that he dived). In the 1971-72 season, he scored so many times from the spot, reported in the newspapers as 'Lee One Pen', that he became affectionately known as the 'Chinese Mandarin of Maine Road'.

During these years, I followed City wherever I could. This was not without its dangers. At home, one could time one's retreat from the ground to avoid the packs of marauding opposition supporters. Travel to away games was a different question. It was a matter of pride to wear my blue-and-white hand-knitted scarf. And it was a matter of perverted honour for opposition supporters to seek to steal it. At the Baseball Ground, a group of Derby County supporters surrounded me and gave me the choice of surrendering my scarf or 'We'll kill you.' With insane stupidity, I hung on to my scarf and got rescued by a police officer.

Book here for success: Tony Book, captain of the all-conquering City side of the late 1960s.

Later on, at Liverpool, in 1970, I was not so fortunate. A family discussion resolved that I should take my scarf because Liverpool had the reputation of having wonderful supporters. I travelled for the first and only time on the football 'special' train, to be greeted at Lime Street station with an avalanche of bricks and missiles from the waiting Liverpudlians. Realising that to sport my scarf would be dangerous, I stuffed it inside my jacket. In a torrid game, City lost 3-0 and Wyn Davies was sent off for head-butting John Toshack. On the long walk back to the station, I was surrounded by a pack of Liverpool supporters. They asked me where I came from. In a reply reflecting both my dim-wittedness and my social science training, I responded by querying why it was they wanted to know this. There the conversation ended. I was beaten about the head, kicked and robbed of both my scarf and my money. There was not a police officer in sight. One passive onlooker tried to console me by explaining that decent Liverpudlians abhorred what happened, but were powerless to intervene. A few minutes later, another home supporter spotted my bloodied face and asked if it had been inflicted by Liverpool fans. When I replied 'Yes', he punched me in the face, shouted 'Good!' and ran off.

In all of this, the outstanding memory is of my own stupidity – both in taking my scarf anywhere near Anfield and in uncritically swallowing the television football pundits' one-dimensional, mawkishly sentimental, account of Liverpool Football Club and its supporters. No doubt this myopia was the outcome of sustained and privileged access to boardrooms, players and directors' boxes.

The golden era of Mercer and Allison came to a shabby end with the ousting of Mercer, who, like Trautmann before him, had been guaranteed a job for life by the board. Allison assumed full control, before being lured back to London by Crystal Palace in 1973. When he returned in 1977, there was no Mercer to restrain his gambler's instinct: the slogan was 'Spend, Spend, Spend', as he became the Vivienne Nicholson of football. The role of the supporters in all of this was to watch in stupefaction as Allison dismantled a good team and spent millions on establishing a worse one. This crazy spending policy contaminated all of us associated with the club. To declare one's allegiance, as I did in the foreword to something I wrote at the time, was to invite ridicule. One reviewer commented how unwise it was to display lack of judgment so early in the text. It was also traumatic watching the rapid departure of talented players from Maine Road. The first words one of my friends said to his new-born son in 1979 were in the form of a question: 'Do you think City were right to sell Peter Barnes, Sammy?' Sammy's reply is unrecorded. And, queueing to renew my season-ticket at this time, I witnessed an irate but loyal subscriber handing over the money and calling on the club officials to tell 'him' (Malcolm Allison) to take more care of it next year. Some hope!

Life after Allison was quieter, not least because the club were saddled with £4 million-worth of debt. Managers came and went and City continued their yo-yo progress from First to Second Division and back again. John Bond, Billy McNeil and Howard Kendall all came and went. Kendall's arrival at Maine Road was greeted with ecstasy. The whole ground rose to salute him as he walked on to the pitch before the home game against Norwich City on Boxing Day 1989. My father-in-law, an opera enthusiast who hadn't been to a game since 1939, enquired as to why everyone was cheering the balding man in the suit. Within a year, we were all asking the same question. When Kendall's departure, back to Everton, was announced in a BBC news flash, I really believed that the BBC must have got their facts wrong. When he compared his spell at Maine Road to a diversionary 'affair' from his more permanent 'marriage' to Everton, I, like many others, felt mildly abused. Objectively, however, Kendall saved City from relegation and restored high standards of professionalism to an ailing set-up.

From the post-Allison period, certain things are chiselled on my memory. One is the Cup run of 1981, in which John Bond steadied the Allison inheritance by adding Tommy Hutchison and Bobby MacDonald to the team. After Rodney Marsh and possibly Freddie Hill, Hutchison was the most skilful player seen at Maine Road for a generation. MacDonald was a fine full-back in the Billy Leivers tradition. Paul Power scored a thunderous winning goal in the Semi-Final, at Villa Park, against the much-fancied Ipswich Town. I remember joining the City fans behind the goal in going berserk. The Centenary Final of 1981 will probably be remembered by most for Ricky Villa's decisive goal for Spurs. For me, however, the vital memories are two-fold: the tricky task of writing a lecture while queueing for Replay tickets at Maine Road (the Replay was better value than the lecture); and being on the £10 benches, with friends I had known since childhood, celebrating Steve Mackenzie's wonderful goal.

A less pleasant, but equally vivid memory, is of travelling in 1984 to Stamford Bridge with a friend who is a Chelsea supporter and an expert on suicide. We had good seats for the League Cup-tie between Chelsea and City, but were surrounded by thousands of apparently crazed partisans. 'If I were you,' Steve suggested, knowing my voluble tendencies, 'I would keep very quiet in here tonight.' I needed no convincing. I sat in silence, listening in astonishment to a succession of racist, anti-semitic, songs. They were sung with a venom and a fervour which gave me some inkling of what a Nuremburg rally must have been like. It was occasions like this which deterred me from regular attendance at games, so that, by the end of the decade, I had become something of an armchair supporter. My allegiance remained undiminished, however, and on rare weekends in Manchester, my father would put up only token resistance before accompanying me to Maine Road.

When my son, Benjamin, was born in 1991, my father presented him with a City scarf and I pictured, in my mind's eye, father, son, and grandpa making the great trek to Moss Side. 'This is where grandpa and I sat when City beat Burnley 7-0 in 1969 and Francis Lee scored a belter,' the dream continued. Benjamin listened in awe to the tales of derring-do. In the cold light of day, I am not so sure. Since the experience of being beaten up at Liverpool, I have been determined that the celebration of a fine tradition will not avert my gaze from the seamier side of the game. I have seen enough of contemporary football crowds to question the wisdom of exposing small, or even medium-sized, children to their caprice. When it comes to my own offspring, I will take no chances.

Furthermore, even if it turns out to be safe, is it fair to impose the son of an exiled Mancunian to an apprenticeship of northern suffering? I now know just about enough about parenthood to understand that, in the end, Ben will decide for himself. If he decides to take up his City inheritance, I will teach him all I know about Manchester City and the wider football tradition. I will have to trust that – unlike me – he can quickly rise above the parochial and appreciate football genius regardless of the colour of the shirts. If he shows no interest, I will shed no tears.

Derby day in Manchester: Dennis Tueart takes on Martin Buchan.

14

Go Go County!

Harry Fletcher

29 October 1958: Edgeley Park was a grim place. Stockport were playing the RAF. Dozens of memories of the ground, the fixtures and the characters are indistinguishable now, but that night was almost certainly the birth of a 35-year fascination with an unfashionable cause.

On the night, the significance of the fixture was lost on me. The airforce fielded a team of youngish players from bases in Stafford, Wellesbourne and Harper Hill. The programme notes welcomed 'the team (and accompanying officers)'. Further games followed against Western Command and the Midlands Services League. The crowds were safe and small. The dads said they were watching the future; the sons were confused, unaware that most of the service sides were two-year conscripts, soon to return to fame and Football League sides.

Humble record

Yet 1958 was no great landmark. During the previous 75 years, Stockport County hadn't won that much.

Formed as Heaton Norris Rovers in 1883, County adopted their present title eight years later. Few outside Stockport will know that they also took on the rather confusing nickname of the 'Hatters'. They were Third Division (North) champions in 1921 and 1936. They won the Fourth Division in 1967 and finished second in that division in 1990. Promotion never lasted more than a season or two. Indeed, the overwhelming majority of the last 108 years has been spent in the lower depths of the Third (North) or Fourth Divisions. Only one County player was ever capped for his country: goalkeeper Harry Hardy played once for England in 1924. Between 1970 and 1989, County managed to finish in the top half of the Fourth Division on four occasions. The highest place during that inauspicious period was eleventh. But County do jointly hold the record League win of 13-0, against Halifax in 1934. And they went 51 games without defeat in the mid-1920s.

In the more recent past, Stockport held Liverpool to a draw at Anfield in the Cup in 1965; George Best turned out for them on three occasions in

1975; and Eric Morecambe insisted, in his foreword to the 1978 *Roy of the Rovers Football Quiz Book*, that both Des O'Connor and Mike Yarwood had had trials for County in the early 1960s.

County, writes Alan Rowlands in Bert Trautmann's biography, 'had performed without any great distinction since their formation, occasionally finding the right form to linger around the promotion area for a while, but since 1959 when they had been relegated from the Third Division, a place in mid-table was regarded as something of an achievement'.

Supporting County, then, has hardly been exhilarating. There is no persistent air of expectation associated with clubs that have mass followings. There has always been a sharp contrast between the almost arrogant assumptions of the Old Trafford regulars and the self-effacing souls of Edgeley Park. There are no London 'Hatters' or European support groups. Stockport has always been a local club; it projected itself as a family club long before it became the fashion; but, first and foremost, it has always been a struggling club. Most of its fans, while desirous of achievement in the long run, would want it to stay that way.

A re-examination of my 30-odd years of inconsistent fascination for the club suggests that there are a handful of prerequisites for persistent support for Stockport – or, perhaps, for any basement team, particularly if the fan is in exile. London has collected hundreds of supporters from unsuccessful clubs. Witness a recent terrace meeting at Brisbane Road of supporters from York, Grimsby, Ayr, Rotherham and, of course, Stockport.

By half-time, the meeting had concluded that basement fans do not really ever expect to win anything: to do so would destroy the long-term empathy with the underdog. These basement fans therefore need and expect to be giggled at and labelled as no-hopers by prosperous football peers feeding from domestic and European success. No hope, however, does not correlate with despair or depression. Quite the reverse: it's enjoyable pain. Despite living with defeat, missing promotion, worrying about re-election and now the prospect of demotion to the GM Vauxhall Conference, there is always a hunch that a change of fortune is just around the next game or two or three. The optimism at Stockport goes back to its formation in 1883. The sense of self-sacrifice that comes with it is part of the package. The basement fan is not attracted to the anonymity of the capacity crowd, the lure of the Premier League or the aura of Roy Race and Melchester Rovers PLC.

For the committed County supporters of the 1960s, for example, Old Trafford or Maine Road was an occasional welcome treat but never a serious threat to grass-root loyalties. On a personal level, Old Trafford was not an early option. Many Mancunian parents forbade attendance at City or

United, fearing, no doubt, a crushing in the crowd or some other terrible mishap. If not diverted into piano lessons or some other 'constructive' distraction, the unfortunate children of such parents were steered, under supervision, to Edgeley Park. Even then, it was safety first for me and my school chums in south-east Manchester – initially from Ladybarn Secondary Modern and then from Burnage Grammar – who were never without a chaperone.

My first real encounter with a competitive match was in 1959 and it was a Cup Final. The first leg of the Cheshire Bowl, to be precise. The finalists were Stockport and Crewe. Other teams were rumoured to enter the competition, but most years it was those two who made the Final. County won 1-0. No one particularly famous played that night, although Trevor Porteous, at No. 4 for Stockport, re-appeared for the club, throughout the next 25 years, in a whole range of capacities, including captain, coach, player-manager and physio – in all, an extraordinary tale of club loyalty. The outcome of the second leg of the Bowl, played the next night, is long lost and forgotten.

The politics of optimism

By 1960, Stockport were several seasons into their 30-year wilderness. The side saw a succession of managers, the latest occupant being the 25th since 1945. All had thankless tasks, few achieved any success, most were motivated by the politics of optimism. This optimism remained a recurrent theme in the manager's notebook and the chairman's notes, the columns in the club programme wherein the steady succession of managers and chairmen persisted in rallying the faithful.

Thus, in the manager's notebook in 1962, Reg Flewin reported that, 'Although often disappointed when negotiating for new players, I always had confidence in the present playing staff pulling themselves out of the bad run which has more than been proved in recent games against Brentford and Aldershot.' Three months later, Reg was driven to reflect that, 'After the run of misfortune we have suffered since the beginning of the season it was about time Dame Fortune smiled kindly on us.'

A year later and Reg Flewin had gone. Trevor Porteous, survivor of the Cheshire Bowl, had taken the job. With unique justification, after holding Liverpool at Anfield, he wrote: 'It could be that we have now reached the turning point in our fortunes and can only hope for this to be proved true.' It wasn't, of course. But, by February 1965, optimism was back with a vengeance. Ejected by Manchester City in the abrupt manner that Rob Behrens describes, Bert Trautmann was wooed to Edgeley Park. Pleased with his capture, the chairman proudly boasted, in his notes, that 'Bert, our administrative manager, is shortly to begin a series of out-and-about visits to factories and clubs to talk football and let you know what we are aiming to do.'

In the same match programme, the manager now thought County worthy of Second Division football, 'at least' – even though he found the team's current League form 'pretty depressing'. But the earth did move. Bert switched matches to Friday nights to tempt City and United fans to contemplate dual support. He adopted the club's first slogans – *Go Go County* and, perhaps a shade predictably, *Friday Night Is County Night*. Attendances did rise appreciably, despite continued bad results. Bert described his task as 'formidable', adding, 'Super optimists that we are, there is enough confidence in the club that it can be done.' The memories are good.

Groups of sixth formers from Burnage School, wondering if anything really could improve, would arrive at Edgeley Park in uniform. Arguments would ensue with elderly turnstile attendants about schoolboy status and levels of payments. Bert would appear from his office to settle the disputes himself. No one was ever turned away, no matter how much we outgrew our blazers.

The crowds rose to 6,000 – even 7,000 – during those months. It seems odd now, as I re-examine my programmes and cuttings, that Stockport still finished last in the Fourth Division, once more applied for re-election and kept League status because of big-team support. The optimism was still in abundance, the chairman promised success, Bert brought in Manchester City players and County even toured Germany in the close season. But the excitement was short lived: by the end of 1966, differences over selection procedures, and no doubt much else, led to Trautmann's departure to Munster. In 1967, though, Stockport did clinch promotion; but, two seasons later, they were back where they had been for years and where they were to stay for decades.

By late 1969, the new coach, Matt Woods, was writing of 'things not going so well' and 'of the need for determined optimism'. It was not to be. Attendances fell to earlier levels and media interest reverted to the limits of the local newspapers. The next manager, Brian Doyle, decided not to forecast fame or results. His decision was one of the wisest in Stockport's history: the next 20 years were spent in the northern doldrums, with re-election, or the threat of it, the seasonal reality.

The only recurrent theme discernible from the club notes was now that of survival, although the pattern was much the same for all small northern clubs. The good players left; few were transferred in; modest fundraising

" LET OFF STEAM " here by all means,
but for STEAM CONTROL go to
L. L. PRICE (PIPELINES) LIMITED
VALVES, FLANGES, PIPE FITTINGS, for steam, water
and gas. COPPER and BRASS TUBES. COPPER COILS etc.
" Brascop House ", 33, Buxton Road, Heaviley, Stockport
WE HAVE THE LARGEST STOCKS IN THE AREA   Phone STO 4821

STOCKPORT COUNTY A.F.C.

OFFICIAL
PROGRAMME

PRICE - - 3d.

WEDNESDAY, 29th
OCTOBER, 1958

COUNTY v.
R.A.F.
Maintenance Command

C. & C.
for
Club Orange & Club Lemon

★ **CANTRELL & COCHRANE**
LIMITED

★ **Welkin Road, Lower Bredbury,**
Stockport

★ Phone WOOdley 2136

was paramount. The ground itself, in the shadow of the Manchester to London railway line, was always in urgent need of repair.

Hooligans, racists and the police

The phenomenon of soccer hooliganism largely passed County by. There were signs of potential trouble in 1965-66, at the time of the slogans, the hype and the hope of Trautmann, with his Manchester City connection. My memories are quite clear of parental disapproval for the boisterous 'Cheadle Enders' and of discussions, outside the directors' entrance, of the need for concerted action to stamp out the darkly threatening behaviour. I remember a well-dressed man, presumably a director, telling young fans of Peterborough's defeat and therefore County's gain, being jeered at and abused in return. It was unpleasant, unseemly and incomprehensible. The chairman was forced, half way through the season, to issue an ultimatum:

> It concerns the youthful fans who give voice to their County feelings behind the Cheadle End goal. Unfortunately, they have caused some nasty situations in recent games, which has resulted in the police having to evict a few of them. This kind of support we can do without … Some of the behaviour concerned – including the throwing of missiles and the chanting of obscene verses – will have to stop.

These were strong, and indeed risky, words from a club in need of every paying customer it could muster. Maybe the tirade and the disapproval worked: little else of a disorderly nature is recorded in subsequent programmes to hand. The manifestation of the hooligan challenge was firmly up the A6 at Old Trafford. The limited disorder at Stockport was a distant echo of the Stretford End. The imitation was sadly predictable: the chant, the missiles, the abuse, the minor pitch invasion and the fighting outside. Most of it was drink-related, all of it outpourings of masculinity. The participants, to be kind, were youths with limited forms of expression. At Stockport the imitation took hold at the precise time that marketing, public relations and media attention gained a foothold.

Cheshire media interest increased, rather than reduced, the attention-seeking behaviour. The police nationally had no alternative but to respond. No doubt the Cheshire Constabulary reacted in a similar way to the rest of England and Wales. I have no first-hand knowledge for, by 1970, Stockport had been left behind. However, personal witness accounts of police officers and hooligans, over the next 15 years, suggest that the nature of the police response to organised thuggery at least helped perpetuate the scale of the activity.

From exile in London, support for Fourth Division Stockport proved difficult. County's visits to London were rare: the smaller south-east clubs were clustered in the Second and Third Divisions, a function, perhaps, of local and regional economies.

As I mentioned earlier, some of London's unattached tended often to get together, during the 1970s and 1980s, at London's fashionable football spots: the 'lower terraces' at White Hart Lane or the 'Clock End' at Highbury (to which Syd Jeffers extends such a warm, albeit partisan, invitation below). In the process, we witnessed the triple horror of violence, racism and tough policing – leading, eventually, to our alienation from soccer as a spectator sport.

The violence I associate especially with Tottenham. I think, for instance, of being among home supporters, returning south from White Hart Lane. Ahead, concealed in a church, were six or seven Liverpool fans. It was unclear whether the Liverpool ambush was by design and intent or the consequence of some earlier feud; but the attack was vicious. For some time a pattern had developed at Tottenham: in the High Road, after the match, opposing fans belted each other; and, if that was not possible, both pelted the police. For the unattached exiles, seeking entertainment, the Liverpool incident turned Tottenham into a no-go area for many years.

The racism was especially rife, in the 1970s, at Upton Park, where the baiting of Clyde Best was a disgrace. But neither the racist taunts nor the racial violence were peculiar to London. In 1980, three or four of us, loosely attracted to the fortunes of Portsmouth, travelled to Northampton for the final game of the season. A win put Pompey in the Third Division. Afterwards, the town centre was awash with visiting fans, focus pointed inward, backs draped in Union Jacks. A youngish black man turned a corner into the throng. The mob stared for a second or two, then attacked. In a moment the incident was over, the victim scarred by the injustice of it all for years.

At times, the police acted oddly, if not with hostility, to the confrontations. Following a rather dull match between West Ham and Derby in the late 1970s, the police policy was to funnel all the spectators onto the far pavement. The fans moved slowly. Individual officers became aggressive. Suddenly, and without provocation, an officer armlocked a longish-haired youth, to my right, and frog-marched him into an awaiting blue van. The van was engulfed by protesters, but the police refused to listen to our concerns. The outraged public hung on; witnesses were offered; a solicitor was found; the lad was bailed. The court acquitted him; justice was done. The police officer seemed puzzled: why had neutral spectators gone to all that trouble – hanging around the station, turning up in court, giving evidence? We, ourselves, were not sure: something about the underdog?

Several years later, a group of fans now into their thirties travelled by train to Villa Park for an FA Cup Semi-Final. Outside the station, we were herded down a narrow, police-lined pathway to the ground. Our party hung back and attempted to leave in search of a restaurant. But the inspector would have none of it. Protestations and tight legal points – we had two lawyers among us – were ignored. The officer was abusive: a price of attendance was strict control of match-day freedoms, he explained. Several minutes later, 3,000 angry and thirsty fans were penned into an area at the back of Villa Park. Windows were broken, items were pinched, fans baited the Birmingham police.

Incidents like these were repeated all over the country each week for over a decade. The exiles turned to gardening and childcare on Saturday afternoons.

It may be that the heavy police response to the unacceptable behaviour of a small, but criminally intent, group contributed both to falling attendances and to a loss of confidence in the impartiality of the force. Much of the problem appears to have been transferred elsewhere: into domestic strife; into other sports; or into joy-riding and community riots. We neutrals are older and more subdued. For some of us, the boyhood loyalties have been rejuvenated.

Stockport are in the Third Division now – or Second, in the new vocabulary of the Premier League and the 70 also-rans. The latest manager, Danny Bergerra, seems to inspire. In May 1992, County played at Wembley twice within a week. Thousands of fans chanted 'There's only one Danny Bergerra' – for hours on end. The police smiled benignly. Sadly, the super-optimists lost both ties. But that need not matter, for I hear that confidence at Edgeley Park has never been so high.

Full references to the Trautmann biography and the *Roy of the Rovers Football Quiz Book* are given at the end of this book.

15

Faith in the City

Jack House

Two dates are of ultimate significance in my life. On 2 September 1944, newly returned from wartime evacuation, I was taken for the first time by my Dad to Ashton Gate, the home of Bristol City Football Club. There I saw Bristol City defeat Cardiff City 3-0 in a wartime League West match. Even at this remove, the winning team trips fairly easily off the tongue: Ferguson; Preece and Reilly; Clark, Roberts and Brinton; Collins, Chilcott, Owen, Thomas and Hargreaves (2-3-5, of course).

So began a love relationship with the Robins which has now lasted for nearly half a century. During this period, I have seen them scale the heights. Who will ever forget that opening Division I match in 1976-77, when newly-promoted City humbled mighty Arsenal at Highbury? And I have seen them plumb the depths. Who, apart from those of us involved, can appreciate the anguish we endured when they were relegated from Division I to Division IV in successive seasons between 1979-80 and 1981-82?

This love relationship has entailed my travelling by train, car, coach, bus, bicycle, foot (and on one occasion even by boat) to some of the extremities of the land, including Carlisle, Newcastle, Norwich, Plymouth and Wrexham, in support of the Robins.

The second date of ultimate significance was 31 October 1981, the feast of All Hallows (or Hallowe'en). The venue was the Church of Saint Francis of Assisi, Ashton Gate, situated practically within spitting distance of City's ground. There, amidst all the symbolic ritual which the Catholic tradition in the Church of England espouses, I was ordained a priest and licensed to serve in the parish of Bedminster, one of whose main geographical focuses are the pylons which have so often shone on the Robins.

Bishop Freddy Temple, then Bishop of Malmesbury, who presided at my ordination, was a confirmed Manchester United supporter, but I consoled myself with the fact that at least United wore the same colours as City. And, in any case, I had taken steps to ensure that, among those who laid priestly hands on me, were two fellow Cityites, Roger Thomas and Iain Whyte.

Thus, over the past 11 years, my ministry as a priest has involved me in seeking to serve my fellow-parishioners in Bedminster – as together we have shared in the highs and lows of human experience, birth, marriage, divorce, unemployment, suffering and death – and in trying to focus each and every one of these within the context of the universal assertions and claims of the Christian faith.

Partisan or pastor?

It has on occasion been suggested to me that my commitment to Bristol City and my vocation as a priest are wholly incompatible or, at least, would seem to entail a degree of role conflict. Thus it is alleged that my loyalty to the City is, by its nature, an intensely localised commitment, involving as it must a refusal to acknowledge the validity and claims of any other club – especially of City's arch rivals, Bristol Rovers.

In my view, no self-respecting City supporter would ever set foot inside the Rovers' headquarters for any reason, be they, as in former years, Eastville Stadium, or, as now, Twerton Park at distant Bath. I am in no doubt that the very worst thing that can ever happen to the City is to lose to the Rovers – a fact which some of our imported managers of recent years have not fully appreciated, if their somewhat inane comments in the local media are to be believed. On the other hand, my vocation as a priest requires me to minister to all, irrespective of age, sex, race, creed – or even football preference.

The holding together of these two vistas, the rabidly partisan and the universal, is indeed the source of very real tension for me. Yet such tension, and its resolution, is, I believe, of the very essence of being both a lifelong, one-club football supporter and a priest, intent on serving one's parishioners to the best of one's ability.

The focus of ministry of a caring parish priest lies within a local congregation, which in turn gathers into itself the life of the local community and then dares to declare that this life, in all of its manifestations, is of very real significance. Thus, when Bristol City won promotion to Division I in 1975-76, the first time in 65 years that the Robins had got back into the top echelon of English football, it seemed wholly appropriate for me to organise a Mass of Thanksgiving at Saint Francis. The local community deserved an opportunity to reflect upon, and celebrate, this long-awaited triumph.

The Mass was duly held on the Sunday following City's promotion-clinching victory over Portsmouth. In fact, Radio Bristol having got wind of what was planned, the service became a minor *cause célèbre* – an object of some controversy both within and without the congregation. Some 16

'Divided City' – Rovers' Meyer bisects City's Peacock and Williams in the 1955 Ashton Gate derby.

seasons later, as I re-read my homily on the need to provide an opportunity to offer thanksgiving to God for an achievement which many of us long-suffering supporters had thought not only unlikely, but a sheer impossibility, I would not have second thoughts about repeating the enterprise. Oh that the opportunity would present itself again!

Two further opportunities to express the corporate commitment of the congregation to the City – for it must be appreciated that other members of the Saint Francis congregation have been, and still are, as fanatical in their support as I have been – arose in 1978 and 1987. The first event was the 25th anniversary of the consecration of the present church building, which we decided to celebrate by the making of a banner to be carried on ceremonial occasions. It was generally felt that, in addition to symbolising our allegiance to Saint Francis of Assisi and all things Franciscan, this new emblem should indicate in no uncertain terms our allegiance to the City. The banner was designed by a lifelong friend, teaching colleague and fellow Cityite, the late Dick Williamson. The centrepiece portrays Blessed Francis with outstretched arm and perched on his hand there is – yes, you've guessed it – a robin!

Before Rosemary, my wife, could make the banner, its design needed the imprimatur of the Diocesan Advisory Committee – some of whose members needed persuading that the robin had an honoured place in the traditions surrounding the many dealings of Saint Francis with his feathered sisters and brothers. Now, when we walk in solemn procession behind our banner, as during the annual Glastonbury Pilgrimage each year, we declare to all with eyes to see our everlasting allegiance not only to Blessed Francis of Assisi, but also to Bristol City Football Club.

The second occasion was the centenary of the consecration of the original Church of Saint Francis of Assisi, Ashton Gate (subsequently destroyed in the wartime blitz). The Church Council decided that we ought to have a set of centenary kneelers for the altar rail, so that the faithful could the more reverently and comfortably receive the bread and the wine of the Holy Communion during the Sunday Mass. Ivy Chidgey, a member of the congregation, a one-time season-ticket-holder at Ashton Gate and, to wit, my own mother-in-law, set to work and made a kneeler with a robin in the centre, which she inscribed with the initials 'BCFC' and the motto 'Up the Robins'. Each Sunday now there are a number of communicants who kneel on that kneeler as they share in the eucharistic feast. As I am distributing the host, I sometimes glance out of the corner of my eye to see if there are any queue-jumping attempts by those who hope that the City kneeler might bring them just that little bit extra of divine unction.

Matches and dispatches

The marriage of parishioners, including the actual conducting of weddings, looms large in the ministry of a parish priest in the Church of England. The fact that, all other things being equal, the couple have the ultimate say in the timing of their wedding has meant that, on occasion, I have had to rush straight to the City ground, in my clerical gear, as soon as a marriage service has finished.

If the wedding takes place during the football season, I am always careful, in my welcome to the families and guests, to express a hope that this special day for the couple will be properly crowned by the City's winning. And, on the comparatively few occasions when necessity has meant that the marriage service coincides with a match at Ashton Gate, and a roar has indicated that a home goal has been scored, I have momentarily stopped the service to remark that a couple could not have a more memorable start to married life than that provided by the Ashton roar *fortissimo*.

With some couples I have been able to bring my commitment to the City to bear upon the situation in a very personal way. I found out from Peter, who was to marry Carol, that most of his family and friends were coming from Manchester and were avid United supporters. After extending to them a warm and loving Franciscan welcome, I qualified it by reminding them of the 1-0 defeat inflicted by United on City in the 1908-09 Cup Final – the Robins' only appearance in an FA Cup Final and a result for which I have never forgiven United. At the marriage service of Susan and Andy, a keen Norwich City fan, I drew attention to the hardiness of the robin, an all-weather bird – compared with the seeming fickleness of the canary. Andy had better change his bird, I suggested, if his marriage was going to succeed.

Of course, as a parish priest I am by law obliged to officiate at the marriage service of any parishioner who chooses to marry at the parish church. Thus it was that I found myself standing in front of Jayne and Greg, knowing full well that the groom was an avid Rovers fan, hailing from the Eastville side of town. I went to considerable lengths to stress that my willingness to conduct the service was an obvious sign of my following the Gospel injunction to love my enemies.

People tell me that these footballing barbs help to break the ice and to make the service into a much more humorous, happy and, I trust, meaningful occasion.

By the same token, my support of the Robins, and my daily experience of sharing in the deepest commitments and emotions of parishioners who have been fellow Cityites, have been on occasion, I hope, a means of bringing comfort and solace into the sadness, sorrow and even despair which accompany the passing of a loved one. When appropriate, I refer, in my funeral homily, to the fact that the departed one had been an Ashton Gate regular and how appropriate it is that the local municipal cemetery, which will be the last resting place, overlooks the ground.

I recall, for instance, three such homilies: for Bill Garland, father of Chris, one of our local lads who moved on to Chelsea, before returning to play for City in their First Division spell; for David Hopegood, whom I had known since we were brought up together as lads in the same street of terraced houses near to Ashton Gate; and for Dick Williamson, whose design for our new church banner I mentioned earlier.

I was able to note that the wreath on the casket containing Bill's earthly remains was made up of red and white carnations – Bill supporting the Robins to the last. I could remember how David, who had followed City through thick and thin, would sit, every Saturday night in the bar of the *Rising Sun*, in solemn judgment on the day's performance of his beloved Robins. And, paying tribute to Dick's loyal support of the City over many years, I could reminisce about going with him and his son, Steve, to see First Division City lose 3-0, in an FA Cup replay in 1977-78, at Third Division Wrexham. I could especially recall how, in the midst of our abject despair, Dick had tried, in his usual gentlemanly manner, to cheer us up by reminding us that it was only a game. His efforts had, of course, been of no avail.

As far as I am aware, I have never been asked to officiate at the funeral of an out-and-out Rovers supporter. My sense of Christian charity would doubtless enable me to be objective in what I had to say, much as when I was engaged to conduct the funeral of a leading member of the local Tory party. A Rovers' connection, albeit it an obscure one, was almost introduced into the service for Clive Fowler, a City season-ticket-holder and popular manager of a local, south Bristol team. The unwitting culprit was, in fact, David Bull, who had been deputed by Sue, Clive's widow, to find a reading in memory of a football manager. When David told me that he wished to use 'The Lost Captain', a tribute composed upon the death of Herbert Chapman, I was obliged to point out that this eulogy had been republished in *Football Ambassador*, a book given to me as a lad in the 1940s. It was the autobiography of the late Eddie Hapgood, of pre-war Arsenal and England fame, who had been a trialist with Rovers in 1927. There were two good reasons for ignoring the connection. First, when David designed the Order of Service (or 'Programme', as he and Sue felt Clive would have wanted it to be called), only the Highbury connection appeared in the credits. Moreover, I could content myself that Hapgood had had the good sense to refuse Rovers' terms and to sign for Kettering instead.

Whether the life of the resurrection, to which I commit those whose funeral services I conduct, has red and white as its predominant colours I know not. I am convinced, though, that if it is to be a life worthy of the term, then it must have in its essential experiences the joys and the ecstasies and the feelings of deep emotion in which I have shared over the years in supporting the City.

Gospel of hope

A parish priest is sometimes viewed as some sort of middle man who can do a 'fix-it' job with God, by engaging in the necessary invocations and manipulations. Thus, it has been assumed by some Cityites that one of my ministries ought to be to pray for the success of the Robins on the field of play, somehow ensuring that my dream of City being promoted and Rovers relegated in the same season be realised. In fact, I do pray regularly for Bristol City Football Club. The club is among a number of other community groups and organisations, listed in *A Prayer Diary for Bedminster*, for whom prayers are offered on specific days of each month in our local churches. This prayer is essentially for the well-being of those who direct, manage, are employed by, play for or support the Robins.

The success or otherwise on the field of play must, I feel, be left to the natural ability, developing skills and sense of commitment of the present day successors of Billy Wedlock, Don Clark, John Atyeo, Chris Garland and Norman Hunter. As a man of faith, I continue to wait in hope.

The full reference to the Hapgood autobiography, cited in this chapter, is given at the end of the book.

16

Joy of the Rovers

Cyril Gibson

A number of older Bristolians who no longer watch professional football will tell you that they still regard Rovers as *their* team because of the loyalties engendered in the early 1950s. The side that won the Third Division Championship in 1953 had eight players from the Bristol area including 'Twinkletoes' Harry Bamford – who died so tragically in a scooter accident in 1958 after playing 449 games for the Rovers and who would have spurned a pass back to his goalkeeper even from his own goal-line – and Geoff Bradford who, in the 1953-54 season, had scored 18 goals – including four hat-tricks – by 1 November, before his leg was broken by a very bad tackle at Home Park. He also scored another hat-trick in his come-back game against Stoke on the last Saturday of that season. The other outstanding player in that team – Jack Pitt – is still giving good service to the Rovers, as groundsman at Twerton Park, at the age of 72 (a day older than I).

It will probably be a long time before Rovers even play Liverpool again in a League match, let alone beat them at Anfield, as we did in 1955-56, when we finished 6th in Division II – our highest-ever position in the League (repeated in 1958-59). The early 50s were our glory years, particularly in the FA Cup: in 1951, I saw Rovers draw 0-0 at Newcastle in front of a 63,000 crowd – one of the years United won the cup (three times in five seasons) with outstanding players like Jackie Milburn. Five years later, we won 4-0 against Manchester United, who fielded five of the players later involved in the Munich air disaster of 1958. This was probably a greater achievement than beating them 2-1 at Old Trafford in the League Cup in 1972, even though that team included George Best and Bobby Charlton.

Let me tell you more about my loyalties to Rovers during a life-time in Bristol. Unlike most contributors to this collection, I have not needed to find ways of watching home games from afar – unless you count my machinations to fit football into a competing schedule of trade union meetings. But, then, as you will see, I am far from alone in my continuing loyalty to Bristol Rovers.

Constant loyalties in different worlds

I have been watching the Rovers since 1928, when I first walked the mile or so from home to Eastville Stadium with my father and his friend, Bert. I recall listening in wonderment to them talking about football and resorting occasionally to mysterious bilingual expressions learned in the trenches. I cannot, of course, recall the particular things that were 'all san fairy ann' to these two First World War veterans; but their conversation, as we walked to my early Rovers' home games, is illustrative of a different world from the one we are living in today – just as the football is so different from the days of leather balls, no substitutes, and centre-forwards who were allowed to charge goalkeepers without being penalised. I still remember Jack Havelock – ex-regular soldier – who used to delight in trying to knock keepers into the net in the early 1930s. Ironically, the last goal I saw scored in this way was by the City's John Atyeo, in a local derby at Eastville in the 1950s. Our goalkeeper, Ron Nicholls – the Gloucestershire opening batsman – caught the ball on the goal-line and could not have been charged had he stood firm instead of showing his shoulder to the oncoming Atyeo.

My loyalties really formed in the 1930s when Rovers were the under-dogs for most of the time – although in 1933-34, when we regularly fielded our five Macs, we did a famous double over them, 3-0 away and 5-1 at home. I saw both games but didn't realise at the time (or I have since forgotten) that this was our first-ever derby double in the Football League, in fact almost the only one. In the inter-war years, we beat the City only six times in 22 League games; and, in all competitive games over the years, they have won twice as many games as we. Our best derby period was in the late 1980s, when we were undefeated in 10 successive League games against City until they beat us 1-0 in 1990-91 – in the last minute after we had missed a penalty. And we did, of course, thrash them when we pipped them for the Third Division Championship in 1990.

Rovers' being for so long the under-dogs helps to explain the fervency of my unwavering support. I have enjoyed watching teams at all levels and for many years I saw nearly all the Reserve Team home games and more recently, since retirement, I have watched the Youth Teams. A part of the pleasure has been making my own assessment of the youngsters I think will make the grade and then watching them progress from Youth Team to Reserves and, I hope, to the First Team. It is always good to be proved right – except, of course, that some of the predicted successes, most notably Gary Mabbutt, have moved on to star elsewhere.

Reserve games are now played mid-week; but my season-ticket for

Bristol Rugby gives me a good excuse for not going to enemy territory – not that I need one. There is only one soccer team in Bristol for me and I can't honestly say that I would have cried if the City had folded when they went bankrupt in 1982, leaving a number of unpaid debts when the company was re-formed, nor if they had been relegated from the Fourth Division (where they spent 1982-83-84) – although demotion was not, of course, automatic in those days.

In the late 1950s, I purchased a few shares in Bristol Rovers Football Club. These entitled me to go to the Annual General Meeting and to take issue with those directors who were associated with the Stadium (Greyhound) Company, which owned the ground and virtually controlled the club. My criticisms date back to the directors' misguided parsimony in 1955-56. Their post-war policy of 'No Buy. No Sell' had been successful, so long as our team of the 'Glory Years' remained intact. But then, in 1955-56, Rovers had a chance of promotion to the First Division – until Geoff Bradford again broke a leg. Yet, despite low wages and gates averaging 24,000, the board refused to buy a replacement. The chance was lost; and, as I have already explained, we have only once done as well, since, as in that squandered moment of 1955-56. Hence my criticisms of the directors at many an AGM, with the Greyhound interest remaining dominant until the early 1980s.

Then I became more closely connected with the club. In 1985, it faced a very serious financial situation; and it could easily have folded the following year, had it not been for the hard work done by the new board of directors who took over in March 1986, under the chairmanship of Denis Dunford. The situation had been eased in 1985 only by staff redundancies, leaving all the administrative work to be done by Gordon Bennett – managing director and a life-long supporter – and Angela, officially a part-time assistant (although almost full-time) whose tremendous enthusiasm, experience and patience were invaluable.

Following the redundancies, Denis and I were asked if we could help out in a voluntary capacity. He took on some of the accountancy duties and I helped out with some of the administrative responsibilities, including match returns, hiring of the artificial pitch at our training ground, distribution of season tickets and controlling the YTS records.

I remained a Rovers volunteer for about five years – until I was 70 and the club's financial position had improved. This interesting episode gave me a good insight into the work associated with running a professional football club, particularly as, for two months, Angela and I had to hold the fort in the office while a successor was appointed to replace Gordon

Exultation in exile: the great Bristol promotion clash of 1990, when Rovers pipped City for the Third Division Championship, took place – in these ground-sharing days – at Twerton Park, Bath.

Bennett, who had moved on to WBA. Although I was happy to help out with the various new demands, it was understood that my additional duties strictly excluded any that had to be performed on match days. I left those to the directors: I wanted to see the match.

Having been to The Hawthorns for a YTS meeting and seen something of the facilities there, I don't imagine Gordon ever worked a 100-hour week for the Albion or slept in the office after working late, as he was reputed to have done sometimes when with the Rovers. He has since moved on again to Norwich City, as youth officer. His last big job for the Rovers was to organise the move to Bath when the new directors decided that they could not afford the terms demanded by the Greyhound Company for a new lease. We must be the only League club in the country with our ground 12 miles away from the office and, halfway between the two, a training ground (hired) with a Portakabin for the manager's office.

Trade union competition

My football allegiance was well known to my office colleagues, so that when I retired, I was given a specially-designed card with players in the Rovers strip shooting the ball into the net while the Reds stood watching. And in my trade union, NALGO – on whose South-Western District Council I served for 30 years, which included five years on the National Executive Council (NEC) – my loyalties were not only widely known but were, on occasion, significant. Thus, throughout the 'Glory Years' of the 1950s in which I have rejoiced above, I was well-placed, as branch secretary, to have my opposite numbers get tickets at their end for our all-ticket home cup games.

I paid the price, of course, in all those Saturday meetings – of a sub-committee in Exeter, the full District Council all across the region and the NEC in London. Rovers' first-ever Saturday home game in Division II – against Derby County, newly relegated from the First Division – clashed with the quarterly meeting of the Exeter sub-committee, which normally started at 2 pm. My request to change the time of the meeting was supported by Laurie Milsom, who had played in goal in the early 1920s for Torquay. The morning start enabled my branch colleague and me to be back in time for the whole match. It poured all through the game and all through my raincoat. My suit was so wet it had to be sent to the cleaners but we won 3-0, so all was well.

The full District Council meetings were more problematic and the NEC even worse: when I couldn't get back from London for a home game, I had to settle for watching QPR, the nearest club to Paddington Station. Although

I never left before the end of a District Council meeting, I sometimes had to drive up to 100 miles to see a home game. On 14 December 1963, a meeting at Bridgwater clashed with a local derby at Eastville but I didn't get to either. I hit black ice on the outward journey and finished up in Weston General Hospital with head and neck injuries. When my wife came to visit me late in the afternoon, I had difficulty in lifting my head off the pillow. But I was able to read, in the paper she had brought, that at half-time the Rovers were leading 3-0 (F/T 4-0). I still recall my reaction: 'Bloody hell. I've waited all these years for this and I've missed it.'

I had also missed the FA Cup victory at Ashton Gate in 1958 when we beat them 4-3 before a crowd of 39,126 – the largest-ever gate for a Bristol local derby. By this time, my partisanship had intensified to the extent that I was no longer willing to go to Ashton Gate – not even for local derbies.

Crackers' corner

This refusal to enter the City's ground is a principle shared by many a Rovers loyalist. I want to introduce you, for instance, to some of the fellow-enthusiasts who foregather, during summer months, in what we have come to call 'Crackers' Corner' – at the County Ground in Bristol, the home of Gloucestershire cricket. I must first tell you, though, about a former colleague who died last year at the ripe old age of 89. Born within a stone's throw of Eastville Stadium, Bill had supported Rovers all his life. Despite his age, he travelled to Bath, on a special bus organised by the club, up to a week before his death. I am told that, at his funeral service, the organist played *Goodnight Irene*, the club's theme song from the glory days. I doubt whether Bill could remember how to get to Ashton Gate.

I have to confess that there are a few oddballs in our 'Crackers' Corner', including some who follow another soccer team and two who are rugby supporters, one of whom – normally a very moderate person – finds it as difficult to find anything good to say about Bath RFC as I do about the City. Leaving them aside, I want to tell you more about the Rovers' fans in the group, of whom four have each been to at least 90 of the current League grounds – not counting the new 'DIY-kit' ones, discussed by Eugene Ring above. If we have several claims to be crackers, we can also claim to represent a cross-section of attitudes – ranging from a rational tolerance to intense hostility – on matters concerning Bristol City, including the vexed question of going to Ashton Gate.

At one extreme, we have Steve S. and Steve H. – both of whom have served on the Supporters' Club Committee – who refuse to go to Ashton for local derbies. Steve S. won't even go to home local derbies because of the tension and goes off on holiday instead. That is surprising, for, in his younger days, he used to watch both teams on alternate weeks and became a fervent Rovers supporter only when he moved to the east side of the city. Both Steves regret that the Rovers failed to buy Ashton Gate when the City were in financial difficulties. An offer was refused but they feel that the City should not have been allowed to form a new company, evade their financial obligations and stay in the League. They would have been happy to see the City disappear altogether.

Mike D., who travels 45 miles from Cheltenham to watch Rovers teams at all levels, has been to almost every League ground and to 400 non-League grounds. He refuses not only to go to Ashton but also to local derbies at Twerton: he just doesn't like the City, although he accepts that there is no logic to his attitude. He would go to Ashton (reluctantly) if the Rovers shared the ground.

Like me, Sally and Mike adopt an intermediate position. Although they feel the local media are biassed towards the City, they do not mind Bristol's having two clubs. Sally's father took her, at the age of 11, to see her first League match in 1953, when he felt she ought to see the game which would take the Rovers to the Second Division for the first time in their history. She was hooked and when she married Mike, one of the considerations as to where they should live was that it should be within walking distance of Eastville. Sally acknowledges that there is no rational explanation for their obsession that Rovers have to be the top dogs in Bristol and admits cheerfully that, other than local derbies and the few games played at Ashton following the fire, some years ago, in the Rovers' stand, the only visits they have made to Ashton were when the City were in the First Division – and then only to games they felt reasonably hopeful of seeing the City lose. Mike and Sally stopped going to away derbies when crowd problems increased, although they also resent putting money into the City's coffers.

Nigel, a former chairman of the Rovers' Supporters Club Committee, and Malcolm, who was, for a short while, assistant secretary of the club, are at the other extreme in that they consider competition in the city adds spice to our football life. So neither would wish the City to go out of business. Nigel used to go not only to away derbies but even, occasionally, to other matches at Ashton Gate. Now, though, he objects to the bad spirit fostered by some supporters in each camp and so he boycotts away derbies.

Malcolm, who gave up being assistant secretary because he wasn't seeing enough football, saw his first match in 1963, when he was seven. At one time he went to all away matches, and for 17 years he didn't miss a home game. He always goes to Ashton for local derbies. When the City were in the First Division from 1976-80, he went regularly and would do so again to see the better visiting teams. Not only does he like having two teams in Bristol: he is in favour of their sharing a ground. He argues that any initial hostility by Rovers' fans would disappear once they had experienced the vastly improved facilities at Ashton. Post-war history supports his view that the success of one Bristol team acts as a spur to the other. Like Nigel, he feels that rivalry between supporters of the two clubs is now more intense than he has ever known it; but, as long as it is friendly, he considers it healthy. Last year, Geoff Twentyman, Rovers' Club captain, said that friendship between players in the two clubs had probably never been better. And he praised those City supporters who sent 'Get Well!' cards to Rovers' player, Vaughan Jones, who broke his leg in the first minute of his come-back match, in September 1991, after returning from a leg operation. Many supporters, in both camps, will remember the on-field rivalry between Jackie Pitt and Ginger Peacock in the 1950s and the boxing match which led to their both being sent off and laughing together about the incident.

Malcolm's views on the benefits of two clubs in the city are shared by Mike Jay, author of the club's official history – *Bristol Rovers FC*. Mike would like the City Council to provide an all-purpose stadium, which both clubs and other sporting groups could share (assuming, of course, that City were prepared to move). It now seems possible that a business consortium might build such a complex to provide a home for the Rovers and other local bodies. Mike Jay went to Ashton only twice when City were in Division I. And, if the Rovers lost their League place, he wouldn't watch City but would watch more non-League football. Probably, like the rest of us, he would be prepared to follow Rovers in the Vauxhall Conference.

The pendulum swings

Last season started badly. We lost 1-0 away to City in the League and 3-1 in the first leg of the Rumbelows Cup Second Round. But Rovers went through on away goals with a 4-2 second leg win at Ashton. Our Christmas box arrived in the home League game, when, having gone a goal down, we came back to beat them 3-2. And Rovers finished eight points and four positions above City.

It seems safe to predict that, as long as there are two teams in this divided city, the pendulum will continue to swing between them. Yet I would so like it to get stuck on our side.

Come on you Blues!

This chapter has drawn upon two histories of Bristol Rovers: by Mike Jay; and by Jack Steggles, from whose *Joy of the Rovers* I have borrowed the title of this chapter. Full details of each publication are given at the end of this book.

Joy of the Rovers – enthusiasm at Eastville, January 1954.

17

'You Don't Look the Type'

memories of being a young woman watching Bristol Rovers

Cherry Rowlings

I was introduced to football by my father, though he was far from being a regular spectator and, as far as I can remember, made no attempt at all to persuade or cajole me into taking an interest in the game. In fact, if anything, it was the reverse; I wanted to go and see 'real' (i.e. professional) football and he, along with my mother, was reluctant to take me until they deemed me old enough.

One man and his dog – and me, too, please!

I was born and brought up in Bristol, a city which had – and still has – many advantages but which, I reluctantly came to recognise, was not a centre of excellence for football. We lived almost in the centre of the city, but marginally closer to the north side and therefore marginally closer to the Rovers. Besides, it was easier to get to their ground at Eastville: you went on the local steam train; whereas going to Ashton Gate, to watch the City, entailed a long walk, which was mostly uphill on the way back. My father, coming from the suburbs south-east of London, had no loyalty to either Bristol club but was used to watching Crystal Palace ('poor old Palace') and Chelsea ('lucky old Chelsea') and Fulham (which did not come with a label like the other two clubs; or maybe I have forgotten it). So it was really convenience that took us to the Rovers, though at the time I was fiercely certain that we had gone for the better football.

However, before I saw the Rovers, I was introduced to 'live' football (as opposed to radio commentary, there being no televised games then) through watching amateur football in the Downs league. My father, our dog and I would walk up to the Downs, that large, relatively flat, expanse of grass near the Zoo, which most visitors to the city will know. Goalposts seemed to sprout overnight on Fridays to make it possible for a flourishing league to exist on Saturdays. We watched Clifton St Vincent's, named after St Vincent's Rock by the Clifton Suspension Bridge. They were one of the better teams who played on one of the flatter pitches; whether this explained their better play or was a reward for success, I do not recall. But I do remember their black-and-purple strip, which seemed very sophisticated to me and much preferable to the black-and-white Newcastle United look-alike strip of their close rivals, Clifton Villa.

It was here on the Downs that I learned a number of things about men and football. The most powerful lesson – graphically captured in the imagery of Tessa Davies below – was about the sheer physical strength of men. Young men, they will have been, though to me, at the age of seven or eight, they were of a senior generation. We stood, of course, on the painted touchline, along with maybe 30 or so other regulars and had to beat a hasty retreat, dragging the dog with us, if a sliding tackle or a tussle on the sideline brought us within touching distance. The sound and sight of two men, chasing a long ball and converging, so it seemed, on a spot just in front of me was both frightening and fascinating. There was no way, I knew, that my friends or I could ever match that physical display.

I learned, too, that some things were hard to understand about men playing football. The example I remember most clearly concerned the 'Saints' and their centre-forward, Colin Mitchell. He was a tall, well-built player, fair-haired if I remember correctly, and good at scoring goals with his head and his feet. He seemed clearly destined for higher things, yet he stayed with the Saints. I could not believe he had not been offered something better; Rovers and City scouts kept a regular eye on Downs League football and he must have attracted their attention. My father thought it possible that he had decided that the Downs League was what he enjoyed or what he thought he was best at and that perhaps, therefore, he was not interested in going elsewhere. I found it hard to believe that anyone might not want to play for the Rovers – or even for the City – just as later, and paradoxically, I was to find it tough that a player's loyalty to his club was not above being bought by a wealthier one.

While Colin stayed put, other Downs League players went. The one I remember most clearly was Ray Mabbutt, whose move from the Saints to the Rovers more or less coincided with mine as a spectator. He had a solid spell with the Rovers, never reaching the heights later to be achieved by son Gary but nevertheless making an important contribution.

Eventually being allowed to go with my father to the Rovers was something of a relief. One of the reasons was that I attended a primary school where contact between boys and girls was at a minimum in the classroom and the playground. But outside, any girl who could be accepted as a member of one of the boys' gangs was definitely 'something'. As a

Looking the type – the Wembley way.

child I did not find it easy to make friends, let alone achieve such social conquests. I discovered, however, that some acceptance could be gained through conversation about football; and, while this in itself was not sufficient for admission to the innermost gang circles, it did provide a respectable level of inclusion at an age when that was very necessary.

Whether I was really accepted, I am now not sure. I could argue a point of view and had therefore to be taken notice of, particularly since the most powerful of the boys was a City fan and was duty-bound to defend his team against attack. But I knew I was considered an oddity – unlike any of the girls in my class and clearly something that the boys were unused to dealing with. As I grew older, I found that this uncertain position remained, especially when first meeting people and sharing my love of the game.

The magic of Rovers

I well remember my first sight of the Rovers. It was a Football Combination game, against Spurs Reserves. Along with the real smell from the nearby gasworks, the imaginary smell of sin always seemed to be lurking around Eastville, adding an extra thrill to being on the terraces: the ground was the home of greyhound racing and evidence of betting was all around. I pondered the significance of something which I was too young by law to be allowed to go and watch, even though my father talked of the gracefulness of the dogs, particularly over hurdles, and the friendly atmosphere at meetings. Today the gasworks have gone and – for reasons explained by Cyril Gibson – the Rovers share Twerton Park with Bath City.

Having made the transition to League football, I was a fairly regular live follower of the Rovers from the mid-1950s through to the early 1960s, when I left Bristol. Thereafter my attendance at games became more sporadic and has reflected my place of work: Oxford; Crystal Palace (I worked in Croydon); and Stoke. Perhaps because I had lost the attachment that comes of regularly watching what could be regarded as 'my' team, the pleasures of these other games were different and certainly less intense. Pete Alcock elaborates on this phenomenon in his chapter below. However, when I returned to Bristol during the 1980s, my attendance at the Rovers was also less regular. Exposure to First Division football had made me less tolerant of the game in the lower divisions, especially for the period when Rovers languished in the Third.

The magic of the Rovers is therefore, for me, the time of those earlier, teenage years at Eastville. Those years include important footballing memories, with a strong Rovers side often holding their own against the leading Second Division opposition – helped, no doubt, by their familiarity with the rather heavy Eastville pitch. Having no wish to replicate Cyril Gibson's fuller history of those years, as told in the previous chapter, I want to concentrate on three issues: just a few of my favourites, with special reference to the question of loyalty that I raised earlier; some of the visitors who attracted me; and some of the problems – at which I hint in the title to this chapter and which the title to the next chapter despairingly embraces – of trying to remain a female football fan.

First, then, my memories of particular players. I was watching when it was still not unusual for a player to be a footballer in the winter and a cricketer in the summer. The Rovers seemed to have a particular link with Gloucestershire (no doubt related to their northerly position in the city and their erstwhile location near the County Ground, where Cyril Gibson and his cronies foregather – he tells us above – to watch cricket and debate the Rovers). He recalls goalkeeper Ron Nicholls, but I particularly remember inside-forward Barrie Meyer – like Nicholls a wicket-keeper – who played for the Rovers first team when still in his teens and who could excite the crowd with his running both on and off the ball. Perhaps because of his involvement in cricket, he did not 'train on' as a footballer to the extent that initially seemed possible; or perhaps he was one of those players whose talents were less likely to be nurtured in a home-spun team such as the Rovers.

For the team was then as it is now – with little money for spending on players and heavily dependent on the skills of the scouts at identifying promising amateurs or schoolboy players. Unlike the City, who have always had more money and more patronage, the Rovers were and are a local team, their players from Bristol, the surrounding counties and South Wales. This has been both their attraction and their handicap; and increasingly, like many clubs in their position, they rely on being a nursery for the likes of those talents Cyril Gibson reports watching in the junior ranks, *en route*, via the Rovers first team, to stardom elsewhere.

I was lucky to be watching at a time when staying with a club was more common. Thus the left-wing partnership of Dai Ward (nippy and quick to pounce) and Peter Hooper (who could end a fast run down the wing with a precise pass into the centre and was also an effective taker of free-kicks and penalties) had a long time with the Rovers while also being capped for Wales. Another member of their team, Geoff Bradford, whose goal-scoring feats are recalled in the previous chapter, is another example, I suspect, of a player whose game would have benefited from a better pitch and a more favourable footballing environment.

The advantage for the crowd, of course, was that these long-serving players became familiar figures with playing personalities that evolved over time. When one of them, Harry Bamford, died in the scooter accident that Cyril Gibson recalls, there was a strong sense of loss which even non-football fans can still remember.

The Second Division of those days offered some talented visiting players and, more rarely, teams. The individual who stands out for me was Johnny Haynes, whose presence in the Fulham team made their visits to Bristol required watching not only at Eastville but at Ashton Gate. His skill and precision have rarely been matched: Glen Hoddle is probably the most recent possessor of such ability with the long pass. And then there was Liverpool, enduring a spell in Division II. Their team at Eastville in 1961 included one Ian St John, just signed and at quite a price for those days. The Rovers crowd, mindful of this, was quick to criticise and carp; but my father and I reckoned we knew talent when we saw it and thought that Liverpool had made a wise buy. The next season, they were promoted: a loss to Second Division crowds but just in time, as Eugene Ring explains above, to greet his arrival on Merseyside.

Trials of a female fan

Being a (young) woman on the terraces – we never went in the stand, regarding sitting down to watch the game as a sign of weakness – was in many ways a grown-up version of what I had found in primary school. My experience of football crowds then was that they were, as a crowd, friendly – quick to offer a better vantage point to a still-growing child, to give assistance if another spectator became ill or to urge the less inhibited to moderate their language when a 'lady' was present. Fighting was almost unknown and when it did occur, it was usually at local derbies and involved only two or three men whose consumption of alcohol and belief in their team had combined to get the better of them. Abuse, too, was normally directed only at the referee or opposing players – the latter again likely to be more prevalent at derby matches, in which rival players were seen to be resorting to their familiar tactics of trying to terrorise their opponents.

I was never then aware of being afraid of the crowd – not like now, when the neo-fascist behaviour (not only on the London terraces whence other contributors especially report it) is both frightening and distressing.

I was, however, wary of individuals or, rather, of men as individuals. Twice I went unaccompanied to matches, but that was enough. I did not want to be 'chatted up' by young men watching near me and I was angry that I was subjected to this, while lone young men seemed to be able to watch the game without anyone trying to force conversation on them. Going with my father protected me from this (though not from the occasional 'touching up' by a man standing behind me). The other women I saw in the crowd, who tended to be older than I was, were usually with their boy-friends; perhaps it was the unusual spectacle of a woman without a 'minder' that appeared to constitute an invitation for comment and chat.

If my sex made my experience of being a spectator different, I was aware that it was not just this. My age had an impact: had I been a boy in my early teens, I would probably have been in the Boys' Enclosure, watching with my contemporaries. So also did the fact that my voice was enough to show that I came from one of the 'posher' parts of Bristol – a distinguishing feature that probably compounded my difficulty in entering into the usual exchanges on the game that take place between neighbouring spectators. I was already unsure as to how far I should enter into these casual exchanges of observations, questions and information, lest I appear to be 'forward' or 'leading someone on'.

This is a situation familiar to most women at different times in their lives and one means of managing is to address comments to other women. But there were not many women in the crowd and those there were tended, as I say, to be clearly engaged with their male partners. I also learned that, if two women began to dispute a point, then there was always the danger that nearby men would start to listen and take sides. On one such occasion, I felt it was like being at a cock-fight, the other woman and I being, in more senses than one, the two birds who were goaded and encouraged by surrounding men.

It is now 30 years or more since I was watching Bamford, Bradford, Ward, Hooper and their team-mates: Petherbridge, Warren, Pitt. Since then, as I indicated earlier, my attendance at the Rovers has been infrequent and, at other clubs, sporadic. In middle age, I am less likely to attract attention on the terraces. By contrast to when I was a teenager, I am almost invisible to the young men who would previously have been inclined to chat me up or pass comments. In this respect, I feel more secure.

Otherwise, though, much has been lost, in that the crowd and – as Harry Fletcher demonstrates in his chapter – the crowd-control strategies em-ployed by the police are infinitely more hostile. As to whether I am more accepted as a football fan, I am still aware of the surprise, albeit momentary, that this arouses in others. I am still obviously not 'the type' – an opinion voiced, as Jean Thomasson and Tessa Davies have both experienced, more by other women than by men.

However, I am approaching an age where, according to the stereotypes, I am allowed a harmless eccentricity. Watching football and – now that I am again away from Bristol – following Bristol Rovers no doubt qualifies as mine.

Women and children first: as this and other chapters demonstrate, female fervour – here captured at Colchester in 1950 – is far from new.

18

Why Can't a Woman Be More Like a Fan?

Tessa Davies

I want to 'come out', here and now. I'm not a 'real' football fan. I can't be because I'm a woman, I don't go to any live games and, worst of all, I watch all my football on the telly. I have no history of being passed over heads at the 'Gasworks End' nor can I recount noble stories of rain-soaked dedication in following a gritty Third Division side. In truth, if you're after more confessions, I don't actually support any particular team. There, it's all out in the open and, before your fingers flick to a chapter whose author has more points on the 'footie cred' scale, let's pass a critical eye over just what constitutes a genuine fan.

I would argue that the 'true supporter', as defined by the footballing establishment – and also, sadly, by some of the alternative, fanzine culture – is by and large a man. The devoted lad who is rooted to the terraces, season after season; who may well cancel his wedding day, should it coincide with a Cup-tie; who could name a first-born after first team players; and who is capable of struggling with relegation over lager and curry. After years of struggle against institutionalised sexism, we women fans have learned that, as long as we adopt these norms of fan culture, we *may* make the grade. Those unable or unwilling to be initiated into the rituals are pooh-poohed as phoneys, members of the arm-chair brigade – never a true fan. For us who are unwilling to become 'ladesses' – or, indeed, for us at home looking after the lads' children and cooking the lads' sausages – the only way we can participate in the game we love is to watch it on the telly. And make no mistake: we do love the game.

A genetic quirk?

According to my mother the source of my devotion is a gene, and a defective one in her view, inherited from my football-mad father. For my part, the explanation lies less with biology than with a child's desire to stay up late on a Saturday night, so as to experience that unknown 1970s TV hinterland of 'after the Mike Yarwood show'. The manic chimes of the *Match of the Day* theme provided further enticement to open negotiations with weary parents. More often than not deals were struck, sandwiches cut; and my dad, still fresh from the Swindon Town terraces, would emerge from his newspaper and ready himself for yet more footballing delights. Whatever 'wizardry' or 'artistry' – football pundits always used those words in the 1970s – presented itself, it was never, in my father's view, a patch on Don Rogers, the much-loved Swindon Town winger who destroyed Arsenal during the Town's famous League Cup victory of 1971. Don the maestro apart, I could never fathom my father's favourites. Leeds United were 'animals', Arsenal 'lucky sods who always scored in the last minute' and Liverpool and Manchester United 'bigheads'.

I quickly began to enjoy these televised snippets and became fascinated by the banter of the 'panel' at half-time. It was an altogether different and more excitable world than my previous experience of televised sport: Alan Weeks at the swimming and the braying voices at Hickstead. In the past the rich and rhythmic rise and fall of the results announcer at the end of *Grandstand* made football seem like one of life's great mysteries. Where on earth was Cowdenbeath? Why did Torquay always seem to have an evening kick-off? Wouldn't they be too tired by then? So here I was, late on Saturday nights: I should have been in bed, but the mystery was unravelling and I was hooked.

My father, blessed with three daughters and previously doubtful of any companionship in footballing terms, encouraged my interest by taking me to a pre-season friendly: Swindon Town v Sampdoria. My initial impression was that the players themselves looked more like bison than men, with thick brown thighs glowing with liniment. It was an introduction to an alien and, of course, very male world. The terraces were alive with growls, oohs, aahs, men swigging from bottles and shouting insults, sharing jokes, passing sweets. And this was a new and animated version of my father, very different from the one at home who lived behind a newspaper. I still have a photograph, taken on our return: me shining and beaming, bursting with rosettes; my father looking pale and diminished, his post-match boozing restricted by parental responsibility.

As years passed and my interest in football showed no sign of waning, my mother continued in her search for some genetic explanation of this aberration. Her intricate stories of our Welsh ancestors unearthed not only assorted grandads and uncles who might have played for Wrexham, but also a story, full of tabloid appeal, had it not happened 90 years ago. As it was, my romantic illusions surrounding the game were fuelled by the revelation that my Great-Aunt Nancy had got into 'trouble' as a result of a passionate

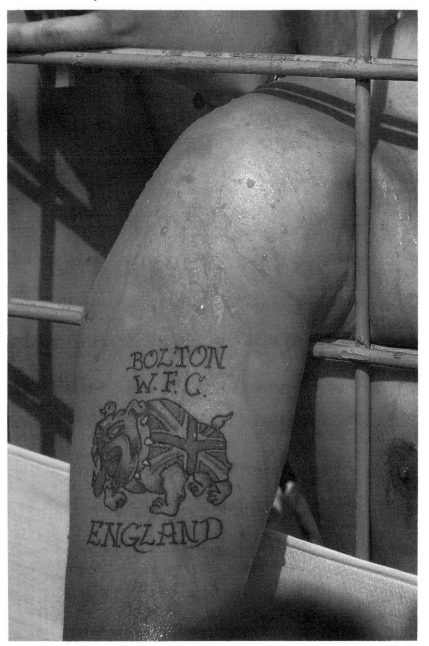

'Why can't a woman …?'

affair with the manager of Millwall Football Club. The poor woman had been deserted by the cad but gave birth to a son. While the boy was in infancy, his mother died and her immediate family absorbed the orphan into its care. Some years later, the errant manager returned to claim his heir but my formidable great-grandmother, mindful of the man's desertion, chased him away down the street with a yard brush. This all goes to show that Millwall may be tough, but nothing that a Welsh district nurse and a broom could not handle.

In early adolescence, my height and width made me feel more comfortable in the male world of football than amidst the assorted waifs and stringbeans who sprang around the school gym like antelopes. Unfortunately, girls *did not* play football – a rule we did not, as I remember, question – so I played netball; put the shot; was centre-half at hockey; and was, in terms of physique and skill, more of a Jack Charlton than an Olga Korbut. Not only did we never think to question the rigid gender division of PE sessions but I don't remember having a single conversation with my friends about football. My contact with the boys, scornful of my knowledge, was restricted to desperate attempts to swop Esso World Cup coins in order to complete the full England squad of 1970. Why was it that I always had six Paul Madeleys and never once a single Martin Peters? The boys were suspicious that a mere girl should even care about such a discrepancy.

A woman's place

By 1979, I was training to be a nurse in Oxford. The vagaries of the planning process had resulted in the bewildering spectacle of the nurses' home being placed adjacent to the Manor Ground. The warden of the home – who must have been bitten by a football fan while in her pram, for I can think of no other justification for the extent of her paranoia – would fly into a frenzy every other Saturday. Wielding a gigantic bell, she would stride the corridors imploring us to stay in our rooms with the doors and windows bolted. When Manchester United came for a Cup-tie, we were all convinced that she might call in the local militia and play out the last scenes from *Zulu*. Having failed to find a nuclear bunker to protect us for the duration of the game, she contented herself with a warning that Manchester United were 'particularly nasty' and that, as well as the usual security precautions, we should on no account even look out of the windows for fear of provoking them into an orgy of lustful destruction. We took our cue, climbed over the wall and invited the marauding Mancunian hordes down the pub.

There are very few similar excursions to the pub these days. In fact, there are very few excursions anywhere other than the swings, school and the shops now that I am a mother of two small children. Although I now live ten minutes' walk from the Dell in Southampton, I've not yet made it to a single League game. Even if the Dell were to install creche facilities, the demands of four-year-old Scarlett and one-year-old Harry, plus a part-time job, leave little spare time and energy to devote to the live game.

As compensation, I devour any televised football and particularly love the thrill of international games. I despise the racism and xenophobia erupting in many areas of sport, fuelled by the rampant nationalism endemic in contemporary global politics. I sometimes question, therefore, my own passion for the England team to succeed. Perhaps we should accept Orwell's premiss that patriotism *can* have an acceptable face, an emotion more to do with feeling secured at the roots than with superiority.

When the day of the match dawns, I pepper the daily humdrum of Postman Pat and poos with thoughts of 'How are the lads feeling?' I hope Lineker's toe holds up. A sudden panic! 'What if Des Walker falls under a bus on the way to the stadium?' The evening kick-off approaches. My partner, Roly, returns from work, eager with questions – 'Any team news, yet?' – and the children are hurried to bed and shamefully short-changed for stories. Should we eat before, during, at half-time or after? In the event, our appetites are arrested by nerves. But here are Tel and Jimmy trying to calm us. I'm temporarily side-tracked by the thought that one day Tel will punch Jimmy. But not tonight. They are out of the tunnel and the camera scans faces. And here are the lads, a strange-looking assortment of Bash Street Kids, capped by a Handsome Prince. I glance out of the window and want to berate, Alf Garnett-style, all the people carrying on with their 'normal lives', without thoughts of the match. I'm mystified by the late-night shoppers on the horizon. How can they think of Debenhams at a time like this? One kick and we're off ... the phone rings. I'd ignore it but you never know: 'Oh hello Tessa! There's nothing on but the bloody football so I thought I'd ring for a chat.' I garble my apologies and confess to my obsession. 'Oh I'm surprised! You don't seem like the type,' the female caller snipes. 'Presumably because I don't wear a Union Jack tee shirt and spit in the street,' she swears I retorted.

The response of the caller is not untypical. I know other women fans who are equally dismayed by the amount of flak they receive from astonished friends. There is a certain breed of ideological puritan who, despite their mountain bikes and wholegrains, regard any interest in sport as a symptom of underlying political 'dodginess'. One gets a great deal of practice, in football circles, in handling sexism, but I find the wrinkled-nosed disgust of my 'sisters' hard to take. I have been accused of collusion and some women question my involvement in a sport that is so openly sexist and 'macho'. Somehow, if you like football then the man of your dreams must be Rab C. Nesbitt.

Fortunately, such attitudes are becoming stale. Somewhere, someone seems to have given the nod to feminists like myself. It is OK, after all, to be into football. Anyway, it's part of the wider struggle, isn't it? Why do I sense this change in attitudes? Is it that football has become just another trendy pastime like 'wild men' weekends and Thai food? Is this trendiness bolstered by the recent practice of high-profile TV and media types, acceptable to the 'right-on' brigade, coming out as football fans? Or is it that the delicious Gary Lineker has shown that you can be an ace footballer *and* a 'new man'? Whatever the reasons, this wider acceptability of football has seemingly assisted in raising the profile of women's issues in the game and we are told that more and more girls want to play football at school.

Is the future female?

Let's hope that many schools have a higher regard for equality of opportunity than those in Southampton in 1985. In seeking one hundred 10-year-olds to adorn its centenary celebrations, Southampton FC asked 10 local schools to provide 10 children each. Only one, Bitterne C of E Middle School, responded with a mixed parade of five girls and five boys. Each of the other schools selected ten boys.

I was interested to learn the extent to which these children of the 1980s, young girls born into a decade of supposed rapid progress for women, had retained their interest in football. I was able to trace and talk to two of them, now aged 16: Sophie McCartney and Victoria Quayle. It became clear that, 15 years after my own school experiences, very little had changed. Victoria provided a poignant reminder of the rather sedate behaviour expected of girls: 'We wanted to enjoy ourselves as much as the boys. People expected us to play girlie games. We were still being girls, but we wanted to have fun as well.'

And that was a school where the staff had a commitment to gender-equal sports and were prepared to argue their position with Southampton FC. It seems that it was the boys who disrupted these good intentions: Sophie and Victoria recall their being dismissive and resentful of the girls' interest in football. The girls remember the struggle to play football as being part of a continuing battle to achieve equal status with the boys in the school. Later on, at an all-girls senior school, which prided itself on directing girls away from traditional exam subjects and job expectations, the pupils were prohibited from playing football on the grounds that 'It's not a girls' game.'

Both still retain an interest in football but feel that more encouragement needs to be given to females, both by schools and clubs. They were unaware of Channel Four's under-publicised coverage of women's matches, but felt that the media had a key role to play in raising the profile of women in all areas of the game. More optimistically, both agreed that younger friends were already benefiting from the battles they had participated in and that women officials, administrators and even managers were within the bounds of possibility.

It is interesting that women often stress the vital role television could play in increasing the involvement of girls in all areas of football by providing role-models. We are beginning to see – and hear – women fronting sports programmes, but we also need more widely publicised coverage of women's games (without perhaps the leaden commentary), women commentators and women pundits. It is too early to predict the effects for women of the ducking and diving of media moguls that clinched the satellite deal for live games. As a dishless citizen, reliant on TV coverage, the impact on my own participation could be catastrophic.

If girls and women are beginning to gain credibility as players of football, are they yet accepted as credible fans? I would conclude that, despite the long history of women's involvement as supporters, many of us are not. This is not just because our love and knowledge of the game is not taken seriously. As fans, our careers often follow a very different path from the terrace-bound traditions enjoyed by men. Despite the gains of feminism, most women still have primary responsibility for childcare and the domestic sphere *and* they undertake paid work. These duties leave very little of the spare time, not to mention the economic freedom, vital if one is to maintain the credentials of a true fan.

Because we cannot compete on equal terms, the definition of what it is to be a football fan needs to be expanded. Add to the above the absence of childcare facilities in football grounds, the dearth of any decent toilets and refreshment facilities for adults and children alike, and many women are clearly unable to experience live football – the supposed life-blood of the genuine supporter. Plans for the installation of civilising, American-style, facilities are often dismissed by purists as attempts to hijack the traditional game as part of the conspiracy to hype, market and package. Presumably, football wouldn't be football without someone peeing on your head.

Well, lads, if that's what you want, you can keep it. And I'll just stick to my TV.

19

Good to be a Gooner

being the confessions of a black, middle-class, male academic with a romantic working-class affectation and a season ticket for the Arsenal

Syd Jeffers

Unlike some of the other contributors to this collection, I did not have a religious conversion to football atop a No. 19 bus, nor was I taken to Highbury as a boy by a football-supporting parent. I suppose this means it was my own fault that I became an Arsenal fan. I am a self-made Gooner.

On becoming a Gooner

Oh to ... Oh to be ... Oh to be a Gooner!
(popular Arsenal chant)

I was born and raised in West London, so by rights I should have been a Chelsea, QPR or Brentford fan. The boy at the end of my quiet *cul-de-sac* in leafy Ealing was a member of a family of Italian Soho butchers. They were all great Tottenham fans; so, playing football against their garage door, we took turns at being Gilzean, Chivers and other Tottenham stars of the period. Luckily, I grew out of this.

At primary school, we played football manically with a battered tennis ball every break-time: 30-a-side and strictly no girls allowed. But my own very mediocre playing career was cut short when, against the advice of my headmaster, I was allowed to pass on to the local grammar school. There I was to play once for the first-year team, as a reserve on Wormwood Scrubs, before a rather portly gent, who used to take us for games, suggested that, as I was already nearly six foot tall, I should play rugby. And so I did for the next six years.

During this period, I watched *Match of the Day* at a friend's house where – along with radical politics, posters of Che Guevara, badges and joss sticks – they were all into football. The mother, something of an artist/radical (Liverpool); the eldest daughter, my first crush (Man Utd); the eldest son, into Diana Ross (Leeds); and my best friend, who always beat me at snooker (Derby County). I remember praying in front of the telly that England would win in 1966. And I remember, quite vividly, Charlie George sliding to his knees having scored in some FA Cup Final or other, although I was not really concerned at the time. I had no allegiance to football. I was merely a passive spectator. I liked watching football on TV, but I was no fan.

While I was at Sussex University, my Derby County-supporting friend came down from Liverpool University and took me to see Brighton pull back from 1-3 to draw with Liverpool. But it was not until I came back to London and managed to get a room in a short-life housing association place round the corner from Highbury, that I became a fan. Having initially ignored the fortnightly crowd that descended on the area, like flying ants, disappearing from sight at 3 pm, to become a periodic cheer and groan audible from the back garden, I decided to explore. I went alone, out of the door round two corners onto Gillespie Road, and followed the crowd through a tiny turnstile. I had become part of the national myth that is football.

Emotional gambling and being a supporter

Where's your double gone?
(Tottenham chant, upon winning the FA Cup Semi-Final,
14 April 1991)

Champions, Champions, Champions!
(Arsenal chant, upon winning the League title on Merseyside,
26 May 1989)

That was nearly nine seasons ago. After going to the occasional big game in the first couple of seasons, I became a habitual user and was soon on my way to becoming an Arsenal junkie, a Gooner.

As a fan you stake some lesser or greater part of your self, your psychic economy, on the fortunes of your team. If, like the Arsenal, your team hardly ever loses at home and is lucky enough to win something big, like the League Championship (1988-89 and 1990-91), you are likely to be onto a safe bet.

The periodic losses and disappointments ruin a day, perhaps a week-end – almost a summer in the case of the Wembley Semi-Final against 'the scum', on 14 April 1991, and a winter against Benfica, on 23 October 1991

– but build credibility. Being able to take the downs as well as the ups is an essential part of the job spec. of the 'true' supporter. It differentiates you from the fair-weather fans who rediscover their footballing affections when it suits – like the gloating Tottenham kind who ring you up after you've been humiliated by Wrexham (4 January 1992), even while the team and the manager are still on the pitch trying to think up excuses.

After the Semi-Final defeat at Wembley, I walked defiantly through the crowd of deliriously happy, blissfully unaware Spurs fans to reach my bicycle. A Spurs supporter, unlocking his own bike, tried to be charitable: 'Well, you can't win everything; you've got to leave us something.' I was so choked it was five minutes before I could catch him up and bring myself to acknowledge this small act of charity.

Contrast the momentous night we won the League title on Merseyside in the last minute of the last match, on goal difference. Oh joy! I watched the game on telly with friends in Finsbury Park. After the jumping up and down subsided we went out: I felt drawn to the ground and was sure others would be, too. People came out of their houses and flats and were gravitating towards Highbury. BMWs were driving up and down the Blackstock Road, honking their approval, fans stopped buses to wave back at bemused passengers (future converts?) and supporters were generally drunk on the exhilaration, climbing the scaffolding around the marble halls of Highbury itself.

This spontaneous outpouring of celebration and shared joy – repeated again, less spontaneously, for the civic receptions held that year and the season afterwards – felt like a tangible manifestation of the dominant romantic notion of 'community'. One wonders what similar feelings must have been experienced, for so many years, in Liverpool. I was high on it all summer and a lot of people in North London had a stupid grin on their faces all summer, too. It still raises a warm glow just thinking of that moment when Mickey Thomas beat Grobbelaar at Anfield (26 May 1989). Jackpot!

Social cachet

Yuppies, yuppies, give us a song
(North Bank chant to the executive boxes, upon their completion)

If its contribution to the 'community' – exile from which is a dominant theme of this book – is an obvious function of football, the game has played several other parts in my brief career as a fan. Going regularly to the football

'Georgie Graham's Red Army.'

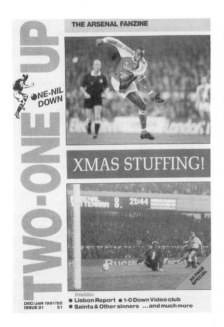

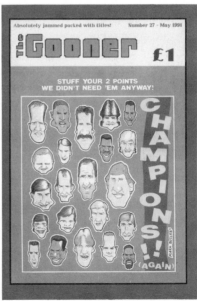

'The vibrant fanzine culture has been strong at Highbury.'

allows you to play host, offering to take visitors, guests from abroad, estranged and would-be girlfriends and even my father (in a variation on the familiar dad-takes-son-to-the-game formula) to the match.

Having begun by going to the Arsenal alone, gravitating to a particular position on the North Bank half way up, in line with the left-hand line of the penalty area, one got to recognise the regulars who likewise returned to their own spots, week in and week out. I migrated to the East Stand when I started to take friends, who, not being six foot six tall like me, did not enjoy the same view of the game from the North Bank, or who felt a little intimidated by the size (not the behaviour) of the crowd itself.

Standing on the East Stand terrace, right up against the perimeter wall, has had its advantages. Kids would be lifted over the wall by their parents or elder siblings, to be deposited in the three-foot-wide wooden trench between the wall and the back of the advertising hoardings.

This was ideal for three reasons. The little trench was about five feet from the sacred turf itself and left the youngsters safe from the sometimes rowdy celebrations that accompanied the goals. It was in the field of vision of the TV cameras, which meant that you were quite likely to be on TV: I was often spotted and recognised by friends, and even strangers, which was quite flattering. And you could make fleeting contact with the players – in the form of wishing O'Leary and Limpar a 'Happy New Year'; and by catching a ball, which you refuse to throw back directly to a particularly ugly and aggressive opponent.

Going to the game is like going to the theatre, poor people's opera, patronised by all tiers of society, literally. From the ordinary punters in the largely exposed concrete stands, to the slightly better-off in their partially covered plastic seats, to the recipients of corporate hospitality – insulated, in their fully glazed and carpeted executive boxes, both from the weather and from the crude vulgarity of the crowd.

One can of course rough it. This enables you to appear suitably earthy and to trade street cred. Bumping into the rough-looking bloke, who always stood three people down and one across from me on the North Bank (RIP), in the upper tier of a West End production of Lorca's *The House of Bernarda Alba*, I could enquire 'Don't you go to the Arsenal?' 'Of course, I've got a season ticket' – the ultimate fashion accessory.

Indeed, being a supporter, following a club and – more specifically – being a 'mad Arsenal fan' give you access to identities with a certain currency. It allows you to trade approving nods with kids in the street who clock your Arsenal ski hat while you cycle around the West End. And it enables you to make male small talk (is there any other kind?) with fellow-academics who, you discover, share your weakness for a rather romantic working-class affectation: supporting a team and being a bit of a lad after all.

In fact, the rituals at work are a bit as one imagines the Masons to be: adult males partaking in arcane exchanges over somewhat meaningless symbolic events, dressing up in the regalia for the occasion and conversing with one another in a semi-private language. A little guilty that their cover as liberal or progressive 'new men' will be blown away as they reveal themselves reassuringly to each other, as 'lads' underneath that apparently professional, adult, veneer.

Women are mostly excluded, but sometimes join in the game, half-kidding and teasing the boyishness of it all, but observing the rules of engagement: my team right or wrong; I can remember your last embarrassment if you mention mine; and so on.

The academics' football 'habit' seems to be especially addictive in the field of race and social theory (my own specialism), whose prominent members tend to be fairly 'out' about their fondness for the game. Thus I had a credible excuse to skip the afternoon session of race and politics workshops at Birkbeck College in Bloomsbury. The host, John Solomos, would understand, as he is a 'mad Baggie' (see Roger Bullock's chapter for a translation).

And I remember a conference, on race in 1989, at which Barry Troyna (Spurs) gave a paper with a Tottenham shirt on. Of course, I put him off his stride by taking a picture with flash. When he looked up dazed and asked 'Why?' I casually raised my Arsenal clip-board and said, 'Because of the shirt.' At the end of that session, I witnessed his being taken to task by Professor John Rex (Coventry City). There was much finger-wagging, which the uninformed might have perceived as a predictable confrontation between an older Neo-Weberian and a younger, more radical, Neo-Marxist. But I couldn't help seeing it as a re-run of the 1987 FA Cup Final.

Racism and ritual anti-semitism at Highbury and Stamford Bridge

... The Tottenham run away. They're Yids ...
Yiddoes, Yiddoes, Yiddoes

Back on the terraces (not for long, thanks to satellite TV decoders and lordly pronouncements on the safety of standing as opposed to sitting at football matches), the sense of a shared identity is expressed more verbally and immediately.

There seem to be about five or so basic chants that all clubs share that are customised locally, like the one that repeats the name of the manager and colour of the team – as in 'Georgie Graham's Red Army'. There are also one or two special chants that are more exclusive to that club, like our own imaginative 'Arsenal, Arsenal, Arsenal' or the ironic 'Boring, boring Arsenal' chant that we reserve for games when we have thumped the opposition 7-1 (Sheffield Wednesday, 15 February 1992).

Every team has a particular rival, the habitual enemy. Ours is Tottenham and they have a special place in the Highbury hymn book. The chanting at the start of each game is usually directed against them. Indeed, you really have to be a big club to be even recognised in your own right. When the opposition run out to warm up – or if the away fans, herded into a small corner of the Clock End opposite the North Bank, have the temerity to sing up themselves – this merits a round of 'Who the fuck, who the fuck, who the fucking hell are you?' – followed by the Arsenal chants and the anti-Tottenham one.

This last chant is very pernicious in that it is a core chant proclaiming not just a ritual antagonism towards Spurs but a ritual, and frighteningly casual, anti-semitism. The chorus of one of the chants goes:

> *Hark! Now hear the angels sing.*
> *The Tottenham run away.*
> *They're yids!*
> *And we will fight for ever more,*
> *because of Christmas Day*
> *Yiddoes! Yiddoes! Yiddoes!*

Being black and a bit of a professional sociologist, I was struck early on by the fact that the racism, which the likes of Harry Fletcher (see his chapter) had led me to believe to be 'rife' on the terraces, did not seem to be that evident. Indeed, at Arsenal, you would see not only a lot of black players on the field but plenty of black supporters off it. There seemed to be a certain amount of integration between fans and no particular racial antagonism. Those monkey chants that you still hear on TV (Holland v Germany, European Championship 1992, for example) and which follow black players around like a bad smell, were not to be heard at Highbury by the time I started to go.

In fact, the monkey chant seemed to have been transformed into a positive chorus that accompanied a goal. Just as black people and youth generally had appropriated and transformed many abusive labels and stereotypes, this chant (never, of course, restricted to the football terraces) seemed to have returned to them as a more general youthful assertion of identity.

Racism was apparently alive and well, though, in the ever-popular and repulsive form of anti-semitism. I suppose that, if you look towards Tottenham from Highbury, the very visibly 'alien' Orthodox Hasidic Jewish community around Stamford Hill marks out the ethnic border of Tottenham. Oddly enough, my regular companion at Highbury, who has been a fan since childhood, tells me that other clubs had traditionally used the same chant against Arsenal. When I went to Stamford Bridge, the 'Shed' – long infamous as the alleged home of Neo-Nazi thugs and skins, who so shocked Rob Behrens (see his chapter) – did indeed repeat the Yiddo chant.

What worries me is the way that this casual, ritual anti-semitism is reproduced at Highbury and elsewhere. The management have made isolated efforts to distance themselves from it and recent legislation makes it a criminal offence (as the Prime Minister reminds us in his chapter below). But this is all patently ineffective. Commentators on TV always ignore the monkey chants, and the most obvious and audible racist cries from the crowds, in the hope that they will simply go away; or, if they are too intrusive, we get attempts to disguise what's going on, with references to 'that unfortunate behaviour'.

The North Bank's last stand: 2 May 1992

You'll never take the North Bank
... Stick the Bond right up your ... Arse ... en ... al!

The last chant I must mention is 'You'll never take the North Bank'. This is because they have. 'They' being the directors of the club, against the wishes of many of the fans. The opposition to the flattening of the North Bank took many forms. The last home game of the 1991-92 season – a handsome, and somewhat flattering, 5-1 annihilation of Southampton, which allowed Ian Wright to score a hat-trick and so pinch Gary Lineker's Golden Boot award for top First Division scorer – saw a peaceful, but vocal, post-match demonstration by a good number of fans. Unfortunately, this was unceremoniously cleared by the police after an hour or so.

The vibrant fanzine culture, which has done much to revive football, has been strongly represented at Highbury by several titles: *One Nil Down, Two-One Up*; *The Gooner*; *The Arsenal Echo*; and *An Imperfect Match* were full of discussion about the infamous Bond Scheme. Mostly fans felt that they were being passed over, priced out and pissed about by the directors and their business mates in the executive boxes. The growing tension between fans and the club directors expressed in, and sometimes by, the fanzines was evident with threats of litigation and closure.

An Independent Arsenal Supporters Association was established and organised peaceful demonstrations of opposition to the Bond scheme. These took the form of black balloons let off during a game; the waving of a red card, saying 'Stuff the Bond!'; the stand-in at the end of the season; and collaboration with rival fans facing similar difficulties, notably at West Ham.

Unfortunately, as Martin Lacey forcibly laments, the fans don't have any real say in the running of the clubs; and, as TV rights and sponsorships take football away from the supporters on the terrace to the spectators in their armchairs, fiddling with their decoders, the game looks set to change quite radically.

And yet, as the title of this book proclaims, 'We'll support you ever more.' This means, I suppose, that regardless of the above – the anti-semitism; the lack of power; the growing sense of exclusion by ability to pay; the ironic chauvinism; and the straightforwardly aggressive macho stuff – the fans will continue to support their teams.

As I write, I have already shelled out £162.50 to renew my season ticket and have thus renewed my commitment to find ways of fitting my holidays, leisure and social life around the football season.

See you on the Clock End!

Good to be a Gooner.

20

Turning to Wednesday

Pete Alcock

This book is about football support and loyalty; and, as all football supporters know, support and loyalty are inextricably intertwined. To support a football club requires loyalty to that club through thick and thin – no more, no less. Yet my story is one of changing loyalty, of turning from one club to another. How can this be explained? And how could it possibly be justified?

Loyalty as activity

My explanation of this process of turning – and, through describing my experience of that process, my justification of it – is that loyalty is not a *passive* state of affairs. Loyalty is inextricably linked to support. And support is not passive; it is an *activity*. Indeed, it is the active nature of support which makes it so important – and so enjoyable. It is through participation in the activity of support that loyalty is forged; and through renewed participation elsewhere, loyalty can therefore, perhaps, be changed.

Central to my understanding of support, and certainly to my experience of it, is the distinction between the *spectator* and the *fan*. I know – for I have been both. The spectator attends football matches to watch the game, to admire the skills and to follow the ebb and flow of opportunity. This is much the same as watching a major match live on television – a development that has brought spectating to a much wider audience, but which, as genuine spectators will testify, is no substitute for being there oneself. The fan, on the other hand, attends a football match to see his or her team win. Of course, fans admire skills and appreciate the spectacle of the game. But they do not see fortune and opportunity; they see only success and failure. Or, rather, they do not see it: for 90 minutes and beyond, they live it.

For those who have been both spectator and fan the difference is easily recognised. A 2-1 scoreline, with the losing team pressing hard in the last ten minutes, is an exciting finale for the spectator. For the fan, whose team is winning 2-1 at this stage, it is a seemingly endless endurance test, to be borne with heart thumping and teeth clenched. Both are enjoyable experiences; but they are not the same. And for me there is no doubt which is the more desirable.

I am a fan – a supporter. I started out as a fan. Then I tried to be a spectator. But, while acting as a spectator, I once again became a fan. It was not an inevitable conversion. Yet it was entirely explicable – and, I believe, quite justified in the circumstances.

From black and white ...

As a youngster, my experience of learning to love football was also an experience of learning to be a fan. I was brought up in Newcastle, in the 1950s and 1960s, where young male children had only one primary recreational activity – they played football. And where, as soon as they were old enough, they were allowed to go to the match. Well, for me, it was a case of being *allowed* to go, rather than being encouraged, let alone taken: my father was not interested in football – he was not a Geordie – and one did not have such expectations of mothers.

The 'match' meant, of course, Newcastle United at St James's Park. From the age of 11, I went to St James's on a regular basis, in most seasons not missing a home match. I tried, too, to make it to away matches, in particular the highly-charged trip to local rivals, Sunderland. The 1960s were an exciting time for Newcastle. Relegated in 1961, they returned to the First Division in 1965 and won the European Fairs Cup in 1969 – one of four successive English wins before this competition gave way to the UEFA Cup.

Throughout my teenage years, United were my first love and my first priority. My only successful emotional relationship was with a young woman who also became a fan. I quickly learned to relish the atmosphere, the tension, the heartbreak and the glory. And I learned that 90 minutes on the terraces was a participant activity: it involved knowing everything about the team, such as injuries or potential transfers; it entailed shouting and chanting to encourage them to greater effort; and, of course, it meant caring primarily about only one thing – the *result*.

As all true fans know, the dourest 1-0 victory is a result; an exciting 4-4 draw is an opportunity squandered. Try explaining that to a spectator. And the team (or the 'lads' in the north-east) are never beaten. Sometimes, perhaps often, they fail to win. Or they give away silly goals. But the talk in the bus on the way home was always about those mistakes; never the greater achievements of the opposition.

I learned all these truths growing up as a fan for Newcastle, going to the

'Wor Jackie': Jackie Milburn, legend of Pete Alcock's first love, Newcastle United, playing at Stamford Bridge in 1955 – John Major's first season as a fan there.

match, sharing the tension, being part of the crowd. Then, at 18, I left home and went to Oxford to study. Of course, my support and loyalty continued, even though it had to be explained, and justified, to new friends, some of whom supported – with equal passion, they claimed – their own distant 'home' teams. But I was no longer part of the crowd.

I had always played football, too. Now I started to play regularly for college teams and in local leagues on Saturday afternoons and/or Sunday mornings. In my early twenties I moved to Sheffield and continued playing. Local league football is a fascinating experience from which I got immense pleasure – but that is another story. What it meant was that my weekends became dominated by playing, at the expense of watching, or supporting, football.

On the occasional free Saturday, however, I did attend matches in various places. Wherever possible, I watched Newcastle's nearby games and tried – without always succeeding – to join the travelling supporters. In Sheffield, I watched both Wednesday and United. In those days, the latter were playing the better football and, if anything, I went to Bramall Lane the more often. At these games, I learned what it was like to be a spectator. As a player and long-time admirer of football, I could enjoy the individual, and the team, skills; and, as a spectator at a live sporting event, I could appreciate the atmosphere and the tension. But it was appreciation; not participation.

Throughout this period, I still felt loyal to Newcastle. Friends would ask me, or rib me, about their fortunes. In 1974, they reached the FA Cup Final – for the first time since that historic period in the early 1950s, which Cyril Gibson recalls in his chapter. Not being in the town, I could not get a ticket, but I went to stay with old friends in Newcastle to watch on TV. Newcastle lost 3-0. As I can now admit, they were completely outplayed by Liverpool. It was a sorry evening in Newcastle town centre.

In 1976, Newcastle were back at Wembley for the League Cup Final. This time I was more determined – or better connected. A Sheffield colleague, who was also from Newcastle, got us tickets. This was my first trip to Wembley for a football match. I still felt myself a fan – albeit with a touch of nostalgia, for this was the first time since leaving Newcastle that I had travelled with United supporters. They lost again – to Manchester City. It was only 2-1 this time; but I still felt the pain as I travelled back to Sheffield, where almost no one cared.

... to blue and white

By the mid-1980s, I had stopped playing regularly in the local leagues: in my late thirties, five-a-side seemed an easier game. I also had a 12-year-old stepson. His friends and he were naturally (it seemed 'natural' to me, anyway) interested in football and, in particular, in the local team. As Jack House and Cyril Gibson have demonstrated, allegiances in a divided city tend to be rather more complex than mine had been. But, for my son, the 'local' team meant Sheffield Wednesday and he wanted to go and see them. So I took him.

Moreover, I had friends in a similar boat. Longstanding loyalists to their respective 'home' teams – Bristol City and Wolves – they now had children who wanted to see Wednesday. Over the next few years, we went increasingly frequently – with various collections of children and their friends. At this time, Wednesday, under Howard Wilkinson, were relatively successful in Division I. But they did not play the most attractive football. As a knowledgeable spectator, I could see the limitations and the faults. But my son, my friends' children and their friends could not or did not care to. They went to see Wednesday win. When Wednesday did not win, they were manifestly disappointed. When Wednesday did win – indeed, even when they scored – the youngsters were obviously ecstatic. Just as I had been at much the same age at St James's Park, they were becoming supporters. They were not just attending; they were participating. They quickly began to ask about, and to know about, the players and the club. They relished the success and tried to explain away the failures.

For my friends and me, who had known what it meant to be a supporter, these were familiar developments. Gradually, though, we began to realise that we were part of these developments. We took the children to the games, we answered their questions (so had to know about the team), we shared their success and commiserated with their failure. As we went together to more and more matches, it became more and more obvious that we were being touched, indeed being taken along, by them. What I began to realise, then, was that the activity of support, in which our children were engaged, was an activity in which I too was engaging. As my friends and I watched more, and knew more about the club, we discovered that we too cared about their fortunes. We could not remain spectators; we became fans.

Like me, my friends had so far maintained their distant loyalties. But now, they confided, they supported Wednesday. Not that they needed to confide: it was obvious, from the subtle – and the not so subtle – changes in conversation, behaviour and emotional anxiety, that their loyalty had turned. And it had become obvious to me that mine had turned, too. The moment of truth came in 1988, when Wednesday were due to entertain Newcastle in the traditionally highly-charged Boxing Day fixture. Although the season was barely half gone, both teams were struggling and badly needed the points. The game therefore promised to be an interesting one for the spectator. Long before the day arrived, however, I had realised that I could not be a spectator at this match: I wanted Wednesday to win. It was not a classic game for Boxing Day. Newcastle won. It is a cruel game, football; but the die had been cast and I was not going back.

On to Wembley

So now I was sure that I had turned to Wednesday. I was going regularly to matches – something I had not done since my teenage years in Newcastle. My son was by now 16 and finding other ways of occupying his Saturday afternoons. But I was not going for him anymore; I was going for myself. I was a born-again supporter, enjoying anew the thrill of football in a way that I had never been able to sustain as a spectator.

This was a turbulent time for Wednesday. They were changing managers and changing styles. Relegated to the Second Division in 1990, they came straight back. And, in that promotion season of 1990-91, they reached the final of the Rumbelows League Cup. They were playing Manchester United. Together with my fellow-converts, I managed to get a ticket. So once again, I went to Wembley with the other fans.

This time, of course, Wednesday won – against the odds. It was their first major trophy for almost 50 years. And it was a nail-biting experience, with Wednesday defending a 1-0 lead, as the minutes ticked so slowly away. But, needless to say, it was a wonderful day for us fans – for the crowd of which I again felt very much a part.

Staying loyal

We new Wednesday fans now have season tickets at Hillsborough. We share the tunnel vision and prejudice of the true supporter: how could we manage to lose that game; why is the international potential of this or that player not openly recognised; how can referees be so consistently one-sided? Each game is an ordeal – but one to be relished in a way that, as a spectator, I never could. Yet I do retain the strains of my earlier loyalty. I look for Newcastle's results with particular interest. And, if there is no clash with Wednesday, I try to attend their visits to nearby teams. At these games, though, I now feel that I am a spectator; and I am looking or listening, at half-time, for Wednesday's scoreline.

I do not regret having turned, because I cannot. What is there to regret? As I said, for me being a football supporter is an active process: it is about commitment through participation. And, through participation, my commitment has changed. This change was prompted initially by my son; but I do not think that he, or his local roots, were the real cause. The real cause lay in the real process of going to the match and recognising that the real excitement of being there depended upon caring about what was going to happen – the enjoyment of being a fan, rather than a spectator.

I suppose it is possible for people to remain, or to become, only spectators. And I suppose it is possible for fans to remain loyal – as so many of my fellow-contributors claim to have done – to a distant team, even though, in some cases, they rarely see them. But those for whom this is possible are missing out on what is, for me and thousands of fans like me, the great attraction of the football match: watching your team through the ups and downs of the season; living every other Saturday in expectation and fear; and being one of the crowd.

This prompts me, therefore, to ask whether loyalty can be sustained at a distance and against the attraction of the now local team. If, as I have suggested, loyalty is an activity, then there is an inevitable tension here. And my own experience, albeit stimulated by the new-found loyalty of a new generation, is testimony to the pressure that new loyalties can bring.

What price my current loyalty, then, in the face of any future move? Indeed, what price any loyalty once it is subject to the pressure of supporting without participating? Could I turn again? Like any cautious social scientist, I will not pretend to be able to predict what will happen – only to set out what can. Loyalty *can* be turned, I know.

21

No Turning from Liverpool

Geoff Fimister

It was in 1963, sometime between the release of *She Loves You* and *I Want to Hold Your Hand*, that I became aware that my home city of Liverpool was the centre of the Universe. I was 14 at the time. It is difficult to convey to those who were not there the impact that the Beatles' sudden and immense fame had on the city. There was a sense of pride and achievement even among those who didn't like the band (I can remember my Mum and Dad, who had no time at all for 'beat groups', sitting next to me watching them on *Sunday Night at the London Palladium*). Beatles' records seemed to blare out from every city centre shop – even, somehow, those shops which didn't sell records. The place was awash with tourists of all nationalities, looking for sights and souvenirs. Stories abounded, some apocryphal and some true (it was hard to tell which was which), of the visitors' alleged willingness to believe anything the locals told them – such as the tale of the two American girls rescued by the police from the Mersey Tunnel after having asked two lads for directions to the Cavern.

Beatles in parallel

It seemed only natural that the football club which bore the city's name should be ascending on a parallel curve – how could it be otherwise? And Liverpool FC's renaissance indeed paralleled the rise of the Beatles. The club had spent most of its history in the First Division, but had sunk, in 1954, to the Second. Then, in 1959, came Shankly; and in 1962 – the year *Love Me Do* (the Beatles' first record) was released – came promotion. In 1963, Liverpool finished a respectable eighth in the table and were FA Cup Semi-Finalists. The next season, they won the Championship and consequent entry into Europe, where they remained, almost as of right, until the Heysel disaster 20 years later. In 1965, they finished only seventh in the League, but won the FA Cup, defeating Leeds in the final.

One could not help noting with approval (unless, perhaps, one was an Evertonian) this sporting reflection of the city's musical success. But it was in 1965 that I first began to identify myself as a supporter. It was the European Cup campaign, followed on TV, that did the trick. I was struck by a combination of some excellent play and the excitement of the cliff-hanging finish to the Quarter-Final: after three draws with Cologne, the match was won on the toss of a coin (this being before the days of penalty shoot-outs) and even the coin had to be tossed twice, landing edge-down in the mud at the first attempt. Sadly, Liverpool went out to Inter Milan (and some genuinely dodgy refereeing) in the Semi-Final, but I was hooked: although music would remain my first love, I henceforth took it for granted that Liverpool was my team.

In 1966, this current of achievement took the club to the final of the European Cup-Winners' Cup (to be defeated by Borussia Dortmund) and to another League Championship win. And so it was to go on. Three of that successful team of 1966 made it into the 22-man squad for the World Cup – although only Roger Hunt played in the Final itself. I watched the Final on a friend's TV and then went to a party which lasted all night. The party was not specifically planned to celebrate the outcome of the game, but you could see it that way if you wanted to. I remember it mainly for some excellent records and for a young woman named Suzanne.

Of more interest, for our present purposes, were the few days leading up to the Final. Liverpool Trades Council was involved in some kind of exchange arrangement with its counterpart in Kassel, in Germany, which meant that at this time, of all times, it had on its hands a bunch of young Germans who needed entertaining. My mate, Dave Martin, and I were the nearest thing to interpretation facilities that the Trades Council had available, in that we were involved in the Labour Party and studying German at school. We thus got the job of accompanying our guests on various coach trips, visits and dinner engagements, using our pidgin German to facilitate international goodwill. Most of them were football mad. And as they were due to go home the day before the Final itself, we felt we should arrange for them to watch one of the Semi-Finals on TV at some suitable venue. The England v Portugal game fitted more easily into their programme and Gilmoss Labour Club was booked for the occasion. Our guests were, of course, expected by the locals. West Germany had beaten the Soviet Union the previous day, so we knew our friends' home team would be playing the winners of this game. We arrived at the club to find that the TV set had expired. Consternation! A fleet of cars was quickly assembled, to screech off to nearby Dovecot Labour Club, where our guests were not expected. The last-minute arrival of a bunch of excitable youths passed unnoticed at first – until they began to cheer on the Portuguese in German. I well recall the saucer-eyed astonishment to be seen around the room, as I peered out cautiously from behind my pint. I need not have feared: good humour, as well as the England team, prevailed.

Aside from the excitement of the 1966 World Cup, for me enhanced by the fun and games with my German charges, I have never been much moved by the fortunes of national teams: there seem to be neither the commitment nor, let's face it, the *teamwork* of club sides; and, although I often watch such matches on TV, my involvement rarely rises above idle curiosity. I do have a, probably irrational, tendency to favour national sides with Liverpool players; but that provides a lot of nationalities to choose from, and, of course, requires neutrality when they are playing each other.

Rival attractions

People, especially young people, have (consciously or unconsciously) to make choices that determine which of many alternative paths they will follow. I could have been a football fanatic, had my later enthusiasm been activated at this stage, but other influences intervened – notably music.

Rhythm & blues, rock, folk, jazz and the various exciting hybrids between them, became the chief objects of my teenage enthusiasm; and, in Liverpool, you didn't have to rely on records – you could go out and see it happening. Thus, if I had been asked in 1965 which was the more spine-tingling, Liverpool's FA Cup run or the guitar-playing of the Rolling Stones or the Byrds, then I'm afraid that Keith Richards's muddy fuzz-tone or Jim McGuinn's 12-string Rickenbacker would easily have trumped Ian St John's Cup-winning header. Likewise, throughout the late 1960s, even though I now regarded myself as a Liverpool supporter, it was not Anfield on a Saturday afternoon, but the Cavern or the University Students' Union on a Saturday (or any other) night, that absorbed my spending money and my spare time.

Of course, there were other distractions: the usual search for teenage romance; the necessity to do some work at school and then at Liverpool Polytechnic; and the demands (not just as a German-speaking tour-guide) of an active political life in the Labour Party – but it was ever music which most diverted me from other pursuits.

In 1970, I went to Loughborough University. Loughborough came as a major culture shock: about the only thing it had in common with Liverpool was that it began with 'L'. Musically, it was disastrous: there were more good bands on in Liverpool in a night than Loughborough could muster in a year. My partner, Anne, soon got a teaching job in Derby, so we moved

Proud to be a Scouser: Liverpool and Everton fans in post-Hillsborough unity before the 1989 Cup Final.

The Kop – 'centre of the universe'?

there and I commuted. It could not truthfully be said that Derby was a joint which jumped – a fairly strong trad jazz scene apart, it was musically not much livelier than Loughborough – but one feature did seem familiar: football. This was the era of Brian Clough at Derby County and the local enthusiasm and sense of going somewhere in the world had something of the feel of Liverpool's rise nearly a decade before.

I did not begrudge Derby their success, unless it was at Liverpool's expense (which sometimes it was – notably in 1972, when they just pipped Leeds and Liverpool to win the Championship). Indeed, I now greatly regret not having participated by getting myself down to the Baseball Ground. In those days, though, I would not bother to watch a match, even on TV, if Liverpool were not playing. Although I had initially been attracted to the club, at least in part, by the quality of their football, a new dimension was becoming significant: I was an exile – a displaced person. I missed the excitement of Liverpool as a city, I missed the music and my sense of Liverpudlian identity was under threat. Even the Beatles had broken up. But throughout the 1970s, one thing was a constant point of cultural reference: Liverpool FC ruled, not only OK, but magnificently. Admittedly, the turn-of-the-decade seasons were relatively quiet: fifth in the League both in 1969-70 and 1970-71; and no cups. But Shankly was meanwhile signing Kevin Keegan, Steve Heighway and John Toshack; and great things were in store.

This did not yet spark my later obsessional interest in the team's fortunes. It was more a quiet sense of satisfaction: an affirmation of identity. We moved in 1973 to another great footballing city – Glasgow – but the excellent local jazz scene diverted me again (although Liverpool's 1973 League Championship and UEFA Cup victories, followed by the FA Cup in 1974 – news of which was not entirely suppressed by the Scottish media – again brought a warm glow to the exile).

Later in 1974, we moved to Newcastle. There followed several years of extremely long working hours, which largely squeezed out any spare time for either music or football. However interesting the work, this cannot but have a deadening effect on the soul; and, as the 1970s gave way to the 1980s, the soul rebelled. Although the workload actually got worse, I began to make sure that I got out to participate in Newcastle's varied and vigorous music scene; but I also stepped up my footballing enthusiasm. I began to track Liverpool's TV appearances with greater care. (The importance, to the exiled supporter, of radio and TV is demonstrated by other contributors, notably David Bull and Phil Lee, but I wonder whether this is appreciated by those whose team's ground is but a bus ride away. During Liverpool's

Cup-winning run of 1991-92, I spent £7 on a taxi to get me to a TV set in time to see half an hour of highlights of the 5th Round replay against Bristol Rovers. Had I lived in Liverpool, it would have cost me little more for a ticket to the match.) But now I also began to watch teams other than Liverpool. And then, at last, I started to go to St James's Park to watch the game 'in person' and even to Middlesbrough when a more attractive match was on at Ayresome Park.

This was a qualitative change: although Liverpool still functioned as the exile's touchstone, I was now developing a new love of the game itself. Nor was it only my old appreciation of skilful play: I enjoyed going to St James's Park for the humour and the atmosphere, even when both sides played atrociously (which is far from unknown). And in an excellent game, when I watched Liverpool come twice from behind to draw 2-2 with the home team, I was even prepared to concede that the Geordie side, which had attacked with a will, deserved the draw. My loyalty remains firmly rooted and there is no danger of my undergoing a conversion in the style of Pete Alcock (as described in the previous chapter); but I can see how such seeming stalwarts can be led astray.

The second generation

Newcastle is without doubt a city where football is important. I recall sitting on the edge of my seat, one May evening in 1984, watching Liverpool v AS Roma on TV in the European Cup Final. At 1-1 after extra time, there was a nerve-racking penalty shoot-out, in which Roma were, at one point, in the lead. Alan Kennedy settled it: 4-2 overall. I was due at Newcastle's Shieldfield Social Club for a Labour Party function. Arriving late, I met a local Euro-MP who had been out door-knocking. 'Had a good evening?' I asked from atop my cloud. 'I've just learned,' she said philosophically, 'why there's no point in canvassing in East Newcastle on European Cup Final night.' Most of the population, TV sets carelessly left on, had been 'out'.

The infectious local enthusiasm for the game does weaken old loyalties and bring its converts to the local team from among those who move into the area. But many of us are not swayed. What happens, though, to the children of us exiles, who grow up with one set of pressures at home and another at school and in the street?

My son Alan, now 16, was born in Newcastle, usually accompanies me to St James's Park, but regards himself as a Liverpool supporter. His sister Katie, aged 11, has only recently started to come along: her loyalties are discussed later. My friend and neighbour, Frank Briffa, has, like me, retained his original allegiance – in his case to Arsenal, a cause to which he has converted his partner and a faith in which he has raised his teenage sons and 11-year-old daughter. There have been some lively moments at Newcastle games. Attempts to keep a low profile in watching Liverpool from the home benches have not been helped – as a dangerous shot grazed Bruce Grobbelaar's post or as a visiting defender cut out a threatening Newcastle move – by so-called friends' shouting, over the heads of a dozen or so burly Geordies, 'You were lucky there!' I have to say, though, that the locals have generally been good-humoured on finding us first- and second-generation immigrants in their midst.

There are, of course, exceptions. On one occasion, a very large, and rather drunk, Newcastle fan was sitting behind our contingent, periodically hurling racist abuse at black players on both teams. The visitors, Arsenal, won. As the ball floated over Dave Beasant's fingertips to put them ahead, Frank could not suppress a sort of little jump off his seat. His children, having no such inhibitions, leaped to their feet and cheered, as did two girls a few rows in front. A brief and baffled silence came from the man behind us. Then, 'What,' he enquired, 'are all these fuckin' Arsenal supporters deein', sittin' here, amongst me?'

Sometimes it's serious

One can joke that football supporting is a very serious business; and indeed it is an important part of many people's lives. But when something like Heysel or Hillsborough happens, it puts it all into perspective.

Liverpool started the 1984-85 season badly, probably put off their stroke by the departure of Graeme Souness to Sampdoria. Having dipped, at one point, into the relegation zone, they eventually finished second. This was commendable, but it was not the Championship. Moreover, they were knocked out of the League Cup by Spurs in the Third Round; and lost to Manchester United in the FA Cup Semi-Final. I recall discussing this unsatisfactory state of affairs with some friends in a Newcastle pub. 'Oh, well,' I said, in response to the obvious insincerity of their commiserations, 'it'll just have to be the European Cup again.'

I shall never forget switching on the TV to be confronted with the chaotic scenes at the Heysel Stadium. The decision to go on with the game may well have been wise, but the spectacle was macabre. Of course, with 38 dead, it didn't matter that Liverpool lost, or that the European footballing authorities would impose sanctions. Any tragedy inspires sympathy for the bereaved and the injured and sorrow for the dead, but some events are inevitably closer than others. I felt closely affected by what happened at Heysel. To some degree, this was because I knew Brussels quite well: Anne has relatives there and I have sometimes worked there. Mostly, though, it was because of my identification with both Liverpool the city and Liverpool the club. The generality of citizens and of supporters cannot, of course, be held responsible for that small minority which is evil or stupid or both; but something very personal is moved by such dreadful events.

Accident rather than malice was responsible, only four years later, for the disaster at Hillsborough, but the feelings were in many ways similar. It seemed incredible that something like this could happen again, so soon. Again, I felt personally involved, and took some pride in the dignity and sensitivity shown by Dalglish and his colleagues in the aftermath. Not long afterwards, Anne and I walked up the hill from the Liverpool dockside to the Anglican Cathedral to visit the Hillsborough memorial stone. This payment of respects was, of course, of no help to any of those afflicted, but it seemed important to me.

The future?

It will be apparent from the above that football now competes strongly with music for whatever time I have left over from family and work. The competition became focussed for me just before the Christmas of 1991, when local jazz musician John Silvester invited me to go and see his current group, Too Many Chiefs, at Newcastle's Bridge Hotel: Liverpool were playing Spurs on the same night in a televised League fixture; and I found, at the last minute, that there was no chance of having the match videotaped. What to do? The outcome would have surprised my younger self: I watched the game, with a taxi standing by to speed me to the Bridge in time for the band's second set. It was in the event a very satisfactory evening: Liverpool won 2-1; and the band was excellent.

It seems unlikely that I shall ever go back to live in Liverpool, as my area of work lies elsewhere. Nevertheless, Newcastle United continues to languish outside the top flight, as it has for the past three seasons, so I shall have to start organising trips to Anfield if (give or take the odd fortuitous cup fixture and the Premier League game at newly-promoted Middlesbrough), I am going to see anything much of Liverpool other than on TV.

There may be some hope locally, however. Towards the end of the 1991-92 season, I bought tickets for a routine game with Bristol City, hoping without much conviction that Newcastle would start to pull away from the threat of relegation from the (then) Second Division. By the day of the match, the somewhat unfairly-treated Ossie Ardiles had been ousted as Newcastle manager; the Geordies' Messiah, Kevin Keegan, had been installed in his place; and the game was a sell-out. There was I, applauding Keegan for everything he did for Liverpool, surrounded by about 29,000 cheering Geordies, applauding him for having put Newcastle back in the First Division in 1984. Can he do again as manager what he did before as captain? We shall see. Relegation was indeed staved off in 1992; and, if promotion can be achieved in 1993, I shall once again live within walking distance of at least one Liverpool game per season.

In conclusion, my thesis is this: although exile can be, for some people, an obstacle to continuing loyalty, it can *reinforce* the allegiance of others, providing a point of reference to a lost way of life or to memories which are held dear. For the second generation, loyalties can turn in either direction; although, with successful clubs like Liverpool and Arsenal, it could be the prestige factor which engenders allegiance, rather than merely identification with parental enthusiasms. On the other hand, the magnetism of the atmosphere down at the local ground should never be underestimated.

On the evening of the 'return of Keegan' match, I went with the family down to a steak bar on the banks of the Tyne. Katie sat with her chin in her hand, musing on the game – the first she had ever attended. 'Daddy,' she said eventually, the lights of the river shining in her eyes, 'if Liverpool were playing Newcastle, I'd want Newcastle to win.'

The other side of the Kop? Racist and ghoulish graffiti on the Kop's outer walls. For further commentary on Liverpool whiteness, see p. 22 above.

22

A Struggle for Neutrality

John Hughes

How does a sports journalist – especially if he (or, increasingly, she) has grown up with the kind of commitments to which my fellow-contributors relentlessly testify – stay neutral? After more than 30 years in sports journalism, I like to think it can be done. Yet I still struggle to remain absolutely neutral at the occasional football or cricket match, particularly when my 'home' team is playing a team from the region for which I am professionally responsible.

The journalist's dilemma

As one who earns his living mainly by the spoken word, I have to be careful and professional in the way that I go about my work – especially since I have been, these last 18 years, in the precarious position of a freelance journalist. One misplaced, split-second comment 'on air' cannot be erased: credibility can easily be lost in the heat of the moment.

During those 18 years of self-employment on the South Coast, I have regularly reported on top-class county cricket (with Hampshire winning all four domestic competitions during this time) and on First Division football, mainly from the Dell in Southampton but also from Portsmouth and – in the interlude that Rob Pugh recalls in his chapter – on Brighton, too. The Saints have done me especially proud: even when they dropped back briefly into Division II, they won the FA Cup – an event recorded, with something less than neutrality, in the caption on p. 67 above.

Sports freelances can and do work perfectly well, covering, say, Fourth Division football and Minor Counties cricket. But, as one who attaches great importance to the quality of life, on and off the field, I have to say that I have been more than happy with my lot. What could beat living in Hampshire, close to the New Forest, being paid to watch top-quality sport and mingling, almost daily, with those responsible for that quality? The late, great Henry Longhurst, the man who persuaded me to enter my profession, summed it up perfectly: 'Happy is the man whose work and pleasure are one!'

A clash of loyalties

In fact, I hail from Nottingham and am a life-long supporter of Notts County FC and Nottinghamshire CCC, having been taken from an early age by my father to their respective homes on the Trent – which, as visiting fans know, sandwich the City Ground, home of the unmentionable Nottingham Forest.

Although I showed little interest at first, the likes of Tommy Lawton (whose later exploits with Arsenal were to upset Bruce George) at Meadow Lane and Reg Simpson at Trent Bridge were soon to make a lasting impression and were, ultimately, to shape my career.

The irony of that career, of course, is that I have been obliged, like many a sports reporter, to forge – or to affect – new loyalties elsewhere. At least I do not have to report too often, these days, on the teams I support. Twice, last season, I saw Southampton play my beloved Notts County. In August, newly-promoted County won 1-0 at Meadow Lane; and then, just before Christmas, a late goal enabled them to scrape a point at the Dell. Those four points at the Saints' expense were, of course, to no avail, as Notts went straight back down. While that means two games with Portsmouth, at least the relegation of Rob Pugh's Brighton has stopped me having *four* conflict games in 1992-93.

The respective demotions of County and Albion make May 1991 seem a long way off, for – as Rob Pugh grudgingly recalls – they clashed at Wembley, in the Second Division play-off final. That game epitomised my professional dilemma. Whom did I really want to win? Notts County, the country's oldest club, whom I had supported through so many thin times; or Brighton, a side from 'my patch', who offered me the chance of covering more First Division football? I never did discover whom I backed, but County's triumph, that day, would have made my father a proud man. He was a director of the club for 20 years and such a fanatical 'Magpie' that I was never allowed into Nottingham Forest's ground.

Those who cannot comprehend that kind of behaviour in a 'divided city' would do well to read the views of Cyril Gibson and his friends, on avoiding the 'other ground' in town. In my case, I had, of course, to break the ban when working for a northern newspaper: it was with some trepidation that I made my first visit to the City Ground to report on Forest v Sheffield Wednesday. My father would not have been amused.

In fact, that summer of 1991 was one of double conflict: Hampshire and Nottinghamshire came face-to-face in the Quarter-Finals of the Nat-West trophy. Again, I approached the match with mixed feelings. But Hamp-

Mixed feelings: Tommy Johnson celebrates the first of his two goals in the 1991 Second Division Play-off Final, when John Hughes's native County beat his adopted Albion.

shire's seven-wicket win paved the way for them to lift cricket's equivalent of the FA Cup for the first time. It all meant more enjoyable work for me, besides an unforgettable day at Lord's when Hants pipped Surrey in a thrilling final.

To the life-long loyalist, those confessions will appear self-serving. Yet, when it comes to self-interest, a Saturday afternoon back in May 1979 was the most excruciating I have endured. Quite simply, Brighton had to win their last match, at Newcastle, to clinch their first-ever promotion to Division I. They had already pencilled in a celebration trip to the United States and I was due to accompany the Seagulls, along with a TV crew. Not on duty at St James's Park, I tried following Brighton's fortunes on the radio, but finished up switching it off and pacing around until the match was over. Imagine my elation at the Albion's 3-1 win! The trip was on! And I was on it.

Keeping it in

But I still had to face the TV cameras, 20 minutes after the final whistle: I like to think that I was totally composed and did not give away my personal pleasure that Alan Mullery's men had just earned me a great time, with them, in San Diego and Las Vegas.

Frankly, I am more than a little surprised when reporters, and even broadcasters whose faces are known to the public, let slip their feelings during or after a match. When Southampton beat Manchester United in that remarkable Cup Final of 1976, one of my Manchester colleagues was too overcome to hold a coherent conversation. I felt much the same, seven seasons later, when Brighton's Gordon Smith missed a great chance, in the last minute, to win the 1983 Final against Manchester United (as captured on p. 86 above). But I kept my feelings to myself.

It would have been good to have had Portsmouth at Wembley in 1992. But, as I stressed earlier, I can't complain: after all, I am now a Premier League reporter. Pompey's cup exploits and Southampton's titanic, if less enduring, run provided some relief, in 1991-92, from the Saints' struggle to avoid relegation, while Portsmouth pushed, in vain, for promotion and Brighton took the drop. Meanwhile, as I say, Notts County were going straight back down.

It was, then, a draining season. But I hope my reports and broadcasts gave nothing away. *That's* the secret!

23

Crossing the Floor for Walsall

Bruce George

A friend of mine, a journalist from Bulgaria, was convinced that the stork that delivered her to her parents' house in Sofia was supposed to have deposited her somewhere in England. Having sought to compensate for this navigational error by becoming an amazing Anglophile – no easy task in Communist Bulgaria – she eventually remedied it by migrating to England.

Consigned to Cardiff

I sometimes feel the same sense of injustice at having been delivered – possibly by that same erratic bird – to the South Wales valleys, within the catchment area of Cardiff City Football Club. This consigned me to years of footballing misery and but a few years of joy. Like my friend, I was able to escape to footballing pastures new – albeit to the catchment area not of Old Trafford, Anfield or White Hart Lane, but to within a mile of Fellows Park, the then home of Walsall FC, a team whose history of success makes Cardiff's seem like that of Real Madrid.

Whereas most of the other contributors to this volume have testified to their undying loyalty to the club of their birth, I am compelled to confess that, during nearly 30 years of exile in England, that same inbred allegiance gradually transferred to another club. In political terms, I have committed the cardinal sin of floor-crossing.

I was born in Mountain Ash, a small town formerly dominated by mining, some 20 miles north of Cardiff. The mines have now gone. There, rugby was king. My father played rugby as did his father before him; indeed, my grandfather played for Cardiff against the New Zealand tourists in 1905. Both my junior school and the grammar school tried hard to beat into me an enthusiasm for rugby football. Yet, despite those efforts and despite the great success of the Welsh rugby team – it hurts me to say this, after the catastrophic failure to beat Western Samoa, let alone England – the infant George became a Soccer fan: a deviant from the start!

In fact, there was a period, in my late teens, when I managed to combine three soccer roles: watching Cardiff City; refereeing; and keeping goal for the YMCA in the local Under-18 League.

I must have broken a Welsh record for the number of goals I let in. In one bleak season, Mountain Ash YMCA lost every game bar one – conceding an average of 11 goals per match. There can scarcely be a family in the Valley that has neither kin nor neighbour who scored a hat-trick against us. Notwithstanding, I was invited to play in a Welsh Under-18 trial. The selectors made the error of choosing Dilwyn John, who went on to keep goal for Cardiff. I was left to continue my schooling – and to keep watching City, aka the Bluebirds.

My rugby-playing father, a closet soccer enthusiast, had willingly con-nived in my introduction to Ninian Park. Fortunately I was too young to have witnessed Cardiff City's brush with Moscow Dynamo on their famous 1945 tour. It was Cardiff's Stalingrad: they lost 10-1. Had I witnessed that debacle, it might have had some deep and lasting effect upon my early development. I was later reassured that our guys had not yet recovered from fighting for King and Country; indeed, one of the side had been a Japanese PoW. Even so, I have tried to shut it out of my mind. I was reminded of it, a year or so ago, by a Soviet general, with whom I made the mistake, in between the swigs of vodka, of talking football. He proceeded to rattle off the names of both teams, the three officials and, impressively and depress-ingly, the long list of scorers.

I became a serious supporter at about the age of six, perched atop a crush barrier, a position I continued to occupy until fellow-supporters protested to my father that I had outgrown that privilege: I was bigger than they were. By the time I climbed down from my barrier, City had won promotion – in 1951-52 – to the First Division. One had to go back to the mid-1920s to recall earlier glory days. Every schoolchild remembers the epochal dates in World and British history: 1066; 1492; 1789; 1815, etc. Only Cardiff fans would insert 1927, the first – and probably the only – time the FA Cup would leave England. This is not the time to discuss the validity of the arguments of Arsenal fans that their goalkeeper, Dan Lewis, allowed his celtic origins to override his employers' interests by letting in one of the softest goals ever seen at Wembley (and establishing a tradition later to be followed even more enthusiastically by fellow-celtic goalkeepers north of the border).

Each generation, particularly as it grows older, seems to recall with nostalgia how footballers of their youth were so superior. They really were. It was such a privilege, in the 1950s, to see so many great players and teams. I was honoured to meet, a couple of years ago, when he officially opened

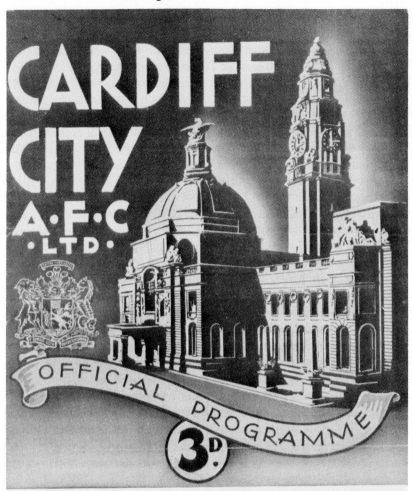

CARDIFF CITY A·F·C ·LTD·

OFFICIAL PROGRAMME

3ᴰ

Football League Division I. Saturday, 12th March, 1955.
— Kick-off 3.15 p.m. —

CARDIFF CITY v. CHARLTON ATHLETIC

Board of Directors—Sir HERBERT MERRETT, J.P. (President), W. G. RIDEN, R. BEECHER
Secretary-Manager—TREVOR MORRIS

Registered Office: NINIAN PARK · CARDIFF.

Walsall's new stadium, the greatest living Englishman: Sir Stanley Matthews.

Seeing all those greats was some compensation for witnessing so many away-wins at Ninian Park, as Cardiff City generally struggled to remain in the First Division. Yet there were great moments I still savour, not least the three consecutive away wins over Leeds United in the Cup. The directors weren't wealthy and so rarely splashed out on the transfer market. I recall one of the exceptions, the vast sum of £30,000 to bring Trevor Ford back to Wales; and who could forget the crowd's spontaneously singing 'We'll keep a welcome' as he ran on to the field for his first game? Trevor was a bruiser who struck terror into the hearts of opposing goalkeepers in the days when they could be shoulder-charged. Cardiff had the policy of bringing back to the Principality Welsh internationals nearing the end of their careers. These included the magical Ivor Allchurch and – with apologies to Neil Kinnock, Tom Jones, Gareth Edwards, Barry John and J.P.R. Williams – the greatest living Welshman: John Charles.

I have mentioned the conflict, for me, between soccer and rugby in which soccer won out. What caused further confusion, and later embarrassment, was that Cardiff City's colours were blue. I can still recall being enthused by the Conservative candidate in the 1950 election: to my eight-year-old mind, his rosette clearly indicated that he was a Cardiff City supporter. I subsequently reached the conclusion that I had more sense, even at that age, than he did: he lost by 27,000 votes. The older I got the clearer it became: not all of those wearing blue rosettes were good guys. On the other hand, I was rather suspicious, as a youngster, of the colour red: despite its association with Wales, was it not the colour of such Cardiff enemies as Liverpool and Arsenal? Indeed, I still remember both the anguish of Tommy Lawton scoring Arsenal's winner in the Third Round of the Cup in 1955, and the physical discomfort of being placed on the luggage rack of the crowded excursion train, returning to Cardiff from Highbury.

I was once asked, in an *Any Questions*-type political meeting, who were the great figures I had most admired as a child. I suppose the questioner was anticipating Attlee, Bevan or Bevin, but was perplexed to hear the names Ron Howells and Graham Vearncombe; but, of course, only the middle-aged Welsh *cognoscenti* would recognise them as Cardiff goalkeepers. In more recent years, another of my idols – the Cardiff and Welsh left-back, Alf Sherwood – became a colleague of my father's and, hence, a personal friend of mine. Alf, who passed away in 1989, was obliged, for many an hour, to share with me both his personal recollections of the great games I had watched and much of the dressing-room gossip that the *Football Echo* dared not print.

The Westminster Wobblers

Having spent most of my gloriously unsuccessful goalkeeping career on disused slag heaps, it was a delight to spend my last decade as an ageing player enjoying the three-fold luxury of playing for a team whose shirts were all the same colour; with a referee and neutral linesmen; and often on Football League grounds, with goalnets and crowds of several thousand.

Not long after my election, in 1974, to the House of Commons, a few soccer-loving MPs and a Lord founded what was to become known as the 'Westminster Wanderers' or – to the hostile hacks of the Lobby – as the 'Westminster Wobblers'. It was a genuinely all-Party team, as reflected in our colours of red and blue with a little orange diagonal depicting the then Liberal Party. One colleague on the political periphery, who was quite a good footballer, so hated the Tories that he couldn't even play in the same team with them, even though – it was I who suggested the compromise – he need pass only to fellow-Labour MPs.

The team consisted mostly of MPs and the said Lord, whose presence appeared to me, at the time, to be the sole justification for retaining the Upper House. Whenever there was the prospect of TV cameras, the demand for places exceeded the eleven available; but for run-of-the-mill games, we had to stiffen the side with parliamentary staff, such as policemen, clerks and lobby correspondents. Most of our games were for charity and we helped raise many thousands of pounds. And we won more often than Mountain Ash YMCA. The North London Vicars, lacking divine assistance; Dagenham British Legion, who had no Montgomery; and Birmingham City Council all succumbed. And we won a number of internationals against foreign parliamentarians, humbling Belgians and Germans at home and hammering the Parliament of the Republic of Ireland in an 'away' fixture at the Islington Astroturf. We played annual grudge matches against the evil parliamentary journalists, so full of outside talent – professional footballers able to read newspapers were deemed eligible – that we usually lost.

We were not averse to slipping in the odd ex-pro ourselves. Malcolm Allison, the late Cyril Knowles and Ossie Ardiles all guested for us. For my final game, the star guest was Linda Lusardi. She kindly donated a typical picture of herself to me with the immortal words, 'To Bruce the goalkeeper with the finest set of hands in the business.' A former Speaker was said to have been seen walking away smiling, clutching his own personalised picture.

The 'Wobblers' gave me the opportunity to achieve a lifetime's ambition of captaining a team at Ninian Park. We played the Speaker's Invitation XI – the selection of George Thomas, now Viscount Tonypandy. We lost the game. Most teams I supported at Ninian Park lost. I greatly impressed the then manager of then First Division Swansea: John Toshack. He tried so hard to score against me, but failed ignominiously. He offered, in the shower, to sign me – but only if I were prepared to be the only 41-year-old apprentice in the Football League.

On to Walsall

In the 1960s I lived in Manchester and lectured at the Polytechnic. Here was my chance, I thought, to support a winning team. After a short period of experimentation, I concluded that neither Manchester City nor United, both enjoying the considerable success celebrated in other chapters above, could be a substitute for failure at Cardiff. Occasionally, I watched Southport during my period as Prospective Parliamentary Candidate in the north-west, polling more – but not many more – votes than the 1950 Election Tory I referred to earlier. Southport lost their deposit, leaving the Football League soon after. One great advantage, though, of living in the north-west was that there were a number of duff teams with Cardiff on their fixture list.

In the early 1970s I moved to Birmingham, a region that then provided fewer ropey opponents than the north-west had done. Then, in 1972, I was selected to fight Walsall for the Labour Party. As I had long disliked Villa, Birmingham and WBA, Walsall FC seemed almost logical as an object of local interest. Mind you, it was not easy. Like Cardiff, they were anchored to the lower rungs of the football hierarchy, although Cardiff had at least enjoyed the highlife of the First Division on three occasions. Apart from a couple of brief spells – 1961-63 and 1988-89 – in the Second Division, Walsall had been destined for permanent Third and Fourth Division status. The ground was the archetypal, turn-of-the-century, corrugated iron 'stadium'; but it had had some great, if sporadic, moments. The highlight was surely Arsenal, kindly presenting themselves for humiliation, in 1933, in the Fourth Round of the Cup. The hero, Gilbert Allsop, who scored the goals, is still alive and has a stand named after him at the new Bescot Stadium.

Subsequent success has largely eluded the 'Saddlers' – apart from the occasional spectacular Cup wins. These have included, even since my arrival, Manchester United, Newcastle, Stoke and Arsenal again (they really do love us) – not to mention the famous draw against Liverpool in 1984.

In the early days of being a Member of Parliament, my support for the Saddlers was still subordinate to my love of the Bluebirds – although the latter had been slowly fading. My divided loyalties starkly confronted me in 1978-79 when, with both teams near the top of the Third Division, they met at Fellows Park. I went to the game, praying for a draw. Cardiff won 3-2 and that was probably my last season of relatively undiluted commitment. As I walked, fairly pleased – though not daring to show it – from the ground, I was spotted by an enraged Walsall fan. 'There he is,' he screamed, in a manner scarcely becoming a civil servant, 'your MP; a fucking Cardiff supporter.'

I was not lynched. And as time went on, what had been a duty gradually became a love. The last real test came on 18 January 1992 when, with me sponsoring the match ball, the two footballing loves of my life met again. The game finished 0-0 and I spent the second half in the splendid dining room, with one eye on the game and the other on a TV, watching Wales win their first rugby match for three years.

Initially, I tended to watch my new team from the terraces – partly from preference but also because of a less than harmonious relationship with the then club chairman. That changed when a longstanding friend and next-door neighbour became chairman, having successfully led a fans' revolt against sharing a ground with Birmingham. There is a longstanding local resentment of 'Brum', a locality described, in the Walsall Official History, as having been, in the 1780s, a 'little Hamlet near Walsalle'.

Despite having frequently been invited, in recent years, to the directors' box, I am still more often found on the terraces. It is a good vantage point from which to watch the lower echelons battle it out, to gauge constituents' views, so freely expressed, on the Labour Party – both national and local – and a fine place to operate an impromptu advice bureau.

In short, I have reconciled my conflicts. Moreover, I am clear about my fantasies: a Labour Government with a 150-seat majority and Cardiff v Walsall at Wembley – not for the Autoglass Trophy but for the FA Cup Final. I suppose I shall have to wait a while.

24

A Blue on the Blues

John Major

When I stand at the despatch box in the House of Commons, on the receiving end of a stream of colourful criticism, I realise how the Chelsea players must have felt in the darkest days of disappointment at Stamford Bridge, on the receiving end of many a sharp-tongued fan. And as I sit in my office with a row of red Government boxes confronting me, I wonder how a Prime Minister can be expected to find time to be a football fan. I also think how tempting it is to leave affairs of state behind: even the dreariest of 0-0 draws on a wet afternoon in December can seem attractive in comparison to those red boxes.

Promises made and broken

If scepticism comes readily to politicians, it comes especially easy to a Chelsea supporter. After all, I have nearly 30 years behind me of high hopes at the start of the season, fading into disappointment with a string of frustrating results by January. It started well enough. My first season at the Bridge was the now legendary Championship season of 1954-55. Chelsea were perhaps the obvious side for a boy from Brixton to follow. Yet my introduction to the sport came more slowly than for most. I was 12 years old before I finally made it to the terraces. My father, although he had a passing interest in football, did not follow it closely enough to encourage me to the Bridge. Nor did my elder brother guide me into the game. My knowledge of football's subtleties developed in the playground. Allowing myself to be described as keen, rather than skilful, I soon realised that I would get more enjoyment from watching others play the game, than they would get from watching me.

When our family moved into Brixton, we were in a large house, divided up into a number of flats. Many tenants came and went, each bringing his or her own influence to the spirit of the house. It was my friendship with two Irish boys, both enthusiastic footballers, which initially encouraged me to go to Chelsea. One of the first games I remember was against Wolves in April 1955, when we were close to sealing the Championship. One of the

Sillett brothers, Peter, who used to play at left-back (his brother, John, was on the right), scored the only goal from a penalty, after Billy Wright had punched the ball over the bar. I remember he scored an unusually high number of goals for a full-back, mainly from the penalty spot or with sweetly struck free-kicks. His penalty against Wolves was put past the international goalkeeper, Bert Williams, before a 75,000 crowd, one of the largest ever seen at the Bridge. Following that, there was no looking back and the Championship was duly won.

I still vividly remember many of the great names of that period. Ted Drake had assembled a fine collection of players in the short period between his arrival at Stamford Bridge and the Championship victory. Roy Bentley, by then coming to the end of his career with Chelsea was, I recall, the club's leading scorer for eight consecutive seasons, a record no one has bettered. Then there was Jim Lewis, one of many amateur players who played for Chelsea down the years. He shared the left-wing with Frank Blunstone, a bargain buy from Crewe Alexandra a couple of seasons before. Chick Thomson and Bill Robertson swapped the goalkeeper's jersey throughout that Championship season. Bill Robertson was still affectionately remembered for his performance a few seasons earlier, when his goalkeeping had almost single-handedly kept Chelsea in the First Division. Having gone 14 games without a win, Chelsea won the last four games, conceding only two goals. Those four games were Bill Robertson's first four for the club. Chelsea avoided the drop by the narrowest of margins on goal average – not the only time in my days following Chelsea that they benefited from careful arithmetic calculations.

Finally, right-winger Eric Parsons recovered from a cartilage operation to play a vital role in that Championship side. In fact, the season was his most prolific as a goal-scorer, but he was also particularly adept at laying off balls for Roy Bentley to slot home. He was one of only two players to appear in every League game that season.

In many ways, there is a close similarity between football and politics. Abrupt swings of fortune are common in both, although there are, thank goodness, fewer teams to beat in politics. After our Championship victory, we endured a succession of mediocre seasons and a rather unexpected drop, in 1962, into the Second Division. Bouncing back after just a year, Chelsea then treated us to the best 10 seasons in the club's history. There were some good years in the League, with third places in 1964-65 and 1969-70, but the period is memorable for Chelsea's Cup glory: League Cup winners in 1965; FA Cup runners-up in 1967 and winners in 1970; and, finally, success in the European Cup Winners' Cup in 1971. There were times then when the words of Harold Macmillan seemed to echo for all us fans: it really did seem that we had 'never had it so good'. By the mid-70s, however, we were on the slide again and Chelsea's problems seemed to mirror the country's. As Britain turned to the International Monetary Fund to bail out our economy, so Chelsea had to go cap in hand to its bankers. The Club was saved from bankruptcy in 1976 only by a twelve-month moratorium with its creditors. The upturn in Chelsea's fortunes in the 1980s was, like Britain's recovery, long overdue and extremely welcome.

After the euphoria of that first season following the club, the disappointing results in the seasons that followed might have dampened the enthusiasm of many a young fan. There is nothing like a string of mediocre home results on wet Saturdays to deter all but the deeply committed. I remember, for example, a long patch of indifferent results in the winter of 1956-57. By then, though, the bug had taken a firm hold. The inconsistency of the side just seemed to add to my enjoyment. I am sure many fans feel like me that much of the special affection for football comes from such unpredictability. For example, in one of the first games I saw that season, we again entertained Wolves. Goals from Stubbs, Blunstone and Brabrook saw us take a seemingly impregnable three-goal lead, which we were still holding with 15 minutes to go. By the time the referee blew the final whistle we were relieved to have held on for a draw.

Time for change

Our decline was perhaps inevitable, given that the Championship side was filled with so many great names coming to the end of their career. Ted Drake was left with no alternative but to build up a squad based around younger players. It was unfortunate for him that he was unable to produce a team to satisfy the fans before he lost their patience and, more importantly, that of the board. Yet he was at least allowed four or five seasons of trial and error, unlike managers of today who are often dismissed after a couple of months of mediocre performances.

One young player I remember from that time is Ron Tindall. He was a particularly versatile all-rounder, not only on the football pitch, but also on the cricket field. He is the only player I can think of whom I watched playing both for Chelsea and for my county, Surrey. He played for Chelsea in almost every position possible, even pulling on the goalkeeper's jersey when the need arose.

The most memorable young player spotted and recruited by Ted Drake was, of course, Jimmy Greaves. I was at White Hart Lane to see his debut, at the age of 17, on the opening day of the 1957-58 season. Jimmy began his prolific goal-scoring career, that very day, in a 1-1 draw. He scored five goals in a match for Chelsea on three occasions. I was lucky enough to be there for one of them and to be entertained, over the years, by so many spectacular goals of his. Two assets enabled him constantly to conjure goals out of nothing: his ability to control the ball and beat a string of defenders; and his knack of finding himself just where he needed to be as the ball was played forward or crossed. One of his most memorable goals was also one of his last, towards the end of the 1960-61 season, in a match we lost 3- 2 against Tottenham. As ever, he was in perfect position when the cross came in and took the ball on the volley from the edge of the penalty box. The ball sweetly struck into the top left-hand corner of the net, in one of those moves that leaves the goalkeeper helpless.

At the other end of the pitch, another young recruit was beginning to make his mark. Peter Bonetti's career with Chelsea lasted longer than any other's (although he was pipped for the record number of appearances by 'Chopper' Harris). When Bonetti made his debut for Chelsea, I was a nervous and rather immature recruit straight from school into a firm of City insurance brokers. Before he retired, I had taken up my seat as the Member of Parliament for Huntingdonshire. In fact, Bonetti played out his last two fixtures in front of the home crowd just after my first election victory in 1979. Needless to say, I was too busy coming to terms with the strange business of being an MP to see either game. Just as I remember a host of magnificent goals by Jimmy Greaves, I recall many magnificent saves from Bonetti. It is perhaps unfortunate that goal-scorers are remembered more readily than goal-savers; but, with a keeper as outstanding as Bonetti, we were never short of breathtaking feats of agility to savour.

I remember, like many other Chelsea fans, bitter disappointment when Jimmy Greaves left for Milan, in 1961, and our astonishment when he failed to return to Chelsea after such a brief spell abroad. Fortunately, Ted Drake had already identified a successor who could knock in the goals: Bobby Tambling shared with Greaves the distinction of scoring on his debut, also when 17, against West Ham United. In all he scored over 200 goals for Chelsea, making him more prolific than Roy Bentley and putting him, perhaps surprisingly, more than 50 goals ahead of Peter Osgood. His finest moment came during the 1962-63 season when Chelsea were struggling to return, at the first time of asking, to the First Division. A goal from Tommy Harmer, the only one he ever scored for Chelsea, had brought us victory in the penultimate game at Roker Park. So promotion from the Second Division now demanded a seven-goal victory over Portsmouth in the final fixture. Bobby Tambling scored four of them. Chelsea, again benefiting from the arithmetic, were promoted by the slimmest of goal average margins.

The main burden of rebuilding a successful team, following Ted Drake's departure, fell to the controversial Tommy Docherty. In the same way that Ted Drake had brought a breath of fresh air for fans in earlier days, so Docherty seemed to do just that for us young fans in the early 1960s. Propelled rather unexpectedly into the manager's office when Drake finally left, he had not only to learn the ropes fast; he also had to teach them to his young team. The promotion-winning side of 1962-63 is the youngest the club has ever fielded. Chelsea could certainly claim to be accessible: one of our more reliable players of the 1960s, John Boyle, joined the club when he simply turned up at the door while on holiday in London. Docherty's success relied in no small part on the partnership he built with Dave Sexton, whom he recruited almost immediately as coach. The genesis of the most famous Chelsea side in its history grew from that pairing.

One of the most exciting players to be developed in that period was, of course, Peter Osgood. Where Greaves and Tambling had satisfied them-selves by scoring one goal each on their debuts, Osgood scored two. Unfortunately I missed the game, a League Cup replay, in December 1964, against Workington at Stamford Bridge, in front of under 8,000 people. It was the fifth season of a competition which had yet to inspire the imagin-ation of the fans – or, indeed, many of the clubs. Thus that season's League Cup winners, Chelsea, won the first leg of the Final before their lowest home gate of the season. Despite his debut goals, Osgood played no further games that season, thanks to stiff competition from Barry Bridges. It was well into the following season before Osgood won a regular place. He was an instant hit with the fans and I have many memories of him displaying his unique, if unpredictable, flair.

Another player establishing himself in the side, at about that time, was Peter Houseman, a highly versatile player whom I saw playing – like Ron Tindall – in almost every position on the field. He also had a famous knack for scoring goals out of the blue on the big occasions – like the first equaliser in the 1970 Cup Final. I recall hearing with shock the sad news of the car crash which killed him and his wife.

Despite the successes of the late 1960s, things were not as settled as they might be at Stamford Bridge. Tommy Docherty had always been an unpredictable genius and began increasingly to come to blows with the rest of the club management. His position was not helped by the sudden death of the chairman, Joe Mears, in 1966. One of the very long line of the Mears family involved in the club from its foundations until very recently, Joe

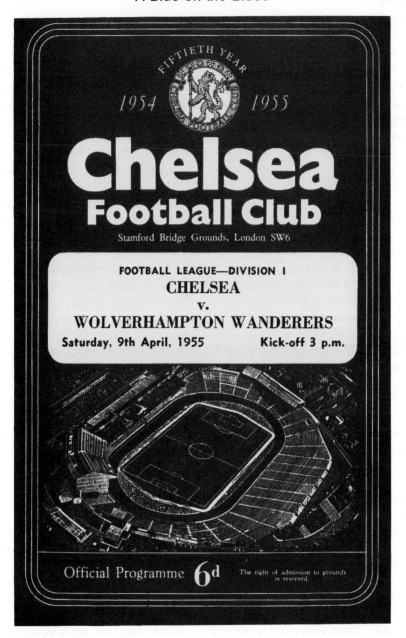

The Championship-deciding game of 1955, watched by John Major, David Bull and 75,000 others.

Mears was a stabilising force at the top. It was perhaps inevitable that his demise would produce the unsettling times it did; and it came as no surprise to us when Tommy Docherty resigned. Given Dave Sexton's close involvement in the building of the side, we were pleased to see him return to try to realise the team's potential. During much of this period, I followed the club less carefully, mainly because I had been posted abroad by my employer. It could take some time for results to filter through to Nigeria from London, but I did my best to keep in touch.

One of the last games with Docherty in charge was the unsuccessful Cup Final in 1967, when we were easily beaten by Tottenham Hotspur. It did not take long for Dave Sexton's organisational skills to begin paying off. In only his second full season in charge, Chelsea swept to the Cup Final and, despite being the less favoured team, beat Leeds in a memorable Old Trafford replay. I clearly remember the strength of that particular side, with Bonetti protected by a fearsomely strong defence in the shape of Webb and McCreadie, Harris and Dempsey. Hollins and Houseman had to face the challenge of Billy Bremner and Johnny Giles, as intimidating a midfield as it was possible to find. None the less, they diligently distributed the ball from midfield to Baldwin and Cooke on the wings or to Osgood and Hutchison up front.

The following season saw our finest period in European football. Our route to the Athens Final of the Cup-Winners' Cup included the defeat, in the Semi-Final, of Manchester City, who were in the competition by virtue of having won it the year before. The Final against Real Madrid took place before the days of penalty shoot-outs; so, when the game was not won after 120 minutes, the team had to stay on in Athens to finish the job two days later.

The early signs of Chelsea's decline came in the following season's defence of our European trophy. Despite a 21-0 aggregate against a Luxembourg side, with Osgood scoring eight, we were humiliatingly defeated by an unknown Swedish side, Atvidaberg, in the next round. We managed to reach the Final of the League Cup, but were disappointingly defeated by Stoke City. By the end of the 1974-75 season, we had sunk to the bottom of the First Division and were duly relegated. Many of the players who had been so instrumental in our success began to drift away. It was a time when following Chelsea became unusually difficult. Managers changed with unfortunate regularity and the club's financial problems grew. Despite winning promotion back to the First Division after just two seasons, we soon found ourselves back in the Second. In 1978-79, we scored fewer points than any First Division team had done before.

Chelsea 1 Huntingdon 1

Throughout many of those years, I inevitably concentrated on developing my political career. It was not necessarily an advantage to someone seeking election to a rural seat in East Anglia to be a follower of Chelsea. On the other hand, I was fortunate to have no direct conflict of interest between club and constituency, of the kind recounted, above, by the Hon. Member for Walsall South. With Peterborough and Cambridge the only local sides, my support for Chelsea has rarely interfered with my constituency interests.

I have been able, then, as a Member of Parliament, to maintain my interest in Chelsea. I was present at many of the games during the 1980s when their resurgence began. I particularly recall the promise shown in the 1983-84 season, when we gained promotion as champions for the first time. A key factor was the emergence of Kerry Dixon who had made his debut in the first game of the season and went on to appear in every League and Cup game we played. Unfortunately, promotion back to the First did not see an immediate return to success. I well remember our slump to the bottom of the First and relegation, amid disgraceful scenes at Stamford Bridge, after our defeat at the hands of Middlesbrough. Just how futile our relegation had been was well-illustrated by our immediate promotion back to the top flight, when we looked like champions almost from the first game.

Obviously, my ability to attend games has been constrained by the callings of Government business. Nevertheless, I still go as often as possible and have attended around half a dozen Chelsea games since becoming Prime Minister. Even on the busiest of Government engagements, I make sure someone is on hand to pass me the results as soon as they are available.

The 1992-93 season sees the establishment of the Premier League and the start of a new era for domestic football in England. It is clear that a great deal of additional money will be available to Premier League clubs through television and other commercial developments. I *personally* hope that a significant proportion of these new resources will be used to improve football grounds in line with the recommendations of Lord Taylor, rather than fuelling an already over-inflated transfer market.

Government and football

While other contributors can similarly express their personal hopes for the future of the game, I am in the fortunate position of being able to do something for football, through Government policy. Sport is, of course, the responsibility of David Mellor, a fellow Chelsea fan to whom I am more than happy to leave most of the decisions. The Government is determined that spectators should enjoy higher standards of comfort and safety and we have encouraged clubs to provide facilities appropriate to the 21st century.

That is precisely why we have helped make available unprecedented funds for football. In the 1990 Budget the rate of Pool Betting Duty was reduced from 42.5% to 40% for a period of five years on the understanding that the full amount saved is used for capital works for the improvement of comfort and safety of spectators at Football League and Scottish League grounds and at the national stadia. As a result, football will benefit by around £100m over a five-year period. Many clubs in all divisions have had major projects approved for grant aid by the Football Trust, which is administering the funds accruing from the Pool Betting Duty concession.

I am particularly pleased with the favourable trend, in recent seasons, towards fewer arrests at, and ejections from, football matches. This has encouraged more people, including families, to go to matches: attendances rose, in 1991-92, for the sixth consecutive season. Football is beginning, once again, to take on the family feel that I remember so well from my youth.

Our return to European club competitions over the last two seasons has been almost trouble-free, and it was particularly pleasing when the Mayor of Rotterdam congratulated Manchester United supporters on their behaviour at the 1991 European Cup-Winners' Cup Final. I hope that the good work by all those concerned – the Government, the football authorities, the supporters and the police – will be maintained and that behaviour continues to improve.

Several measures have contributed to the better atmosphere at our grounds. These include better policing, improved segregation and the use of close-circuit television. More recently, following cooperation between the Association of Chief Police Officers and the football authorities, there have been improvements in the quality, training and competence of stewards. The Football Offences Act 1991 has also outlawed some of the more unacceptable practices that some spectators still engage in. It is now an offence to throw missiles, chant racist or indecent abuse and to go onto the pitch without a reasonable excuse.

Football-in-the-Community Schemes also have an important and positive role. The Government has welcomed and encouraged the various community schemes run by clubs. The greater the involvement the community has with a club the less likely it is that some members of it will damage the club's facilities. The Football League, the Football Association and the Professional Footballers Association have set up, through the Footballers Further Education and Vocational Training Society, a programme of community development in every area of the country, including one at each Football League club.

These measures and the determination of the great majority of supporters to be able to take pride, once again, in our national game have played a part in the success of the Football Association's bid to host the 1996 European Championship Finals. The Government supported the FA in its quest and we will continue to offer diplomatic support in the preparations for the Finals. I am sure that, with hard work and determination on all sides, we can look forward to the successful staging of the first major football tournament in this country for 30 years.

I am generally more optimistic, then, than many soccer fans and I look forward to the Premier League and other changes with less scepticism than some of the other contributors, notably Martin Lacey, express in their chapters. And yet, as I said at the outset, scepticism comes easy to a Chelsea fan. I take refuge, then, writing as the 1992-93 season approaches, in the cliché that we all start level on the first day of the season. And within us all is a feeling that this season is the season for *our* team.

John Major's early hero, Peter Sillett (right), watches Thompson (straddled by Willemse) save from Newcastle's Hannah (left) in a 4-3 win on Chelsea's way to the 1955 Championship.

Reading and Riddles

David Bull

In my introduction to the growing 'literature for soccer', I necessarily referred to several books. And a few contributors drew upon their libraries, too. Full references to these books are given below.

We also offer, here, the answers to two kinds of football riddles – those arising from the use of in-group (fanzine-style) language and those that Bob Holman is prone (or, rather, supine) to be asked in the dentist's chair. If you've not attempted those dentist's riddles and want to do so before you see the answers, hurry back to Chapter 3.

Reading

Arlott, John, *Concerning Soccer*, Longmans Green, 1952.

Arlott, John, *Basingstoke Boy: the Autobiography*, Willow Books, 1990 (Fontana paperback 1992).

Arnold, A.J., *A Game That Would Pay: a business history of professional football in Bradford*, Duckworth, 1988.

Buford, Bill, *Among the Thugs*, Secker & Warburg, 1991.

Canter, David, Comber, Miriam & Uzzell, David, *Football In Its Place: an environmental psychology of football grounds*, Routledge, 1989.

Crossman, Richard, *The Diaries of a Cabinet Minister*, Vol. 3, Hamish Hamilton & Jonathan Cape, 1977.

Davies, Hunter, *The Glory Game*, Weidenfeld and Nicolson, 1972.

Davies, Hunter, *My Life in Football*, Mainstream Publishing, 1990.

Davies, Pete, *All Played Out: the full story of Italia '90*, Heinemann, 1990 (Mandarin Paperback 1991).

Dunphy, Eamon, *A Strange Kind of Glory: Sir Matt Busby & Manchester United*, Heinemann, 1991.

Glanville, Brian (ed.), *The Footballer's Companion*, Eyre & Spottiswoode, 1962.

Hapgood, Eddie, *Football Ambassador*, Sporting Handbooks, 1945.

Hill, Dave, *'Out of His Skin': the John Barnes phenomenon*, Faber & Faber, 1989.

Hughes, Moelwyn, *Report of an Enquiry into the Disaster at the Bolton Wanderers Football Ground*, HMSO, 1946.

Inglis, Simon, *The Football Grounds of England and Wales*, Willow Books, 1983.

Jay, Mike, *Bristol Rovers FC – A Complete Record 1883-1987*, Breedon Books, 1987.

Korr, Charles, *West Ham United: the making of a football club*, Duckworth, 1986.

Lacey, Martin (ed.), *Get Your Writs Out! – another dose of the alternative football press*, Juma, 1991.

Lansdown, Harry & Spillius, Alex, *Saturday's Boys: the football experience*, Willow Books, 1990.

Mason, Tony, *Association Football and English Society 1863-1915*, Harvester, 1980.

Morris, Desmond, *The Soccer Tribe*, Jonathan Cape, 1981.

Murphy, Patrick, Williams, John & Dunning, Eric, *Football on Trial*, Routledge, 1990.

Rowlands, Alan, *Trautmann: the Biography*, Breedon Books, 1990.

Roy of the Rovers Football Quiz Book, Mirror Books, 1978.

Sandercock, Leonie & Turner, Ian, *Up Where, Cazaly? – The Great Australian Game*, Granada Publishing, 1981.

Steggles, Jack, *Joy of the Rovers*, Mainstream Publishing, 1990.

Taylor, Lord Justice, *The Hillsborough Stadium Disaster 15 April 1989: Final Report*, HMSO, 1990.

Tomlinson, H. Ellis, *Seasiders: the first hundred years*, Blackpool FC, 1987.

Wagg, Stephen, *The Football World: a contemporary history*, Harvester, 1984.

Williams, John & Wagg, Stephen (eds.), *British Football and Social Change: getting into Europe*, Leicester University Press, 1991.

Young, Percy M., *Manchester United*, Heinemann, 1960.

Riddles

First the 'unintentional' riddles. I expressed concern, in my introduction, lest our recourse to the in-group language of football exclude non-addicts of the game, which I hope our readership will include. I confess that I didn't understand all of the imagery myself – Rob Pugh tells me that a 'butterfly' supporter is fanzine-speak for a fair-weather fan and Cherry Rowlings assures me that racehorses 'train on'.

The ultimate in-group reference, though, is in the title (for which I accept much of the blame) of Rob Pugh's chapter. Fanzine buffs will get it immediately. If you're not into that cult, then here's how to work it out:

(1) Think back to the 1983 FA Cup Final between Brighton and Manchester United.
(2) Remember the last-minute incident (captured by a photographer on p. 86

above and recalled by John Hughes, in Chapter 22, if you need help) when Gordon Smith had a great chance to win the game for Brighton.

(3) Remember John Motson's false prediction: 'And Smith Must Score'.

(4) Now, even if you didn't know that those words have been cruelly immortalised in the title of a Brighton fanzine, you can comprehend the charitable thought in Rob Pugh's potentially exclusive title.

The other, *intentional*, riddles were those posed by Jim Craig, Bob Holman's dentist (see Chapter 3). The answers are:

(1) Airdrie
(2) Brechin City
(3) Alloa, Celtic, Dundee United, East Fife, East Stirlingshire and Kilmarnock.

The astute reader will notice that, while the former Celtic full-back asked his patients to name only five clubs in his third question, there are six teams in the answer-list. Bob Holman took great pleasure in pointing out to Jim Craig that he had been fooled by the sportcasters' abbreviations: the full name of 'East Stirling' is East Stirlingshire.

The answer to the patient's riposte is that *at least* five English clubs then played beyond their local boundaries: Bristol Rovers (Bath); Chester (Macclesfield); Grimsby (Cleethorpes); Wimbledon (replacing Charlton, who had been doing so, at Selhurst Park); and Maidstone (then still in business at Dartford).

Personally, I'd always thought that Manchester United played in Stretford. And I imagine there could be other boundary disputes and quibbles about definitions if we began to take this question too seriously. So, please treat it as fun – which you may find increasingly difficult to get on the NHS. As Bob Holman writes, 'There may well be others. But these were sufficient to get my own back on Jim Craig.' Why not try it out on your dentist and see?